Hoover Institution Publications

THE ORIGINS OF COMMUNISM IN TURKEY

THE ORIGINS OF
COMMUNISM
IN TURKEY

George S. Harris

THE HOOVER INSTITUTION
ON WAR, REVOLUTION AND PEACE
Stanford University · Stanford, California
1967

The Hoover Institution on War, Revolution and Peace, founded at Stanford University in 1919 by the late President Herbert Hoover, is a center for advanced study and research on public and international affairs in the twentieth century. The views expressed in its publications are entirely those of the authors and do not necessarily reflect the views of the Hoover Institution.

To Jo

Author's Preface

This work could not have been produced without the cooperation of many faithful friends. In the first place, I would like to acknowledge my thanks to all those who helped in locating the often obscure materials that might otherwise never have come to hand. I am particularly indebted to Mete Tunçay of the Political Sciences Faculty of Ankara University for sharing with me the fruits of parallel labors and for his perceptive comments on the text. Finally, I owe a special debt of gratitude to George Rentz and to the staff of the Hoover Institution for their encouragement and cooperation as well as for making it possible for me to consult the rich collection at the Hoover Institution library.

From 1957 to 1962 I was privileged to serve in the American Embassy in Ankara. It should be noted in this connection that the views expressed in this book are mine alone and do not necessarily reflect those of the United States government.

G. S. H.

Westmoreland Hills, Maryland
March 1967

Note on Dates

In the body of the text, dates have been converted into the Gregorian calendar from the variety of reckoning systems in use during the closing days of the Ottoman Empire and up to the calendar reform of 1926. The principal source of confusion in this regard has arisen from the widely adopted fiscal year calendar introduced by the Sultans in 1676. The Ottoman fiscal year, which began on March first of the Julian calendar, was based on the Julian system of reckoning, except that years were dated from the Hegira. This fiscal year thus increasingly diverged from the Muslim lunar calendar also used throughout the period especially for religious purposes. In 1917 this fiscal year system was adjusted to begin on March first of the Gregorian calendar.

In the notes both fiscal year and Gregorian reckoning dates are generally given for periodicals and newspapers. Communist publications often followed the Gregorian calendar; in these cases no fiscal year date equivalents are indicated.

Note on Turkish Names

Until the Name Law of 1934 Turks did not have surnames. Thus, during the period under consideration here all the protagonists were known by their first names, often with identifying place indicators or nicknames. While Turks can usually—but by no means invariably—surmount the difficulties in handling this system, it may be quite confusing to Western readers. It has the important drawback also of obscuring the identity of personalities who later became prominent under their family names. In this work, therefore, where positive identification has been possible, those individuals who lived long enough to adopt surnames have been cited by family name. In only a few special cases (e.g., Yunus Nadi and Nâzım Hikmet), where the family name never came into general usage, popular practice has been followed. When frequent reference to an individual who never adopted a last name has been necessary, the last given name has occasionally been treated as a surname (e.g., Subhi for Mustafa Subhi). Names of Turks from Russia who maintained their foreign citizenship have usually been rendered according to Russian—rather than Turkish—orthography.

Table of Contents

Plates follow page 52

THE ORIGINS OF COMMUNISM
IN TURKEY

Introduction

As to the bolshevists: there is no room whatever in our country for this doctrine, our religion and customs as well as our social organization being entirely unfavorable to its implantation. In Turkey there are neither great capitalists nor millions of artisans and workingmen. On the other hand, we are not saddled with an agrarian question. Finally, from the social point of view our religious principles are such as to dispense us with the adoption of bolshevism.

Mustafa Kemal Atatürk, statement to
General James Harbord, October 15, 1919

Our point of view and our principles, you all know, are not Bolshevik principles, and we never thought and attempted up to now to have our nation accept Bolshevik principles. . . . Our point of view—i.e. populism—holds that force, power, sovereignty, and rule are given directly to the people and are in the hands of the people. Indeed, there is no doubt that this is one of the world's most powerful and basic principles. Naturally such a principle does not contradict Bolshevik principles. . . . Our nationalism in any event is not an egoistic and proud nationalism; and, especially because we are Muslims, we have a community feeling from the Islamic point of view that transposes the limited compass which nationalism circumscribes into a limitless field. Especially from this point of view, the Bolshevik course can seem to be in our direction. Bolshevism represents the view of a class of people who are oppressed in a country. Our nation, indeed, is oppressed and tyrannized as a whole. In this regard, our nation, too, is worthy of protection by the forces which are undertaking the salvation of humanity [i.e. the Bolsheviks].

Mustafa Kemal Atatürk, statement to the
Grand National Assembly, August 14, 1920

Communism in Turkey has attracted little attention outside of Soviet literature. This is not surprising. Except for an initial flurry of anxiety during the struggle for independence, when it was feared that Turkey might slip into the Soviet orbit, there has not seemed any cause for concern. From the first, communists in Turkey were subject to frequent repression. Their top leaders were wiped out in January 1921 while on the way to Anatolia. Since 1925, the Turkish Communist Party has been banned. The tiny nucleus that continued to function was obliged to operate far underground; only from the safety of foreign sanctuary has anyone dared openly to speak in the party's name. Nor were the few front organizations formed over the years by the handful of dedicated adherents more successful in evading the vigilant eyes of the government. Particularly with the deterioration of Turkish-Soviet relations after the Second World War, identification with the Soviet Union seriously handicapped communist efforts to gain respectability. In short, measured by its ability to build an organization capable of competing effectively in the political arena, the Turkish Communist Party must be judged a resounding failure.

With this perspective, both Western and Turkish writers have generally regarded communism in Turkey as a subject more of curiosity than of substance. Dismissing the obviously inflated claims of Soviet authors that a mass movement toward communism was ever in the offing, most Western observers and Turks alike have appeared to accept the assumption that age-old antipathy for Russia rendered Turkey impervious to political ideas from the north. As a result, the view has gained wide currency that communist efforts in Turkey during the early 1920s were carried on almost exclusively by a tiny émigré party based in Baku. Seen from this angle, the Ankara government's original toleration of communist activity is usually explained as merely a device to secure military and financial aid from the Soviet regime in Russia, which had a parallel, but by no means identical, interest in opposing the Western powers. Great prominence is thus generally accorded the ease and the thoroughness with which the Ankara regime was able to root out all vestiges of communist influence once the most critical phases of the Turkish struggle for independence had been safely passed. And in this scheme of things, Turkey's short-lived Communist Party is not commonly credited with any lasting impact on the Turkish scene.

Until recently, it has been difficult to go much beyond this widely held appraisal. Turkey's great national leader, Mustafa Kemal Atatürk, himself devoted no little pains to obfuscating the issue. His public utterances about the communist movement were not altogether consistent, and were always deliberately designed for their political effect rather than for their illumination. The coloring he imparted to Turkish history through his monumental speech delivered in 1927, recounting his version of the struggle for independence, has powerfully influenced all subsequent studies of Republican Turkey. But Atatürk was concerned primarily with building a consensus among the elite in favor of his nationalist reformist movement. To this end, he focused his attention sharply on the Kemalist movement, with himself at the center; he made no effort to present a balanced view of the other forces at work. Yet his stamp of approval on this approach to Turkish history long discouraged Turkish researchers from probing their own records for other evidence.

Nor have the Soviets done what they might have to clarify the issue. For the most part, they have been reluctant to use the extensive Turkish communist materials in their archives, at least until Western or Turkish scholars have given such material currency. Even where Soviet writers have imparted new information on special facets of communist experience in Turkey, their treatment has been much too uneven to prove a reliable guide to Turkish reality.

In the past few years, however, the situation has changed materially. Following the military coup in 1960, the scope of ideological debate in Turkey broadened dramatically. Furthermore, the passing of Stalinism in the USSR and the maturing of the Cold War paved the way for a relaxation of Turkish fears of the Soviet Union. This atmosphere promoted an outpouring of memoirs and documents from former communists and observers of the early party experience in Turkey which for the first time shed considerable light on the communist movement. Today, Turkish students are themselves beginning to delve into the copious original sources—journals and publications of the party—that have been preserved. And after years of relative scarcity an ever increasing flood of material is becoming available.

Thanks to these developments, it is now possible to draw quite a different picture of communist activity in Turkey.

The Turkish Communist Party emerged from the confluence of three distinct strains of communism. In both Western and Soviet literature the émigré movement that Mustafa Subhi organized from among prisoners of war and internees in Russia has received quite undeserved prominence. For while Subhi's organization dispatched agents to operate on Turkish soil, he and his followers never succeeded effectively in dominating the indigenous communist groups. Following the demise of Subhi and his closest associates at the start of 1921, the remnants of their organization were absorbed by the Communist Party in Istanbul. The Istanbul movement, which grew up under French influence during the Allied occupation after the First World War, ultimately became the dominant strain. It produced the main Turkish communist ideologists, whose independence of spirit and pronounced nationalist bias caused the Comintern constant concern during the early years of the party. The third element of the Turkish communist movement unfolded in Anatolia in more direct contact with Subhi's party. Its proximity to Atatürk's base of power brought it almost from the first into conflict with the Kemalist regime and led to the early destruction of this branch of the party.

Communism, to be sure, never succeeded in becoming a mass movement. Yet at one point during the early phases of the struggle for independence, the communists seemed to be almost on the threshold of achieving power. At this time, communist leaders managed to establish a special relationship with key partisan units that formed the main military force of the Anatolian revolutionary movement. These communist-influenced forces posed such a significant challenge to the Ankara regime that Atatürk felt constrained to form his own "official" Turkish Communist Party in an effort to bring this burgeoning communist movement under his control. But this threat remained acute until, following a shake-up of the top military command on the western front, his newly organized regular troops finally succeeded in smashing these partisan units in pitched battle. Hence, contrary to Atatürk's easy assurances to General Harbord, it was not the inherent nature of Islam, nor Turkish tradition, nor Turkey's social structure that blocked the spread of communism. Rather it required the forceful action of a determined nationalist regime to turn back this threat.

Although since 1921 the communists have never been able to muster an imposing political organization, they have nevertheless continued to play a role of some significance in Turkey. As we will demonstrate, communism in Turkey was by no means a completely artificial plant. As an intellectual movement, as a vision of historical development, communism has ever had a considerable fascination for Turks. It grew on the same intellectual soil that nourished the flowering of Kemalism, the revolutionary program that ordered the development of Republican Turkey. For at the time that the First Turkish Republic was formed, a major dialogue was under way between those who saw Turkey's destiny hitched exclusively to the West and those who felt that the East (including principally Soviet Russia) was about to triumph over the "decadent" West. These "Easternizers" were bolstered by the impact of the Russian Revolution, which dramatized the hitherto untested political power of communism; no one in Turkey could be sure at this point that the Bolshevik vision of world revolution would not in fact come to pass. Moreover, in these early days Turkish receptiveness to communist ideas was undoubtedly increased by the warmth of state-to-state relations. Revolutionary Russia, like revolutionary Turkey, took great pains to disassociate itself from its past. At this juncture both were locked in a life or death struggle against the West; both were seeking a magic formula for rapid development in order to meet this urgent challenge.

This constellation of circumstances made it hard for the Turkish nationalist leaders to handle the problem of communism in Turkey. On the one hand, the fledgling Ankara regime initially saw the communists as an indispensable link in securing Soviet aid in the struggle against the Western invaders. But even after mid-1921, when the Communist Party no longer served as a necessary intermediary, treatment of the communist movement remained a delicate issue in Soviet-Turkish relations. Moscow was reluctant to disown those who professed allegiance to communism. At least until the end of the Turkish struggle for independence, the Kremlin apparently continued to use its influence to urge special handling of the communists in Turkey. And in this situation the Turkish communists found themselves alternatively jailed or feted with an almost bewildering arbitrariness.

Unquestionably the inner circle of the Turkish nationalist leadership always harbored profound suspicion of the local communists and sharply distinguished between friendship with the Soviet state and encouragement of the communist movement at home. While Mustafa Kemal Atatürk might on occasion lapse into communist jargon or lavishly extol the Soviet regime and what it stood for, this did not signify any weakening in his opposition to the communists within his own country. In appearance, however, the Ankara government's policy toward communism was confusing in these early years. Indeed, it was often difficult for Turks outside the national leadership to draw the line where Kemalism stopped and communism began.

The communist movement drew its adherents mainly from among those who, like Atatürk himself, saw the ultimate salvation of Turkey in rapid and radical social reform. During the struggle for independence, however, Atatürk recognized the necessity for relegating social reform to a very subordinate position in order not to alienate the conservative elements in Turkey whose support was vital to the success of the nationalist cause. Some of the more impatient devotees of reform chafed under this slow pace. For them, the slogans of communist doctrine offered an appealing answer to their aspirations, a shorter path than Kemalism to carry out their dreams in an effective way. The communist example was attractive also to those of Turkey's educated elite who were highly frustrated at being too far from the center of power to have a sense of personal participation in the Kemalist revolution. Thus it was primarily those who were either outside the Anatolian movement looking in (e.g., those Turks who had been interned in Russia during the First World War) or who were only on the fringes of the nationalist movement (e.g., those in Istanbul and those involved in the partisan movement associated with the Green Army) that strayed into the communist fold. It is to such frustrated and impatient elements of the elite that communism in Turkey has always found its greatest appeal.

After the destruction of the communist power base among the partisans, communism became almost exclusively an intellectual movement. While the party in Istanbul devoted considerable energy to efforts to organize support among the workers, only among the intellectual elite did it accomplish any lasting results. *Aydınlık,* the party's organ in Istanbul, became the center for a vigorous band of radically-minded younger elements who were destined to play a major role in Turkey's ideological development long after the final suppression of the Communist Party. For as Kemal Karpat has indicated in the perceptive chapter on communism in his *Turkey's Politics,* it was exponents of this point of view who first systematically diagnosed Turkey's social and economic problems, offering attractively simple and clear-cut answers for the country's needs. Their prescription for rapid economic advance without sacrificing social justice has powerfully influenced the thinking of development-minded Turks ever since.

The banning of the party in 1925 and the arrest of its leaders, while not completely ending underground activity, did effectively cripple the Communist Party. Kemalist pressure on the one hand, coupled with ideological and personality disputes within the party on the other, led a nucleus of former writers for *Aydınlık* to leave the communist movement. And in the 1930s this group of renegade communists re-emerged to found the *Kadro* movement. The Kadroists attempted in systematic, though unorthodox (in communist terms), fashion to meld aspects of Soviet experience into Kemalist doctrine. For a time their work enjoyed the blessing of Atatürk and of other top government leaders; it unquestionably became one of the most influential intellectual experiments in modern Turkish history. The ideas that the *Kadro* founders brought from their earlier communist experience not only enriched the Kemalism of the 1930s, but have served as a font for much of Turkey's present ideological ferment.

Thus far the term "communism" has been used without any effort to define what it meant in the Turkey of the 1920s. This is no mean task. Communism in Russia in this period was itself in a state of extreme flux. Even after the Comintern finally elaborated its own criteria, the Soviets themselves found it difficult to decide which of the several interrelated and/or competing movements that laid claim to communist orthodoxy was indeed the "Turkish Communist Party." Few of the many in Turkey who sought to capitalize on the name "Communism" had any firsthand knowledge of what was happening in Russia. Even those who adopted the name in all sincerity displayed varying appreciations of what communism might mean—some going so far as to equate it with the religious bases of Islam. Others were clearly opportunists, seeking to exploit the name either to bolster their own prestige or to ensure their control over whatever communist movement developed in Turkey.

Yet by 1925, the end of the period of main concern in this work, this confusion had largely cleared. Both in the Soviet Union and in Turkey, communism had taken on a more coherent character. True, the Turkish communists had not yet openly labeled their organization the "Turkish Communist Party." They still preferred instead to work behind the informal façade of the *Aydınlık* group. Nevertheless, this group was both recognized by the Comintern as its sole representative in Turkey and was subjected to some measure of control from Moscow as well. Communist activity in Turkey therefore came to conform ever more and more strictly to the pattern of the world-wide movement.

The picture of communist activity in Turkey is then exceedingly involved. To bring it into meaningful focus, it is appropriate to start rather far afield: to investigate in brief compass the myriad sources of inspiration that flowed into this main stream. Inasmuch as communism in Turkey was—and, to the extent it still exists, is even today—primarily an intellectual movement, this study must properly begin with a consideration of the radical intellectual currents that took form toward the end of the Ottoman Empire. With this background we will then attempt to unravel the complexities of the groups in Turkey that either called themselves communist or were in fact controlled by members of the Turkish Communist Party. Though this analysis still leaves many unanswered questions, it nevertheless has much to contribute to an understanding of the development of the attitudes and outlook of the Turkish elite today. Such an understanding is essential for any deep appreciation of the modern Turkish scene.

CHAPTER I

Revolution and Reform

Be firm, tireless, and persistent; this business demands always steadfastness and sincerity.
Jean Jaurès, letter to Ottoman Socialist
Party leader Hüseyin Hilmi, 1910

We are revolutionaries, because we want revolution. The first revolution was achieved by ripping the foundations of tyranny from the hands of Sultan Hamid. The second revolution, in turn, will be possible by changing human society from top to bottom, indeed by forming it anew.
Dr. Refik Nevzat, *Beşeriyet*

The last years of the nineteenth century saw social and intellectual developments that laid the groundwork for the emergence of communism in the early 1920s. When Abdul Hamid II assumed the throne in 1876, the problems of bolstering the sagging fabric of the Ottoman Empire had reached critical dimensions. The Empire was on the verge of a disastrous war. Its finances were muddled to the point of bankruptcy. And every day it slipped further under foreign control. With the institution of the Ottoman Public Debt Administration and the flagrant abuse of the "Capitulations," originally granted to foreigners as the boon of a powerful ruler, the Sultan had virtually abdicated economic independence. Indeed, the "Sick Man of Europe" was being kept alive more through the rivalry of the various claimants to his dominions than through any internal vitality of his own.

To meet these challenges, Abdul Hamid set the Empire on a course that, contrary to his expectations, would lead to his own destruction and to a prolonged crisis of legitimacy. His policies, moreover, paved the way for the dramatic upsurge of interest in political and social reform that accompanied the Young Turk revolution and culminated in the Kemalist movement.

Abdul Hamid sought the salvation of the Empire in two directions that ultimately proved incompatible. On the one hand, he recognized that to hope to match the power of the West it would be necessary to undertake a program of selective borrowing from abroad and to reform such native institutions as the administrative and educational systems. At the same time, he was convinced that, having come to the throne by irregular means, he must tighten his own autocratic control. He was especially fearful of the inflow of liberal Western political ideas. These he hoped to exclude by imposing rigid censorship, by establishing a vast secret police and informer network, by exiling known liberals, and by rigorously closing the borders of the Empire. In sum, he was attempting to bring into being a more efficient and much more highly centralized regime, but without making concessions to the political aspirations of the elite on whom he had to depend for the modernization of the country.

These efforts were perforce self-defeating. His new secular schools designed to produce officers who could hold their own against modern Europe became hotbeds of revolutionary ideas from the West. The revolutionaries he exiled abroad maintained extensive contacts within the Empire and flooded his domains with subversive literature, often using for this purpose the extraterritorial foreign postal system over which the Sultan had no control. Even his diplomats abroad served as a channel for the influx of new political ideas.

Among the most significant influences that filtered into the Empire were European, particularly French, sociological theories. These were espoused often with almost religious fervor by the Turkish educated elite. Awed by Western science, these Turks found especially attractive the notion that social development followed regular rules that could be deduced by the scientific methods applicable to the natural sciences. Thus, both in Abdul Hamid's time and especially in the Young Turk period that followed, much effort was expended in attempting to adapt such sociological doctrines as those of Auguste Comte and Emile Durkheim to fit the needs of the multinational Ottoman Empire. It was this positivist sociological approach that prepared the ground for the introduction of Marxism with its pseudoscientific theory of development.

These ideas were still very much in the process of shaking down when the Young Turk revolution of 1908 burst out, bringing in its wake a continuing crisis of regime. During their decade in power, the Young Turks were never truly able to establish their legitimacy. The regime remained to the end a potpourri of competing and increasingly incompatible movements.

By far the strongest political organization to emerge during this period was the Committee of Union and Progress. Originally a secret body controlling the government from behind the scenes, it soon evolved into an open political party dedicated to the Turkification of the multinational Empire. And as its policies encountered resistance, the Committee reacted with increasing harshness. While, in the first flush of rejoicing at the overthrow of the Sultan, freedom of debate was virtually unlimited, after the abortive counterrevolution in the spring of 1909, the Committee gradually moved to suppress criticism. But even after the triumvirate of Talât, Cemal, and Enver pashas finally squashed all vestiges of political opposition in 1913, the grand debate over the future of the Empire continued.

The Young Turk period was one of experimentation. No longer did the traditions that had governed political activity under the Sultans hold sway. The 1908 revolution unleashed a ground swell of concern with social issues which partly caused and partly was itself the result of a dramatic broadening of involvement in political and social activity.

Almost immediately after the restoration of the constitution, for example, a wave of strikes broke out, first among the railroad workers of European Turkey and Western Anatolia, then among other transport and factory workers of these regions. This strike movement quickly gained such momentum that the Young Turks felt constrained as a first order of business to pass a Temporary Labor Law on October 8, 1908, which, though quite restrictive, did accord minimal recognition to the rights of workers. Parliament subsequently enacted a more comprehensive labor act on August 9, 1909, confirming the right of workers to organize under certain restrictions, but restating prohibitions on strikes in "public service" enterprises. This legislation in its essentials was to govern labor activity until after the Republic had been proclaimed.[1]

One of the beneficiaries of this social ferment was the nascent socialist movement, which was to provide a testing ground for ideas and personalities that were later to figure in the development of communism.

Inside the Empire the first to be caught up in the socialist current were the non-Muslim minorities—the Armenians, the Bulgarians, the Jews, and the Greeks. These communities were far more closely bound up with Europe than were the Turks, having already been involved in the international socialist movement for some years before the 1908 revolution. About the turn of the century, the Bulgarian Social Democratic Worker Party joined the Second International and began socialist agitation in European Turkey. Shortly thereafter, the Dashnaktsutiun Armenian revolutionary party adopted a Marxist-oriented program and in 1907 likewise joined the Second International.

Both the Armenian and Bulgarian parties took advantage

of the political freedom introduced by the Young Turk revolution to step up their activity. Only a few months after the event, a group of Armenian socialists from Turkey were received into the Second International as a "subsection" of the "Turkish section," which had then not yet been formed. Under these influences, the Armenian and Bulgarian communities in the Empire in November 1908 elected a small group of self-confessed socialists among their representatives to the newly restored Ottoman Parliament.[2]

For the first few years after the 1908 revolution, Salonika rather than Istanbul stood out as the pre-eminent center of socialist activity in the Empire. Here the large Jewish community played the predominant role. Immediately following the revolution, a number of socialist and labor organizations sprang up, formed largely along communal lines. On October 2, 1908, the Jewish intellectual study group led by Abraam Benaroya merged with the small body of Bulgarian socialists in Salonika to form the Socialist Club. This united organization issued an appeal in four languages calling the working class of the whole Ottoman Empire to join in one common socialist party.[3]

The achievement of such a country-wide unified party was an incredibly ambitious goal, especially given the cracks which appeared in the Salonika movement from the first. Heavily outnumbered, the Bulgarians never felt at ease with their Jewish colleagues. Both the Greeks and the Turks were slow to join. Only the Jews responded with any enthusiasm, and, thanks to their numbers, the Socialist Club became an organization of some prominence in Salonika.

Yet, despite the indifference of the other communities, Benaroya officially proclaimed the formation of the Salonika Socialist Workers Federation in mid-March 1909 and continued the effort to operate on the larger scene. As a first step, the Salonika socialists thus issued a so-called "May Appeal to

All Workers of Turkey," calling for a modest program of political and social reforms. This was followed on June 6, 1909, by a meeting allegedly attended by some 5,000 workers of various nationalites from the Salonika region at which Armenian and Bulgarian socialist deputies protested the government's draft labor law, which provided for continuation of existing restrictions on the right to organize unions and to strike. The Federation's success in fielding demonstrations, proved once again during the celebration of the anniversary of the 1908 revolution in Salonika, encouraged Benaroya to step up his multicommunal propaganda campaign. After a fund drive had raised sufficient money to launch a weekly journal, Benaroya on August 27, 1909, inaugurated the *Amele Gazetesi* (Workers Gazette), published in four languages—Turkish, Greek, Bulgarian, and Ladino. But this experiment proved short-lived. Following the fourth issue, the Greek-Turkish edition edited by the Turkish poet Rasim Haşmet was dropped. With the ninth issue funds ran out altogether and the journal was forced to cease publication. Thereafter the Federation was reduced to printing for its Jewish members a Ladino weekly, *La Solidaridad Ouvradera* (Workers Solidarity).[4]

By this time, too, the centrifugal forces of nationality had broken the Salonika socialist movement into bits. In November 1909 all but a handful of the Bulgarians left the Federation, probably to pass over into the Bulgarian Social Democratic Workers Party, whose leader, Vasil Glavinov, had been sharply attacking the Federation for some time. Torn by these rivalries, the socialists were obliged in 1910 to let May Day pass all but unnoticed in Salonika. Nor were any of the various rival socialist organizations here able to compose themselves sufficiently to accept the invitation of the International Socialist Bureau to attend the congress at Copenhagen in August.[5]

Other socialist groups in the cities of Macedonia and Thrace were equally unsuccessful in sublimating their ethnic antagonisms. For, in the nationality crisis of the closing days of the Ottoman Empire, it was clearly almost impossible even for socialists to bury their rivalries for long.

Immature though it may have been as a political force, the socialist movement nonetheless seems to have had significant influence on the ideas of the "Turkist" movement then beginning to flower in Salonika. Here it was that Ziya Gökalp and his followers made their headquarters until the outbreak of the Balkan Wars. Just at this critical period Gökalp was elaborating the bases for his Turkish nationalist intellectual school which was soon to displace Ottomanism as the prevailing current among the Turkish elements of the Empire. In the process of this probing and searching the Salonika socialists played an important role. Rasim Haşmet, for one, turned Gökalp's *Yeni Felsefe Mecmuası* (New Philosophical Review) and other influential Salonika publications into forums to attack capitalism and to explain socialist concepts. Through these activities the Turkists became acquainted with Marx and the main leaders of the international socialist movement. Gökalp's group evidently found the notion of radical social reform particularly congenial, and devoted considerable attention to reconciling socialist and nationalist ideas. Like most socialists of the day, the Turkists understood socialism far more in its social and economic aspects than as an internationalist doctrine. Their efforts to introduce a radical socialist leaven into the dough of Turkish nationalism contributed significantly to preparing for the future development of Kemalism. Moreover, the mixture they compounded would later facilitate the transition from Turkish nationalism to communism for such major figures as Mustafa Subhi, Ethem Nejat, and Şevket Süreyya Aydemir.[6]

Elsewhere, too, those who had been interested in socialism

even before the 1908 revolution now came out into the open. Almost immediately after the restoration of the constitution, Mehmet Mecit and a tiny group of socialists in Izmir began to publish the newspaper *Irgat* (Worker) in Turkish and Greek as the first step toward forming a socialist party. Mecit was arrested in 1909, however; and, as the atmosphere in Izmir clearly did not promise well for such a venture, this publication was evidently shifted to Istanbul.[7]

Istanbul, the largest intellectual and labor center in the Empire, rapidly became a focus of socialist activity. The movement here, as elsewhere, took root first in multicommunal groups led by Greeks, Bulgarians, Armenians, and Jews. These socialists lost no time in becoming involved in the rash of small labor associations and clubs formed for the most part along communal lines that sprang up following the revolution.

Most prominent of these was the multicommunal "Socialist Center"—probably identical with the 11-member "Social Democratic Party" cited by some sources—which came into being on May Day 1909, with the aim of educating "the labour classes of Constantinople." The Center apparently served as something of a board of directors for socialist activity, particularly among the non-Turkish population. It maintained contact with the Bulgarian and Jewish socialists of Salonika and soon established relations with the International Socialist Bureau in Brussels. At the same time, under the influence of the Center, an active, albeit small-scale, socialist press began to emerge. Toward the middle of February 1909, the Greek socialist G. Constantinides, who may indeed have been involved with the Center, undertook to publish *İşçiler Gazetesi* (The Workers Gazette) in Turkish. This publication, which appeared weekly for most of the rest of that year, was printed in somewhat more simple and more readable style than that of its counterpart in Salonika. On occasion its articles were even reprinted in some of the major Turkish dailies, where they received considerable circulation. The appearance of *İşçiler Gazetesi* was followed soon thereafter by that of the socialist weekly *Nor Hossang* (New Current), which the Armenian Henchak leader Kozikian, a member of the Socialist Center, began to publish with pretensions to lead not only the Armenian community, but workers of all the Empire's nationalities as well. The following June, Socialist Center leader N. Giannios opened the semimonthly *O Ergatis* (The Worker), which is said to have been the Greek edition of *Irgat*. It, too, continued until the end of that year.[8]

Such was the attraction of this heady doctrine that socialist ideas soon came to be debated in the larger circulation Turkish press of Istanbul. By the summer of 1909, the noted grammarian, Ahmet Cevat Emre, was already calling for far-reaching social reform in articles he contributed to the leading daily *Sabah* (Morning). Emre openly equated revolution with progress, and warned that it would be a truly difficult task "to improve the nation." *Tanin* (Echo), whose staff then included future Turkish Communist Party founder Mustafa Subhi, followed suit with articles attempting to explain socialism, "a creed whose nature like that of all social questions is not yet fully known in our land." Even the attacks of the Bulgarian and Armenian socialist deputies against the Young Turk government served as convenient pegs for editorials analyzing socialist doctrine.[9]

Under these circumstances, it was not long before a group of predominantly Turkish socialists began to form in Istanbul around the controversial figure of Hüseyin Hilmi. Hilmi has been much maligned in both Soviet and Turkish accounts as an opportunist who fastened onto the socialist cause merely in order to attract attention. To be sure, this interpretation has much to commend it. It is true that in his later years Hilmi used his position for personal gain and even entered into some sort of secret compact with the British occupation forces. Yet, on the other hand, he did use his resulting ability to play off the British against the French to facilitate the growth of the socialist movement in Istanbul. Moreover, to discredit Hilmi's whole career on these grounds does not do justice to his remarkable persistence or to his considerable organizational achievements. His appreciation of socialist concepts may have remained quite crude, never progressing much beyond facile slogans; but his willingness to champion this cause at no little personal risk cannot be denied. Despite many arrests, he always returned to the fray.

Originally from Izmir, where he had worked as a security official and subsequently published the newspaper *Serbest İzmir* (Free Izmir) prior to the 1908 revolution, Hilmi apparently first became interested in socialism more or less by accident. According to one version, his involvement dated from observing a socialist demonstration while on a trip to Romania. Be that as it may, his interest was strongly reinforced by the influence of his close friend Baha Tevfik, who had been attracted to German materialism at the Political Sciences Faculty in Istanbul.[10]

But it was the French, rather than the German, socialist movement that formed the main source of inspiration for Hilmi and his associates. Before fully embarking on the socialist cause, Hilmi came to Paris to seek—and receive—the blessing of French socialist leader Jean Jaurès for his work in Turkey. From Jaurès Hilmi procured also the program of the French Parti Socialiste along with other books and pamphlets on the French movement to use in drawing up the program for a Turkish counterpart.[11]

The small but active group that Hilmi assembled at this time did not immediately rush to form a party. Instead, it chose first to prepare the ground through a weekly journal called *İştirak* (Collectivism), which Hilmi began to publish in February 1910. On occasion this journal presented rather revolutionary ideas. In its third issue, for example, exhorting workers to unite, it repeated the aphorism of the early Young Turk leader, Abdullah Cevdet:

One must perform ablutions in order to appear in the sublime presence of the queen of liberty. But what a pity that these ablutions must be made with blood.[12]

In general, however, *İştirak* proved moderate in tone and theoretical in content. Even its articles translated from the French often represented a liberal reformist outlook rather than a strictly speaking socialist point of view.

When this rather scholastic fare did not prove financially self-supporting, Hilmi agreed in mid-June 1910 to print a sensational special issue condemning the murder of Ahmet Samim, editor of *Sadai Millet* (Voice of the Nation) . Samim may in fact have been a sympathizer of Hilmi's group, though he can hardly have been a member of the Ottoman Socialist Party as some claim, inasmuch as that party had not yet come into existence. Samim's wanton assassination dramatized the determination of the Committee of Union and Progress to intimidate its critics. In line with this policy, *İştirak* was immediately suspended by the government for its audacity. Undaunted, however, Hilmi and his followers two months later sought to circumvent the ban by publishing under a new title, *İnsaniyet* (Humanity) , a name copied from the Parisian socialist paper *l'Humanité*. But after the government thereupon lifted *İştirak's* suspension, the journal reverted to its former title. And *İştirak's* reappearance in September 1910 was followed in short order by the announcement of the formation of the Ottoman Socialist Party (Osmanlı Sosyalist Fırkası), the first predominantly Turkish organization to espouse the socialist cause.[13]

For all its intellectual vigor, however, socialism was by no means a mass movement. Even in the minority communities, workers did not flock to support the movement, despite the more or less insistent attempts of socialist leaders to appeal to ethnic sensibilities. Particularly in the Turkish community, labor was not yet a force of any magnitude. Few industrial concerns employed more than a handful of workers. Moreover, most workers retained strong ties to their peasant communities. Many worked merely during the slack agricultural season, returning to their villages at harvest time. Even the few tens of thousands of full-time workers remained almost totally bound by the prevailing conservative peasant attitudes. They were largely inured to their hard lot and had minimal expectations. Thus the socialist agitators found it all but impossible to wean any sizable number from their traditional value system.

As a result, the Ottoman Socialist Party drew its membership from a very specialized milieu: journalists (a relatively new profession in Turkey, hence one not yet hidebound by tradition), students (especially those who had been educated in France), and to a lesser extent members of the other free professions (mainly medicine and teaching). Though these elements did not occupy as commanding a position in society as they were later to acquire, the party did wield influence somewhat disproportionate to its tiny size. Despite continual harassment by the government, which forced the party to field a number of journals in rapid succession, its press outlets and members in the educational world were able to carry on fairly extensive propaganda. Notably, however, the Ottoman Socialist Party was unable to command the allegiance of a single deputy in Parliament. For despite the urging of the Turkish socialist leaders, the Armenian and Bulgarian socialist deputies refused to shed their nationalist particularism.

In addition to its organization in Istanbul, the Ottoman

Socialist Party boasted a branch in Paris as well. Here, even before Hilmi's party had taken final shape, Dr. Refik Nevzat had already begun forming a circle of Turks interested in socialism. Dr. Nevzat had broken with the Committee of Union and Progress soon after the 1908 revolution, thereafter falling progressively under the spell of the French socialist movement. Although his group of émigrés agreed to join forces with Hilmi and ultimately recognized themselves as a branch of the Ottoman Socialist Party, the Paris branch maintained virtually complete autonomy. To the end, the views of Dr. Nevzat's band remained considerably more radical than those of its Istanbul headquarters, fitting much more closely into the mold of European socialism. Indeed, the Paris group conducted a nearly independent liaison with the Second International in the name of the party.[14]

The Ottoman Socialist Party was never able to weld its diverse membership into a coherent and well-disciplined body. Its members spanned the spectrum in their varying appreciations of socialism. Some merely identified it with progress and Western culture. Others appeared quite revolutionary. For example, Hilmi's mentor Baha Tevfik approvingly recited Marx's dictum on force as the "midwife" of social change. Hilmi, on the other hand, proved to be one of the earliest proponents of the view identifying socialism with the tenets of Islam. His primary aim was to endow socialism with the stamp of religious authority—though there were others echoing this line who were interested rather in bolstering the faltering prestige of Islam by association with a new vital force. Yet the Ottoman Socialist Party welcomed all these differing interpretations.[15]

Nevertheless, within the party there was general agreement on some fundamental points. First, the Committee of Union and Progress had not lived up to expectations; it must be

made to leave office. (Indeed, some of the more extreme
elements spoke of revolution as the means to accomplish
this end.) This was to be accompanied by a number of basic
social reforms. Prominent among these was the demand that
capital be taken from the hands of the few and shared among
the poor. The party called for progressive taxes, free education, nationalization of major industries, and legislation to
secure workers' rights. Moreover, under the influence of
the noted European radical socialist Parvus (Alexander
Helphand), who emphasized the harmful European economic exploitation of the Empire, the socialists soon began
to attack the Capitulations and to formulate the bases of an
etatist economic policy.[16]

Parvus was the first prominent European socialist to
sojourn in Turkey. After an active and promising career,
primarily in Germany, Parvus had fallen out with the German Social Democratic Party. In the fall of 1910, therefore,
he came to Istanbul, where he immediately became active in
the local socialist milieu, forging close relations not only
with deputies from the minority communities, but with a
wide range of Turks as well. To be sure, Parvus was by this
time already drifting away from the more extreme implications of his theory of "permanent revolution." However, his
continued preoccupation with antiimperialism soon en-
deared him to the Turkists, who were to publish many of
his articles in their *Türk Yurdu* (Turkish Homeland) and
other organs.[17]

With the formation of the Ottoman Socialist Party, the
attitude of the Committee of Union and Progress rapidly
hardened. For some time, the Committee had been suspicious
of the separatist overtones of the socialist movement among
the minorities, particularly in Salonika. Now, as the socialists became more and more active, even going so far as to
encourage workers to strike for political ends, the govern-

ment saw itself faced with a burgeoning subversive conspiracy. In October 1910, therefore, the Young Turk government closed the socialist clubs that had been organized principally from among the minority communities in Salonika and Istanbul. Likewise, the various socialist press organs were obliged to stop publication. Even the persistent efforts of Hilmi's group to change the name of its journal, first to *Sosyalist* (Socialist), then to *İnsaniyet,* and finally to *Medeniyet* (Civilization), were in the end unavailing. By mid-December, though the party was not formally dissolved, its activity came to a complete halt. Hilmi as well as socialist leaders from the minority communities were arrested, fined, and exiled for a time to Kastamonu.[18]

This set back the socialist movement, especially in Istanbul. Farther from the government's watchful eyes, however, in Salonika and other cities of European Turkey the government's action was evidently much less effective. For example, in December 1910 a gathering of representatives of Macedonian organizations convened in Salonika in an effort to forge a united social democratic party. This meeting, which had only the most token representation, if any, from the Turks of the Empire, ended in sharp disagreement. National antagonisms again proved stronger than the internationalist principles of socialist doctrine. To the Young Turks, however, the determination of the minority groups to persist in their work must have argued for increasing vigilance against all forms of socialist activity. Indeed, Benaroya and three colleagues, one a Turk, were arrested on the eve of the Sultan's last visit to Salonika in the summer of 1911 on the pretext that they were plotting his assassination. Benaroya was now exiled to Serbia; and in the ensuing crackdown on socialists from the minority communities, Socialist Center leader N. Giannios was also forced to leave the country.[19]

With the temporary eclipse of the Ottoman Socialist Party

inside Turkey, Dr. Nevzat's branch in Paris came into its own. As best it could from a distance, it took over the function of directing the party, now for all intents and purposes underground. In the fall of 1911, therefore, Dr. Nevzat launched the monthly *Beşeriyet* (Humanity), which was to appear until conditions inside Turkey again permitted the revival of socialist organs. *Beşeriyet* not only expressed the more radical views of the Paris émigrés, but also reported on party activities inside the Empire, even printing a telegram sent by Hilmi from exile. The Paris branch continued also to represent the party at gatherings of the International Socialist Bureau. In fact, on November 5, 1911, it organized a meeting in Paris to protest the start of the Tripolitan War. Moreover, in line with its new responsibilities, Dr. Nevzat's group published its own reform program in February 1912, voicing even more radical demands than had the Istanbul section of the party. This campaign of unremitting opposition to the Committee of Union and Progress was to continue until the outbreak of the First World War put a damper on socialist activity even in France.[20]

Inside the Empire, most of the Ottoman socialists who had escaped arrest soon became convinced that under these circumstances the formation of a united opposition offered the best chance for effective resistance to the Committee of Union and Progress. Yet for all their small number, the socialists could not now agree on which party to support. As a result, many joined the Party of Liberty and Conciliation (or *Entente Libérale* as it styled itself in French), which had been founded by some of Hilmi's close friends. This party, however, never really managed to organize effectively. By 1912, the government had reduced it, too, to nearly complete impotence. Other socialists gravitated into alliance with the Turkist nationalist movement, which began to display increased vigor with Ziya Gökalp's arrival in Istanbul in 1912.

The influence of this socialist influx was especially apparent in the small National Constitutional Party (Millî Meşrutiyet Fırkası) organized in mid-1912 by the editors of the Istanbul newspaper *İfham* (Explanation) and such prominent Turkists as Yusuf Akçura, who had long been interested in social reform. Future Communist leader Mustafa Subhi, who had by this time left *Tanin* to become an associate editor of *İfham,* played an active role in the party. In conjunction with the newly formed Turkish Hearth organization (Türk Ocağı), the National Constitutional Party now launched the National Consumption Society (İstihlak Millî Cemiyeti), a nationalist etatist economic association that gave concrete expression to the teachings of Parvus. A surprisingly accurate foretaste of Kemalist economic policy, this society called for bolstering Turkey's native industrial capacity by the consumption of Turkish goods only. Moreover, though its boycott of foreign products remained ineffectual, it did enjoy some unofficial sympathy among senior government officials, who found this blend of socialist and nationalist ideas particularly appealing.[21]

The socialist movement, however, had not completely lost its old identity. When the chance came in conjunction with the temporary ouster from power in mid-1912 of the Committee of Union and Progress by a group of liberal officers, the Ottoman Socialist Party quickly re-emerged. Hilmi returned from exile. Taking advantage of the more relaxed climate of expression, on June 20, 1912, he revived the party's organ, *İştirak,* first as a biweekly periodical, then as a slim newspaper appearing several times a week. *İştirak,* with a new cadre of contributors, including some Greeks, became increasingly caught up in the wave of Turkish patriotism that accompanied the outbreak of the First Balkan War in October 1912.

Among the minority communities, socialist activity revived as well. Worker clubs and organizations like Benaroya's Federation in Salonika took advantage of this permissive atmosphere to become active again. Having changed its name at Parvus' suggestion to the "Group for the Study of the Social Sciences," the "Social Democratic Party" now also secured permission to reopen in Istanbul. Socialists from all communities joined in celebrating May Day, 1912. Even *O Ergatis* may have reappeared, now allegedly under the direction of a Frenchman named Coupette. And these socialists from the minority communities, too, heartily condemned the prospect of war in the Balkans. In September 1912, they joined with their Balkan counterparts to issue a manifesto not only castigating the European capitalists, but attacking the Turkish government as well for its "religious fanaticism and Mohammedan chauvinism." This resolution was approved by the extraordinary socialist congress in Basel in November of the same year.[22]

From a political point of view, however, this ferment was ill-timed. The Savior Officers were not able to stabilize their regime. By the end of January 1913, the Committee of Union and Progress had again come to dominate the government. Socialist activity was strictly curtailed. And when Enver Pasha and his colleagues imposed their authoritarian rule in June 1913, they put an end to all opposition political activity. Many opposition figures, including Hüseyin Hilmi and most of the Ottoman Socialist Party leaders, were exiled to the interior. At the same time, Mustafa Subhi and his fellow members of the National Constitutional Party were banished to Sinop as part of the wholesale suppression of political dissent. This enforced moratorium on organized political expression was to last until the end of the First World War.

Yet the mash of socialist and nationalist ideas in the Ottoman Empire continued to ferment. If anything, the First World War stimulated the development of Turkish national consciousness. Ziya Gökalp and his associates turned the schools into forums for their ideas. But not only was Ottomanism finally discredited by the experience of the war; noteworthy steps toward social reform took place as well. The educational system was reorganized, a feminist movement began to take shape, and in general, social awakening gained momentum during these years of enforced political inactivity.

Even the triumvirate showed their respect for the power of the socialist movement, at least outside Turkey. Hoping to forestall condemnation by the International Socialist Bureau, whose Armenian section was already strongly lobbying for dissolution of the Ottoman Empire after the war should end, they permitted some "tame" professors who claimed to represent a revived "Socialist Party" to go to the International Socialist Conference at Stockholm in 1917. At the initial sessions in the spring, Medical School Professor Dr. Hüseyin Zade Ali, Law Faculty Professor Nissim Mazliyah, and Dr. Akıl Muhtar represented Turkey. When the Conference reconvened in August, Nissim Mazliyah returned, this time with Salâh Cimcoz. But their efforts were in vain. Though they presented a note to the Conference calling for "a just and durable peace" on the basis of the principle of "no annexations and no indemnities" formulated by the "Petrograd Soviet of Workers and Soldiers," the Conference refused to accept them as delegates. To add insult to injury, this conclave voted a resolution opposing any effort to return the Armenian provinces, Mesopotamia, and

Arabia to Turkish rule, and excoriated the Young Turks for being a tool of European imperialism.[23]

On their return to Istanbul, this "tame" socialist experiment disintegrated. Not until the end of the First World War would this ferment again be able to break surface.

CHAPTER II

The Coming of Communism

We can say without fear that "a nationalist can very well be a socialist." In fact, he can be an internationalist socialist.
"Zenon," İdrak, May 10, 1919

Our country cannot remain aloof from the currents of the times. Neither the lack of organization of the Turkish proletariat nor the claim that Turkey is a peasant country, rather than a country of industry and factories, can lead to the conclusion that the system of socialism which confronts us today resting on completely new and scientific principles cannot be applied in Turkey.
Mehmet Vehbi Sarıdal, Kurtuluş, September 1919

The Turkish Worker and Peasant Socialist Party defends and protects the economic rights and interests of Turkey's workers and peasants according to the principles of scientific socialism.
Turkish Worker and Peasant Socialist Party Statutes, article one

Turkey at the end of the First World War presented a fertile field for revolutionary activity. Defeat had dealt a deathblow to the multinational Ottoman Empire. Gone, too, was the firm restraining hand of the triumvirate who had fled in disgrace. While the Sultan and his palace clique sought to fill the resulting political vacuum, they were fitted neither by experience nor by ability for this monumental task. Moreover, although no Turkish heartland had been captured during the war, immediately after the end of hostilities the Entente established control of key urban and coastal areas. Nor were the Great Powers, preoccupied as they were with the details of their treaty with Germany, in any hurry to work out a final peace settlement with the Ottoman Empire. Further unsettling for the Turks were revelations published by the Bolshevik Russian regime documenting the intention of the Great Powers to divide the Empire into protectorates and spheres of influence.

In these circumstances, the ferment which had been working underground during the Young Turk period came out into the open. The debate over the future of the Empire was renewed, but with a greatly enhanced sense of urgency. No one now argued for reconstitution of the Empire. It was obvious that only the predominantly Turkish areas could be salvaged from the wreckage. Yet in the hopelessness of defeat, many found it hardly credible that the remnants of the once-proud Empire could successfully defy the might of the Western world. These, therefore, saw their hope of salvation only in the protection of a Great Power mandate. On the other hand, there were those who believed that if they acquiesced gracefully to Entente desires, the occupying powers would soon leave Turkey to its own devices. Prominent among this school of thought were the Sultan and his court.

The prospect that Turkish heartland would pass under the control of former subject peoples, viz. the Armenians and the Greeks, injected a new note. As this threat became increasingly clear, the Turkist nationalist movement received powerful impetus. Throughout the country local resistance organizations sprang into being.

Mustafa Kemal Atatürk, although not by any means the originator of this popular upsurge, immediately grasped its significance. Trading on his brilliant military record, he maneuvered assignment as Commander of the Sultan's forces in Anatolia, where he could work away from the close supervision of the Great Powers. His move was superbly timed: just as Atatürk reached Anatolia in mid-May 1919, Greek troops, egged on by the Entente, occupied Izmir. Taking advantage of the widespread anger generated by the Greek landing, Atatürk soon managed to unite the nationalist movement under his unquestioned leadership and to set up a "Representative Committee" tantamount to an independent government in Anatolia.

At the same time, Turkey was by no means isolated from the wave of unrest touched off by the Russian Revolution. Already by the closing days of the war, Ziya Gökalp was describing Bolshevism as "the Red Danger." Others, like M. Zekeriya Sertel, who would many years later emerge as a prominent communist sympathizer, took a more sympathetic view of the titanic force they perceived in the upheaval in Russia. As early as August 1918, Sertel was writing that Bolshevism, "which desires to upset the present social order, destroy European classes, divide wealth equally among all citizens, and end all present political and economic institutions, will compel the European states to end the war" just as it had the Tsarist regime in Russia. Sertel, discerning a wave of worker revolts sweeping over Europe, predicted that socialist groups would eventually come to power all over the world. And he concluded that "only by this path can peace come to Europe."[1]

But news of the troublesome events in Russia came to Turkey more directly as well. Refugees from Russia began to stream through Istanbul in flight from the Soviet regime. Turks who had been taken prisoner or interned by the Tsarist government during the war also trickled back to their homeland in an ever-swelling flood. For example, in mid-1919 two boats are said to have reached Istanbul with a more or less well indoctrinated cargo of "Turkish workers" from Russia. And all these brought tales of the revolution and of the movements toward self-determination in the states along the borderlands of the Russian Empire that were seeking to break free.[2]

The impact of this revolutionary ferment was greatly

intensified by the return of several thousand students and skilled laborers whom the Young Turks had sent to Germany during the war. Many of these had witnessed the social upheaval in Germany immediately after the close of the war; some had even participated in radical socialist and communist activity there. These were the so-called Turkish "Spartakists," a rather loosely applied appelation not connoting any organic relationship with the German Spartakusbund. When they returned to Turkey, these Spartakists carried their revolutionary attitudes not only to Istanbul, but to the principal provincial cities of Anatolia as well, where they contributed to the burgeoning partisan resistance movement and sparked the creation of socialist groups.[3]

In train with these developments, the first group in Turkey that might properly be called communist was organized in Istanbul in October 1918, largely from among the non-Turkish population. Its chief leader, an instructor from the School of Agriculture named Gensberg, was to remain active in the communist movement in Istanbul for some years to come. Associated with Gensberg in this endeavor were such other future communist notables as Serafim Maximos and Kâzım from Van. Maximos was a budding labor agitator of Greek extraction whose activity before he appeared in Istanbul is something of a mystery. Kâzım had passed the war in France, where he had become involved with the Parti Socialiste. It was, in fact, with credentials from this party that he had arrived in Istanbul to begin labor agitation among the railroad workers.[4]

This group spread propaganda in favor of the Bolshevik revolution in Russia and attacked both the Sultan's government and the Entente. It apparently concentrated its work in educational and labor circles, being especially active among workers of foreign concerns like the Istanbul Streetcar Company owned by French and Belgian interests. Indeed, it may have been the activity of Gensberg's circle that prompted the demand by some Istanbul University students—if such an event actually did take place—that Lenin be awarded the Nobel Peace Prize, an incident which Turkish delegate Mustafa Subhi proudly related to the First Congress of the Comintern in March 1919. The police, however, soon got wind of this agitation. The government thereupon reimposed censorship, and in February 1919 arrested Gensberg along with some of his colleagues. With these arrests, the tiny group disintegrated, having sown seeds that would continue to germinate, particularly in the fertile soil of the Istanbul minority communities.[5]

Similar activity, though of a considerably less radical nature at least at first, was under way among the predominantly Turkish population of the Empire as well.

First to organize was an extremely moderate party, the Social Democratic Party (Sosyal Demokrat Fırkası). This party, which was formed on December 23, 1918, by Dr. Hasan Rıza and some former government officials in Istanbul, advanced a program giving considerable attention to labor matters. From the first, however, it demonstrated little vitality. Yet for want of a better alternative, it attracted one adherent who would later make his mark on the communist movement: Zinniatulla Navshirvanov (or, as he was known in Turkey during this period, Ziynetullah Nevşirvan). Navshirvanov's early life has remained obscure, though he is frequently called a Tatar from Russia, a term that was then often used to embrace Azerbaijanis as well. At the end of the First World War, he turned up in Istanbul as a university student. How he became drawn into the socialist movement is a mystery, but already in the early postwar years he was exploring socialist doctrine from a Marxist, internationalist point of view. Approaching Marxism with almost religious fervor, he was apparently driven by a compulsion to tear down the "old" and embrace the "new."[6] His outlook seems so well developed when he made his first appearance that it seems likely that he had been involved in socialist or communist activity, probably in Russia, before arriving in Istanbul.

Shortly after the Social Democrat Party became active, Hüseyin Hilmi reappeared on the scene. In February 1919 he revived his long-suppressed party, this time under the title of the Turkish Socialist Party (Türkiye Sosyalist Fırkası). Initially well received, this party managed to set up several branches in Istanbul and to reactivate its Paris branch under Dr. Refik Nevzat. For a time it was active in Eskişehir as well, where from 1919 to 1921 it apparently published the paper İşçi (Worker).

Associated with Hilmi in the Turkish Socialist Party were some who were rather extreme in outlook. Among the more active elements in the party was Sadrettin Celâl Antel, a former instructor at the Adana Normal School who was teaching in Istanbul at this time. Antel had studied pedagogy at the Sorbonne, where he is said to have come under the influence of Swiss anarchists. His views, like those of a number of future top communist leaders, had been further refined during the Young Turk period in controversy with Gökalp over educational values. Already before the end of the First World War, Antel had begun calling for the introduction of a broad system of secular education to destroy the traditional orientation of the masses in order to prepare them for modern life. With this background, he was soon to find the Turkish Socialist Party too tame for his tastes.[7]

While continuing many of the demands of the past, the Turkish Socialist Party called for much more sweeping social reforms than had its predecessor. Its program now went so far as to advocate the nationalization of the means of production and distribution, though this point was never emphasized in the party's propaganda and could hardly have been advanced with any seriousness. For Hilmi's party was essentially evolutionary in approach; it supported joining with other socialist parties in an international movement as the most effective way of carrying out its program. To this end, the party dispatched delegates from its Paris branch to participate in the gatherings of European socialists in 1919 that sought to restore the international solidarity disrupted by the First World War. Here the Turkish Socialist Party lined itself on the side of the socialists in opposition to the nascent Third International.[8]

For a time in the spring and summer of 1919, Hilmi's Socialist Party held the spotlight in these intellectual circles. Toward the end of April 1919, Hilmi began to publish *İdrak* (Perception) as his party's organ. Like *İştirak* in its last days, this daily concerned itself more with the issues of practical politics than with theoretical analyses of socialism. *İdrak* was especially persistent in attacking the traditional guild organizations still active in Istanbul. Its articles betrayed also Hilmi's continuing interest in identifying socialism with Islam. Moreover, as virtually the sole radical organ of this sort in Istanbul at this period, *İdrak* became a forum for all of this persuasion. In its issue of May 10, 1919, for example, it even published under the acronym "Zenon" Navshirvanov's memorable article "Can a Nationalist Be a Socialist," in which he argued that socialism was an essential requirement of true nationalism![9]

But Hilmi's party was not long to enjoy this privileged position.

Already in the spring of 1919 what was ultimately to prove the most important communist organization in Turkey was taking shape among Turkish students in Germany. Here a group of Turks, heavily influenced by German Marxism, had begun to attempt to adapt to Turkish reality the heady social doctrine they had encountered in Germany. To this end, they began, on the one hand, to organize the so-called Turkish Worker Association (Türkiye İşçi Derneği) among the young workers who had been sent to Germany for technical training. At the same time, they formed a companion political body, the Turkish Worker and Peasant Party (Türkiye İşçi ve Çiftçi Fırkası), and undertook to publish a theoretical journal, *Kurtuluş* (Liberation) in Berlin. The first issue of *Kurtuluş*, which made its debut on May Day 1919, carried the party's proclamation "To the Proletariat of All Countries." This manifesto had a strong nationalist cast, identifying the Turks with the proletariat and condemning the Entente governments as agents of the bourgeoisie.[10]

True to the pattern of the past, the Berlin party enfolded figures of the most diverse outlook. Their only unifying theme was their determination to save Turkey from domination by the West and to see their country take a respected position in the community of nations. Some of this party's members (e.g., Mehmet Vehbi Sarıdal and Nurullah Esat Sümer) might be best described as progressive nationalists, interested in modernizing Turkey. They later became prominent in the Kemalist movement. Others were budding industrialists and financiers, whose education had concentrated heavily on economics. Among these were İlhami Nafiz Pamir (eventually to become Director General of the Sumer Bank), who edited *Kurtuluş* in Berlin, and Mümtaz Fazlı Taylan (later to become a businessman representing Western interests in Turkey), who contributed to the May Day issue a biography of Karl Marx. Besides these not untypical figures, there were, of course, a group of "intellectuals" whose dabbling in Marxism was to prove no passing fancy. For such men as Vedat Nedim Tör, Ethem Nejat, and Hilmioğlu İsmail Hakkı, this experience was to mark their lives, and they were to become drawn ever more deeply into the movement inside Turkey.[11]

Even as the first issue of *Kurtuluş* was still in the presses, most of those involved were preparing to return home. Their task, as they saw it, could be performed only in Turkey. So they joined in the general exodus of Turks from Germany that took place in May 1919.

Once in Istanbul, the group wasted no time in applying for official permission for their party. Initially they met a firm rebuff. But when they submitted a second application, the government interposed no objection. It was, then, with the tacit acquiescence of the Istanbul authorities, rather than with their formal approval, that the Turkish Worker and Peasant Socialist Party (Türkiye İşçi ve Çiftçi Sosyalist Fırkası) came into being in September 1919, the term "socialist" having been added to its title perhaps in hopes of increasing the party's appeal among the educated elite. Without delay, the party revived *Kurtuluş*. It was to appear monthly in Istanbul until the advent of the British military occupation the following spring. Thus was launched the party that, while Marxist rather than specifically communist, was to serve as a rallying point for all communist-oriented elements of the Turkish community in Istanbul. In fact, for some years prior to its final suppression by the Kemalist government in 1925, this organization was to become a but thinly-veiled front for the Turkish Communist Party.[12]

Several of the leading lights of the Turkish Worker and Peasant Socialist Party were destined to play prominent roles in the Turkish communist movement. One was Ethem Nejat, an extremely cultivated educator who had passed the closing days of Abdul Hamid's rule in France and the United States. Though of Circassian descent on his mother's side, he had become a fervent Turkophile and was active in the Turkist

movement in Eskişehir after 1910. At the end of the First
World War, Nejat went to Germany under the auspices of
the Publications Office of the Ministry of Education. Here
he was rapidly drawn into the German socialist orbit and became a mainspring of the *Kurtuluş* group, widely respected
as an elder—he was born in 1887—as well as for his wealth of
foreign experience. He returned to Istanbul in 1919, a convinced revolutionary socialist, but not yet perhaps a true
communicant of Moscow. For to be sure, he had not shaken
off all vestiges of what an associate in the movement termed
his "petty bourgeois" outlook.[13]

A newer recruit to the movement, having joined only after
the Turkish Worker and Peasant Socialist Party had been
transferred to Istanbul, was Dr. Şefik Hüsnü Deymer. Deymer, a Dönme (i.e., of a family of Jewish converts to Islam)
from Salonika, had studied medicine in France before the
First World War. Here he had come under the influence of
the French socialist party, becoming a disciple of left-wing
leader Jean Jaurès, a collection of whose writings he brought
back to Istanbul at the end of his studies. Following his return, he served as a military doctor during the war. Deymer
was a gifted organizer and an accomplished theoretician,
rather than a rabble rouser or spellbinding orator. With his
already well-developed socialist outlook, it was only natural
that he rapidly ingratiate himself with the returnees from
Germany and become one of the principal founders of the
Turkish Worker and Peasant Socialist Party. The same age
as Nejat, he, too, was one of the senior members of the
Kurtuluş group and immediately assumed a commanding
position in the party, becoming its secretary general. Within
a very short time, he had become the acknowledged leader
of the Turkish communist movement, a distinction he would
hold for the next 40 years.[14]

At first, of course, the Turkish Worker and Peasant Socialist Party did not seem markedly different from its rivals. All the various socialist bodies then active in Turkey owed something of a common debt to Marxism. Yet at this period Marxist socialism was by no means thoroughly digested by any of its protagonists. It is doubtful that even those few who then considered themselves communists agreed more than superficially about the nature of the creed they had embraced. Nonetheless, the *Kurtuluş* group enjoyed a certain advantage over socialists of other hues. The admixture of peculiarly Bolshevik traits from Russia and, far more importantly, of radical socialist precepts from Europe contributed just that dash of authority—or snob appeal—that attracted a certain element of the Turkish elite of the day.

The *Kurtuluş* group, indeed, had far more in common with French radical socialism than with Bolshevism. Still largely innocent of the intricacies of Leninist dialectics, these Turkish radical Marxists soon gravitated toward the ideas of Henri Barbusse, the prominent French left-wing socialist. Barbusse's revolutionary philosophy, though perhaps strictly speaking not Marxist at all, seemed to his Turkish audience compellingly relevant to conditions in Turkey. The powerful protest against war voiced in his novel, *Le Feu*, originally published in 1916, made a telling impact on members of this Turkish circle who had seen their country engaged in almost continuous hostilities since 1911. But above all, Barbusse's underlying conviction that "only the enlightened could liberate the unenlightened" evoked a deeply sympathetic response among many segments of the Turkish elite even beyond the *Kurtuluş* milieu. All Turkish Marxists of this period virtually without exception shared Barbusse's impatience and disdain at the shortsightedness and reactionary conservatism of the masses who were to be saved in spite of themselves. Hence the message of *Kurtuluş* was unabashedly and exclusively to the intellectuals—"civil servants, doctors, engineers, writers"—whose duty it was "to equip our young proletariat with an organization and methods of struggle— those most suited to attain the goal."[15]

Under these circumstances, particularly after Refik Nevzat in Paris joined the *Kurtuluş* group in the winter of 1919, Barbusse became a leading influence on the Istanbul Marxists. The leaders of the *Kurtuluş* circle were obviously intrigued by the Clarté movement Barbusse had founded in 1919 to unite "thinkers" of the world "for progress and perfection of ideas in a common front above the hate that politicians seek to continue among races and nations." This was a cause easily comprehensible to Turkish radical Marxists and one in which they eagerly enlisted. *Kurtuluş* now devoted no little space to publicizing the Clarté movement, even publishing its appeal to intellectuals to attend the abortive "First Congress of International Thinkers" which Barbusse had hoped to convene in Bern in mid-1920.[16]

Steeped in this primarily French scholasticism, the leading contributors to *Kurtuluş*, Şefik Hüsnü Deymer and Ethem Nejat, fashioned their lengthy theoretical analyses in a style only faintly reminiscent of the hortatory imperative idiom of Lenin and his followers. Their stated aim of imbuing the proletariat with class consciousness could hardly be achieved through the rather dry intellectual argumentation in *Kurtuluş*, where, for example, pages were devoted to justifying the inclusion of tramps and vagabonds as legitimate elements of the proletariat.* Moreover, despite obvious attempts to simplify their presentation, these writers in their commentaries presupposed such an extensive knowledge of Marxist doctrine as to have been undoubtedly quite incomprehensible

---

* Yet when it came to the hundred thousand refugees from Russia living under miserable conditions in Istanbul camps, *Kurtuluş* bitterly demanded that they suffer for their sins without being provided housing or other necessities of life. *Kurtuluş*, Feb. 19, 1920, no. 5, inside back cover.

outside of the tiny intellectual circle that had produced them. In any event, the government censor would clearly have refused to pass propaganda written in more popular style, exhorting the masses to action. And under these circumstances, besides advertising that the Communist Manifesto would soon appear for the first time translated into Turkish, there was little that the Turkish Worker and Peasant Socialist Party could publish to suggest that it was significantly more radical or dynamic than its competitors.[17]

These were the days when the nationalist movement was unfolding in Anatolia. Its development was in many ways quite slow. The Kemalists exhibited great reluctance to break with the theory of the sultanate and to establish an avowedly independent regime. Thus, although Atatürk did set up a *de facto* government in September 1919 with a mandate from the Sivas Congress, the fiction of the Sultan's supremacy was carefully preserved. In keeping with this, in the winter of 1919 the nationalists participated in the elections to reconstitute Parliament. Here, profiting from the surge of patriotic emotion aroused by the Greek landing in Izmir, Atatürk's supporters swept the lists in most places. But while Atatürk refused to risk placing himself within the Sultan's reach in Istanbul, the bulk of the nationalist deputies did convene in Istanbul, where they participated in Parliament until the British dissolved that body in the spring of 1920.

These parliamentary elections offered the radical socialists new opportunities. Ethem Nejat now insisted that the Turkish Worker and Peasant Socialist Party form a united front with the other socialist organizations in order to enhance the party's electoral chances. His supporters attempted to infiltrate the Turkish Socialist Party, whose leadership was unwilling to fall in with the idea of a united front. Also, the Worker and Peasant party attempted to mobilize worker support through the Turkish Worker Association, which, after its transfer from Germany, had taken root principally among workers of Turkish origin in the government munitions factories. These efforts led to a mass meeting on October 24, 1919, at which members of other socialist and labor groups joined in protesting the two-stage electoral system, calling for its replacement with a system of direct election on the basis of proportional representation. At this meeting a committee drawn largely from notables in the Turkish Worker and Peasant Socialist Party was formed to "do the necessary to defend and preserve workers' rights in the elections" and to "attempt to assure that workers elect three deputies from Istanbul."[18]

But although Ethem Nejat boldly proclaimed that his cherished united front had come into being with this meeting, the other parties refused to prepare joint slates. Thus, while there continued to be much contact among the various socialist organizations, and while individuals did pass fairly freely from one to another (e.g., Sadrettin Celâl Antel and Zinniatulla Navshirvanov entered the Turkish Worker and Peasant Socialist Party at this time and began contributing to *Kurtuluş*), no effective socialist front could be formed.

As a result, in the 1919 elections, all the various socialist parties ran opposing tickets. The Worker and Peasant party even named candidates in provinces other than Istanbul: Ethem Nejat seems to have run in Eskişehir, Mehmet Vehbi Sarıdal in Istanbul, and the foreman Süleyman in Niğde. But in the confused election atmosphere, of all those who claimed the "socialist" label, only Numan efendi of the so-called Ottoman Labor Party (Osmanlı Mesai Fırkası), a body of uncertain composition and orientation, perhaps sponsored by management, was able to win a seat. Numan, though a foreman at the Zetinburnu ammunition factory, was immediately denounced by the Turkish Socialist Party as being neither a "true worker representative" nor a socialist.[19]

Despite the poor showing of the socialist parties in the elections, their activity did have a significant impact. The great fluidity of the political scene in Istanbul at this juncture permitted extensive relations between Turkish nationalists and socialists of all stripes. In consequence, the nationalists continued to be exposed to increasingly radical socialist ideas. The socialists, on the other hand, ofttimes absorbed a nationalist cast—a process of considerable importance for the future of the communist movement in Turkey.

One of the most important nationalist bodies to come under this influence was the Karakol Society, which had been organized late in 1918 by a group including Baha Sait and Dr. Adnan Adıvar. It was a secret society dedicated to organizing guerrilla resistance bands, and later to supplying the nationalist movement in Anatolia with intelligence and arms. By mid-1919, some of its leaders had apparently established contact with unofficial emissaries—possibly Major (later Marshal) Budennyi, who is said to have met with Atatürk in May 1919 in Anatolia—sent from Soviet Russia to report on the situation in Anatolia. A few months later, Baha Sait, whose office served as the Istanbul headquarters of the Karakol Society, became involved in extensive negotiations with Shalva Eliava, a top ranking Soviet officer who traveled secretly to Istanbul early in the winter of 1919 to explore the possibility of providing military assistance to the Turkish nationalists. In fact, Baha Sait, after proceeding to Baku toward the start of 1920, openly styled himself a member of the Turkish Communist Party; and in Baku on January 10, 1920, he even signed a military assistance pact with the Bolsheviks. When word of this unauthorized transaction reached Ankara, Atatürk repudiated the pact. It was at least in part because of this freewheeling relationship with the Soviets that Atatürk took steps in the spring of 1920 to dissolve the Karakol Society.[20]

Another nationalist organization that showed its debt to the socialist movement was the National Turk Party (Millî Türk Fırkası). Established in December 1919 as a revival of the National Constitutional Party, this organization was intended to unite nationalist and socialist groups in a popular front to contest the elections in support of the Kemalist movement. Its program made striking obeisance to international socialist philosophy. The party called for rejection of "imperialist tendencies" and proclaimed that to achieve proper "socialist development" the state should play an active role in economic life and run the major enterprises in the country. It also demanded labor legislation. While the National Turk Party was heatedly attacked by some circles in Istanbul for its support of the Kemalists, it scored minor success in the elections of 1919: Dr. Adnan Adıvar, one of its six Istanbul candidates, was elected. His victory, to be sure, was far less a tribute to the appeal of the socialist cast of his platform than to his own personal popularity and to his espousal of the Kemalist cause.[21]

The opening of the new Parliament controlled by the Kemalists in January 1920 merely stimulated further ferment. Following their failure in the elections, the communist-oriented elements seem to have turned their attention to the labor movement. For at least among the Turkish laborers it seemed possible to channel anti-Entente emotion into the service of the party. Thus, in collaboration with agents dispatched by the Soviets to carry on underground work (no doubt, primarily, in the rapidly growing colony of refugees from Russia), a meeting was held on February 2, 1920, with representatives of the port workers, porters, and bakers unions. This meeting reportedly proposed the formation of a communist group with a central committee including "communist Tatars"—possibly Zinniatulla Navshirvanov—and Turks who had worked in the Crimea. But, whatever the exact nature of this meeting, it appears doubtful that any such organization was ever able to operate effectively in Istanbul. For the permissive atmosphere that attended the opening of Parliament was not destined to last long.[22]

The full-scale military occupation of Istanbul by the Allies in March 1920 brought an end to this period of freewheeling political activity in the capital. Discouraged by their poor showing in the elections and by the failure of their united front, some of the top leaders of the Turkish Worker and Peasant Socialist Party now set off for Anatolia, where they hoped to be able to work in greater freedom. *Kurtuluş* was closed by the British, and for a period the party apparently ceased activity. Those party members who remained behind were obliged to lie low. For the moment, the center of gravity of the nascent Turkish communist movement had shifted from Istanbul. It would not fully return until the Allied occupation finally came to an end in 1923.

CHAPTER III

Russia and the Turks

In the future course of world revolution the Turkish pro-letariat will occupy an honored place.

Mustafa Subhi, speech to the First Congress
of the Comintern, March 1919

The Turkish Communist Party is of the opinion that in the present situation two political groups exist [in Turkey]. . . .
On the one hand, [there are] *the Freedom and Conciliationists* [i.e., supporters of the Sultan's government] *who are the tools of English policy and, on the other, former Unionists* [i.e., the Kemalists] *who are no different, . . . but who appear in disguise. The Turkish Communist Party declares it has no relations with either government.*

Declaration of the Turkish Communist Party,
July 14, 1920

Outside of Turkey in Russia another communist movement was already taking shape. This strain of communism, unlike that developing in Istanbul, was heavily influenced by its close relationship with the Kremlin. From the first, this émigré movement was subject to the guidance and control of Moscow—though as a result of the vicissitudes of the early years of Bolshevik rule in Russia, these Turkish communists had considerable scope for independent action. Indeed, it remained a constant problem to keep their propensity for independence within bounds. But with the help of a cadre of Soviet Muslims and orientalists, these émigrés were eventually forged into an instrument through which Moscow hoped to be able to bring the communist movement in Anatolia firmly under its control.

The guiding light of the émigré Turkish communist movement was Mevlevizade Mehmet Mustafa Subhi, or Mustafa

Subhi as he was popularly known. Subhi was born in the district of Giresun on the Black Sea coast in 1883, where his father was district governor. Moving with his father from assignment to assignment, he attended a series of provincial schools before finally graduating from Istanbul Law School shortly after the turn of the century. The 1908 revolution found him in Paris studying the problems of agricultural credit in Turkey at the École libre des sciences politiques. Here he wrote a thesis entitled "La banque agricole otto-mane," which formed the basis of a report he presented in 1910 to the International Institute of Agriculture in Rome. Subhi at this point was clearly an economic nationalist who believed that a system of private initiative based on the peas-ant was essential for Turkey's independence. Convinced that agriculture would be "for a long while to come the sole re-source of Turkey," he saw it essential to arrest the impoverish-ment of the peasantry, whose "life-blood" was being "sucked away," primarily by foreigners. In this situation, Subhi argued for expansion of the agricultural bank to provide credit at low interest rates to individual cultivators. He held out the prospect that by so doing, the peasant not only would become prosperous, but would be made "faithful to the constitutional regime" as well.[1]

On graduation in 1910, Subhi returned to Istanbul, where he began teaching law, economics, and sociology. While at first sharing the general enthusiasm for the Young Turk rev-olution, soon, like many of his colleagues, he broke with the Committee of Union and Progress. Some sources even claim that he joined the Ottoman Socialist Party at this time. This seems unlikely. His writings of that period—a translation in 1911 of an analysis of sociology by Durkheim's disciple, Célestin Bouglé, and his own bitter protest against the Italian invasion of Tripoli—show his approach to have been still far more that of Gökalp and the Turkists than that of the Ottoman socialists. However this may be, it was his activity in the National Constitutional Party and as a journalist in *Ifham* that earned him exile to Sinop in 1913 in the general roundup of political dissidents. But taking advantage of the lax controls there, Subhi straightway sought to organize his fellow prisoners in what another participant has dubbed a "national Freemason Society" to work underground to bring down the government. For Subhi shared the then widely held notion that the "international" Freemason Society was the force behind the Committee of Union and Progress.[2]

This design obviously could not be carried out from prison. Thus, toward the beginning of 1914, Subhi engineered a mass escape across the Black Sea to Sevastopol. Here the conspirators separated, some proceeding to Europe, others heading toward Egypt, leaving Subhi in Russia, where he intended to publish a paper among the Turkish ethnic groups in the Caucasus attacking the Young Turk regime.

But before Subhi could carry out his plans to organize opposition to the Ottoman government, the First World War broke out. The Tsarist government interned him as an enemy alien, packing him off first to Kaluga and then to the Urals.

Subhi's experiences in these Russian jails were to mark him for life. On the one hand, under the influence of communist agitation among the prisoners, his appreciation of socialist doctrine deepened. He began to espouse a sort of state socialism something on the order of that advocated by Ferdinand Lassalle. This he still believed could be achieved through reforms within the framework of parliamentary democracy. At the same time, however, Subhi was enthralled by the experience of immersion in the atmosphere of revolutionary plotting endemic to Tsarist prison life of this period. It was a natural outlet for the powerful conspiratorial urge in his make-up: in his fancy he probably came to see himself as the "Lenin of Turkey." In any event, by the time of the October

Mete Tunçay, *Türkiye'de Sol Akımlar, 1908–1925,* Ankara: Sevinç Matbaası, 1967

I. Turkish socialist leader Hüseyin Hilmi

Mete Tunçay, *Türkiye'de Sol Akımlar, 1908–1925,* Ankara: Sevinç Matbaası, 1967

II. Early communist organizer Ethem Nejat

III. Communist Party founder Mustafa Subhi

IV. Hakkı Behiç

VI. Yunus Nadi

V. Mehmet Şükrü

VII. Sheikh Servet Akdağ

GREEN ARMY LEADERS

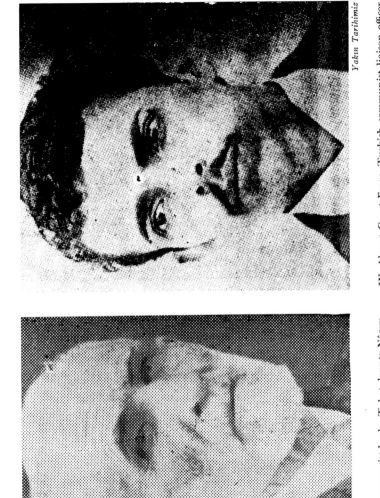

Yakın Tarihimiz

VIII. Ankara communist leader Tokat deputy Nâzım

IX. Ahmet Cevat Emre, Turkish communist liaison officer with the Comintern

X. Ethem, the Circassian, leader of the partisan forces in Turkey

Mete Tunçay, *Türkiye'de Sol Akımlar, 1908–1925*, Ankara: Sevinç Matbaası

XI. Istanbul communist leader Şefik Hüsnü Deymer (right) and Ali Cevdet, Berlin, May 12, 1925

Şevket Süreyya Aydemir, *Suyu Arayan Adam,* Istanbul: Remzi Kitabevi, 1965

XII. Şevket Süreyya Aydemir as a student in the Communist University
of the Toilers of the East, 1922

Revolution in Russia, Subhi was already deeply under the spell of the communist movement.[3]

The revolution brought the problem of the Muslims in Russia to the forefront. Separatist ferment among Russia's Muslims had been apparent even before the Tsar was overthrown. This, therefore, became one of the first matters the new communist regime had to face. In recognition of its importance, moreover, no less a figure than Stalin himself was charged with overseeing this critical area. Following the Kremlin's appeal in December 1917 "To All Muslim Toilers of Russia and the East" to rise up in support of the revolution, Stalin set about to gain control of the burgeoning Muslim separatist movement in Russia. For this purpose, he persuaded Sherif Manatov (a deputy from Bashkiria to the All-Russian Constituent Assembly) and two colleagues to organize the so-called "Muslim Bureau" in Moscow. It was this newly formed body that Subhi joined on his release from prison in the aftermath of the communist accession to power.[4]

For Subhi, the Muslim Bureau represented the avenue to power in the Turkish world that he had been seeking. Thus, while he took part in such ventures as the Tatar paper *Cholpan* (Morning Star), which reflected the views of the "left socialists" among the Tatar and Bashkir communities, he sought also to organize a purely Turkish movement. To this end, Subhi seems first to have founded a Turkish socialist committee to carry on propaganda among the prisoners of war of Turkish extraction who had not yet returned to their homelands. By April 1918, having come to the personal attention of Stalin, Subhi secured backing for a Turkish language newspaper, *Yeni Dünya* (New World), which proclaimed itself "The Turkish Press Opinion of the Central Committee of Muslim Socialists in Moscow."[5] This paper appeared irregularly about once a month, carrying both the theoretical analyses of socialist thought dear to the hearts of

Marxist intellectuals and the sharp attacks on the Sultan's regime which Subhi especially desired. As a result of the latter, it rapidly earned the active protests of the Ottoman Ambassador in Moscow, Galip Kemalî Söylemezoğlu, though few copies probably managed to reach Turkey at this period.[6]

These were days when other foreigners in Russia were organizing to aid the Soviet regime. Under the impress of the example of German and Austrian nationals who convened a congress of their revolutionary organizations of former prisoners in April 1918, Subhi took the initiative to call a similar convention of so-called "Turkish Left Socialists" to meet in Moscow on July 22, 1918.

The 20–30 "Left Socialists" who gathered at this conference were, to be sure, quite a mixed bag, reflecting the varying appreciations of Marxism among Turks in Soviet Russia at that time. Even the staunch supporters of the Soviet Union in this company were divided. On the one hand were ranged activists like Subhi whose main concern was to assemble an effective political machine in order to seize power at the earliest possible opportunity. Opposing were theoreticians who reproached him for concluding tactical alliances with elements who "had scarcely any understanding of socialism."[7] Under these circumstances, and given the presence of a number of participants who viewed the proceedings with considerable scepticism (including the celebrated provocateur Mehmet Rahlitulin sent by the Ottoman Embassy), little lasting accomplishment was possible. Though Subhi voiced the impractical, but irrepressible hope that animated almost all factions for an early "socialist revolution," it proved impossible to agree on a program of action, a matter that was deferred "until the next meeting," scheduled to be held in three months.[8] The sole tangible achievements of the Moscow conference were the proclamation of an "Executive Committee of Turkish Socialist-Communists" to coordinate the various factions on Russian territory and the formation of a "Committee of Agitation and Propaganda." It was not yet possible to announce even in name the start of the "strong Turkish left-socialist organization" Subhi had anticipated in his opening speech.[9]

The disappointment of the Moscow conference did not daunt Subhi. He merely redoubled the pace of his activity. As it increased, so too did his favor with Stalin and his importance in the communist hierarchy. His unswerving loyalty to the interests of the Kremlin at this time, when even some top ranking figures in the Muslim Bureau became infected with separatist aspirations, only further solidified his position in the Soviet power structure. In November 1918, he took part in the first congress of Muslim communists in Moscow, where a Department of International Propaganda for the Eastern Peoples was set up with a special Turkish section. He was elected to the Central Bureau of the Muslim Organizations of the Russian Communist Party; and it was from this position that he first began to elaborate the thesis that the East was the Achilles Heel of the capitalist system. For, while the Kremlin's eyes remained expectantly fixed on Western Europe for the start of world revolution, it was Subhi's contention—one he advanced vigorously at the First Congress of the Comintern in March 1919—that revolution in the East was of central importance in impelling the proletariat of the West to seize power. By revolting against their colonial masters, Subhi believed, the East would deprive the industrial nations in the West of raw materials, thereby generating crises that would inevitably bring down the capitalist system. Thus to Subhi, revolution in the Orient was necessary "not only for the liberation of the East from European imperialism, but for the support of the Russian Revolution as well.[10]

In this scheme of things, return to Anatolia held special

fascination for Subhi. He chafed under the difficulties of communication with the Turkish heartland. Thus, early in 1919 he moved to the Crimea. Here, working underground with the National Party (Millî Fırka), he set up a Crimean Muslim Bureau and continued publication of *Yeni Dünya*. But when, shortly thereafter in June 1919, Denikin's forces retook the Crimea, Subhi and his associates fled first to Odessa and thence to Turkestan. From here tenuous communication with Anatolia was possible at this time through Astrakhan. Despite the disruption of these frequent moves, Subhi's organization persisted in its efforts to disseminate its propaganda in Turkey. Indeed, according to Subhi, two high-ranking communists made their way to Turkey in mid-1919.[11]

Subhi remained almost a year in Turkestan, where he continued publishing *Yeni Dünya*. Here, too, he participated in the formation of the International Eastern Propaganda Council, which aimed to unite all revolutionary organizations in the Orient. Apparently, however, the task of quelling incipient Turkestani dissidence took precedence over his hopes to return to Anatolia. For Moscow had just come to recognize the need for a complete reversal of its policies in Turkestan that had thoroughly alienated the local populace. As part of this effort, Subhi collaborated in infusing more local blood into the Communist Party. And, no doubt owing in large measure to the general improvement in Moscow's fortunes, by the spring of 1920 the Turkestani situation seemed under control.

Soviet policy toward Turkey in this era was vacillating and indecisive. Moscow had not yet shed its illusion that world revolution was just around the corner. Thus preoccupied with the events in the industrialized West, the Kremlin was unwilling to pay much attention to Turkey and the countries of the Middle East and Asia. To be sure, in September 1919, as the Turkish nationalists were meeting in Sivas to forge the bonds of a unified nation-wide movement, the Soviets published an impassioned declaration to the "Workers and Peasants of Turkey." This appeal, however, took no notice of the Kemalists, but merely restated the Soviet belief in imminent world revolution in which the Turks were invited to join. Nor did the intrigues of Karl Radek in Berlin with Enver Pasha reflect any deeper appreciation of reality. From the fastness of his jail cell, Radek was unable to commit the Soviet government to active intervention in Turkey, nor was Enver a figure who inspired great confidence among the Kremlin hierarchy.[12]

The collapse of Denikin's White Army in the spring of 1920 and the progress of Soviet forces toward Turkey's frontier marked a turning point in the fortunes of Subhi's émigré movement.

The Kemalists had long been interested in establishing contact with the Soviet regime. As early as June 1919, almost immediately after landing in Anatolia, Atatürk seems to have met with Soviet Colonel Budennyi, who was on a fact-finding mission in Turkey. Thereafter, Atatürk began sounding out the opinions of the top army command on this issue. While their consensus was cautiously favorable, the commanders emphasized the need for more information about the Soviets before determining any final policy. Following their recommendation, at the end of the summer of 1919 Atatürk dispatched Dr. Fuat Sabit and General Halil Kut to report on the situation in the Caucasus and to make preliminary contact with the Bolsheviks. They, together with such men as former Ottoman Deputy Consul General Yakup, Yusuf Ziya, and Karakol Society representative Baha Sait, soon established a close working relationship with the local underground Bolshevik organizations in the Caucasus. By December 1919, this group of Turks had even initiated irregular contact with Turkestan, where Mustafa Subhi was operating.[13]

As a result of this close cooperation, these Turks fell increasingly under the spell of their communist associates. Indeed, by the start of March 1920, such a staunch Turkish nationalist as Dr. Fuat Sabit confessed to Eastern Front Commander Karabekir, who was in regular communication with the Baku Turks, that he believed it necessary for the Turks of the Caucasus to accept Soviet principles in order to be saved from Georgian and Armenian imperialism. Moreover, when in March 1920 Atatürk encouraged these Turks in Baku to assist the Soviet communist forces in installing a friendly Azerbaijani government that might aid the Anatolian regime, these heretofore loosely associated Turks decided to form a "Turkish Communist Party." With the participation of several "Russian Bolsheviks" they organized a central committee to oversee "operations," publications, and propaganda. This decision was communicated to Karabekir with the request that the Kemalists send a trusted representative to Moscow to coordinate Soviet and Turkish action in the Caucasus. But by the time that Ankara could reply, agreeing to use the Communist Party in Baku as an initial intermediary for contact with the Soviet state until a special delegation could be sent to Moscow, Soviet troops had already "liberated" Azerbaijan and were on Turkey's very doorstep.[14]

It was in these circumstances that Mustafa Subhi arrived in Baku on May 27, 1920, bringing a retinue of followers from Turkestan.

His first concern on reaching Baku was to reform the Turkish Communist Party already existing there to bring it under his control. Dr. Fuat Sabit had by this time departed for Moscow with Halil Kut to carry out the terms of their original instructions, leaving the Turkish communist group that they had thus far largely dominated easy prey for Subhi's machinations. Subhi now replaced the central committee with one in which his loyal followers from Turkestan played a major role. Süleyman Sami, fresh from two years as a teacher in Turkestan, and Mehmet Emin (a Turk from the Caucasus) joined Subhi with Salih Zeki (former District Governor of Zor), İsmail Hakkı (from Kayseri), Captain Nedim Agâh, Yakup, and Tahsin as the new leadership of the party. Subhi also launched an immediate purge of unreliables, striking particularly at former members of the Committee of Union and Progress who had formed an important part of the party's membership. As the party had been woefully deficient in acquaintanceship with the theoretical doctrines of communism, Subhi lost no time in opening a school to train party members in the principles of social revolution. He also dramatically stepped up party propaganda activity, extending the distribution of *Yeni Dünya* in Anatolia, starting a youth publication called *Gençler* (Youths), and publishing several wall newspapers in Baku. In addition, under Subhi's guidance the party undertook an extensive program of translating communist works, ranging from the *ABC's of Communism* and a biography of Lenin to tracts on how to form a Soviet government and instructions for party cells.[15]

At the same time, Subhi was attempting to build up a substantial military force in preparation for an eventual challenge of the nationalist leadership. For this purpose, he incorporated prisoners of war of Turkish extraction into the military unit that he had brought from Turkestan and he sent party organizers throughout Russia to enroll additional recruits. While in Baku, these Turkish troops were directly subordinate to the Eleventh Red Army Command. However, Ali Fuat Cebesoy, who inspected this unit in February 1921 in Baku, concluded that in general its some 1,200 men were quite ignorant of Bolshevik principles, but were eager to return to Anatolia to fight for the nationalist cause. In fact, Cebesoy states that on its return to Anatolia soon afterwards, its personnel served loyally and with distinction on the western front. Once in Anatolia, no doubt, this unit was probably disbanded and absorbed by the then newly formed Turkish regular army, thus losing all traces of its identity as a communist formation. In any event, no evidence has come to light to show that these troops ever attempted to oppose the Kemalists.[16]

As soon as he had refashioned the Baku party to his desires, Subhi moved to extend his influence to Anatolia. Recognizing that the Kemalists were firmly installed as the dominant force in Anatolia, Subhi sent emissaries to Ankara to attempt to persuade Atatürk to permit communist activity in the area under his control. Subhi instructed his agents to offer reassurance that the Turkish communists would support the struggle against the foreign invaders. To this end, the Baku party dispatched Süleyman Sami on June 17, 1920, bearing a letter for Atatürk pledging this support. As a further inducement to Atatürk's cooperation, Sami was instructed to make clear that the "Bolsheviks would channel all the aid they could extend to Turkey through this [Turkish communist] committee." Shortly thereafter a second envoy, Salih Zeki, was sent by a different route with an even more explicit request for permission to organize the party and to carry on social propaganda—though with the assurance that these activities would not disturb the Kemalist defense effort. Moreover, these messages were followed in the middle of August 1920 by a letter from Narimanov, Chairman of the Central Committee of the Azerbaijan SSR, pledging the support of "Muslim communists" for the Turkish nationalist movement.[17]

These assurances to the contrary, the Baku party's true position toward the Anatolian nationalists was marked by considerable hostility. In mid-July 1920, after the arrival of Ethem Nejat and Hilmioğlu İsmail Hakkı, who had apparently stopped off in Anatolia to organize pro-communist groups in Eskişehir, the Turkish Communist Party in Baku issued a strong declaration condemning the deceit of the Kemalists, whose "masked nationalist" representatives (Bekir Sami and Yusuf Kemal Tengirşenk) had just passed through Baku on their way to Moscow as the first official delegation of the Ankara government to the Kremlin. Moreover, Subhi had instructed both Süleyman Sami and Salih Zeki to work intensively to organize sympathizers and to establish a party apparatus without waiting for the Kemalist government's permission. Thus Süleyman Sami, for example, made contact with Veterinary Major Hacıoğlu Salih, who was then working closely with Sherif Manatov, who had come to Ankara from Russia as the representative of the Bashkir Republic. Sami offered financial aid to their group, which was quietly organizing Moscow-oriented communists. In addition, Subhi's envoys invited representatives from every region they visited to a Turkish Communist Party conclave following the First Congress of the Peoples of the East in September 1920.[18]

So active were the delegates of the Baku party that Atatürk became concerned. In Parliament he openly complained that Turkey's security was threatened by this freewheeling communist agitation and propaganda. While, in private communications to Mustafa Subhi, Atatürk reportedly did agree that the Baku leaders might keep in close contact with Anatolia, he apparently refused to allow them to hold their party congress on Turkish soil. Moreover, he strongly cautioned Subhi against engaging in "premature and superfluous actions which could destroy the unity and resistance of the nation," explaining that for this reason "the Grand National Assembly of Turkey was carrying out social revolution slowly and carefully." And in order to protect Turkey's interests Atatürk arranged that Cevat Dursunoğlu and other personalities loyal to him attend the Turkish communist congress in Baku.[19]

The convocation first of the Congress of the Peoples of the

East and then of the Congress of the Turkish Communist Party illustrated a certain dilemma for the Kremlin. On the one hand, Moscow was coming to appreciate the services of the Anatolian nationalist movement in diverting resources which the Entente might otherwise have thrown against the Soviet regime. At the same time, the Soviets felt keenly their diplomatic isolation. The overtures of the Ankara government were the first to hold out the prospect of recognition. Moreover, the Kremlin leaders nourished the hope that Turkey's prestige in the Muslim world might lead large sections of the East, if not into the Soviet orbit, at least into revolt against the Great Powers of Europe. Finally Lenin's doctrine on "national liberation" movements dictated active efforts to woo the Kemalists. And these larger considerations perforce took precedence over the luxury of openly sponsoring movements to overthrow Atatürk's regime.[20]

But while desirous of supporting the "bourgeois" nationalists in their independence movement, the communists were committed to prepare for the day that would come after the victory of the nationalists when a showdown with the Kemalists would be necessary. This was a delicate balance to strike. As the Soviets themselves recognized, this ambivalent attitude cost the communists dear. Though those in the thick of the fray appreciated the need to avoid alarming the Kemalists, it was only too easy to become carried away with their own revoltuionary propaganda. In order to give their nascent movement a feeling of identity, the Turkish communist leaders constantly felt impelled to proclaim in public the need to prepare to seize power after the imperialists had been routed. Naturally such pronouncements did little to inspire trust among the Kemalist leaders.

Far from the heat of battle, at international gatherings like the Second Congress of the Comintern, it was easier for the communists to follow a measured line. It was at this congress that one of the delegates from the Turkish Communist Party in Baku, Hilmioğlu İsmail Hakkı (who was accorded the title "Pasha" in the official minutes), calmly exposed the Communist Party's intention to cooperate with Atatürk's "national liberation" movement:

The Anatolian movement, which is at the present moment headed by the democratic parties, is the best response to that shameless exploitation to which Turkey was subjected by the Entente. . . . The revolutionary government in Anatolia, which is grouping around it all the anti-Entente forces, and which is imbued with a long-standing hatred towards imperialism, is now preparing to enter upon a struggle against European Imperialism.[21]

In Baku, however, it was a different story. There, in September 1920, Turkish communists gathered first for the Congress of the Peoples of the East. This body heard messages from Enver Pasha and İbrahim Tali Öngören, semi-official representative of the Ankara regime, both of whom insisted that the movement in Anatolia was a true revolution and not merely a bourgeois nationalist struggle. Béla Kun thereupon introduced a motion affirming support to the Kemalists as a "national revolutionary movement." However, he warned that this "nationalist revolutionary movement is directed solely against foreign exploiters, and its success is far from signifying the liberation of the Turkish peasantry and workers from exploitation and oppression of all sorts." Thus he directed the Congress to summon "the peasants and workers of Turkey to close ranks in an independent organization," and inveighed against trusting "those leaders of the movement, who in the past led Turkish workers and peasants to the slaughterhouse in the interests of an imperialist group." His warning was underscored by the eminent Soviet orientalist Mikhail Pavlovich Velt'man, who bluntly taxed the Ankara regime for its policy of expansion in the Kars, Ardahan, and Batum areas. He called for the establishment of Soviet power in Turkey as well as in the states of the Caucasus.[22]

The Congress of the Turkish Communist Party, which opened on September 10, 1920, clearly revealed the difficulties inherent in the doctrine of "wars of national liberation." Before this audience, Mustafa Subhi, perhaps in an effort to soften the impact of the excesses at the Congress of the Peoples of the East, took some pains to maintain a balanced line. He warned specifically against the "left-wing" heresy of demanding the immediate establishment of Soviet power in Turkey as well as cautioning against right-wing deviations that would turn the party into a typical "bourgeois-nationalist" organization. The solution he advocated was to urge the formation of a popular front in Turkey. Moreover, even in the proclamation "To the Workers of Turkey" issued by the Turkish Communist Congress, there was no mention of "revolution." This nine-point declaration confined itself to such modest demands as the right to strike, the right to vote, improvement of working conditions, and agrarian reform. Yet at the same time, the Party Congress could not forego reiterating that its cooperation with the Kemalists was only a temporary expedient. Subhi himself confirmed the Congress resolution which declared that its real task was to prepare the ground for the seizure of power by the working class.[23]

This gathering of the Turkish communists also laid bare the gap that separated the tiny hard-core professional revolutionary cadre of the party from the mass of its hangers-on and sympathizers. For in Baku many of the 125 delegates and guests assembled were simply unrepatriated prisoners of war seeking a way to return home. Şevket Süreyya Aydemir, who attended the Congress as a delegate from Azerbaijan and was soon to join the party, graphically described the heterogeneous assemblage in his *Suyu Arayan Adam*. In contrast to the

professionals, mostly from the Istanbul group that had studied
in Germany or the internees from Russia, were those who
called for defending the Sultan-Caliph and for deference to
the religious bases of Islam. Nor did the bulk of those present
perceive any incongruity in the then widely prevalent notion,
expounded by an Imam at the Congress, that Lenin had
modeled his "Creed of Communism" on the principles of
Islam. The Russian woman Stasova, who had been elected
to the Soviet of Action and Propaganda in the East, attempted
to reconcile these sharply conflicting points of view. But she
was over her head amid the welter of dialects and confusion
generated by the speakers: she was even found applauding
appeals for the stricter seclusion of women![24]

Though the Congress thus gave little clear guide to the
party line, it did mark a step in the long process of creating
a coherent and disciplined party organization in Anatolia.
In the first place, it saw the formal linkage of the émigré and
Istanbul organizations. These in future would form the main
line of communist development in Turkey. As witness to
this unity, the Congress elected a unified central committee,
with Mustafa Subhi as Chairman and Ethem Nejat as Secretary General. In addition, it set up a Secretariat, a Propaganda Bureau, and a Foreign Bureau (to handle relations
with the Comintern). But while the central committee hoped
soon to transfer its headquarters to Anatolia—a move for
which it had received permission from the Ankara government in August—for the moment the party headquarters
remained in Baku.[25]

Yet, for all its sound and fury, the Communist Party that
met in Baku was but a tiny nucleus for a unified movement.
It was in no sense a mass organization. Though the Congress
boasted the attendance of representatives of more than a
dozen local communist organizations in Anatolia, in fact

many of these delegates were no more than what today might be called "fellow travelers." Some were simply agents sent by the Kemalists to monitor the proceedings. Others came merely out of curiosity. And the organizations they represented were for the most part equally unsubstantial.

CHAPTER IV

Revolt In Anatolia

The greatest enemy, the enemy of enemies, is not any nation or other; on the contrary, it is the calamity of "Capitalism" and its child "Imperialism" that rule the whole world in a kind of world-wide Jewish sultanate.
                    Hâkimiyeti Milliye, July 20, 1920

Blind imitation is bad in everything, especially in revolution.
                    Hâkimiyeti Milliye, October 13, 1920

Come, comrades, come! Workers and peasants wake up and say that we, too, want to see the humane principles of Bolshevism in our country!
        Nizamettin Nazif Tepedelenlioğlu, declaration
        to "Eskişehir Workers," December 1920

The goal of communism is everywhere the same. Communists the world over help each other.
        Tokat deputy Nâzım, statement at his trial,
        April-May, 1921

In Turkey the Russian Revolution was welcomed as the end of Russian expansionist aims to the south. Particularly with the start of the Turkish struggle for independence, many Turks felt a certain kinship between their revolution and that of their Bolshevik neighbors. Not only did the Turkish intelligentsia tend to regard the experiment in Russia with friendly sympathy rather than alarm, but even extreme Turkish nationalists were inclined to believe that Soviet experience might have lessons applicable in Turkey. On the popular level, it was widely assumed that communism was merely a restatement of Islam, emphasizing the injunction to share one's goods with the poor. Indeed, Soviet observers in Anatolia complained somewhat petulantly about the difficulties in overcoming the general misapprehension that *Das*

Kapital was little more than a translation of the Koran. In these circumstances, it is not surprising that the Russian Revolution and communism encountered little antipathy in Anatolia during these confused days of the start of the national liberation struggle.[1]

Defeat in the First World War had produced a wave of dissatisfaction with the West. This reaction against the political encroachments of Europe crystallized in a school of thought that has been called the "Eastern Ideal." The exponents of this view held that Western civilization had become decadent and would soon be destroyed. In contrast, they glorified the Orient as the center of a new civilization already in its birth pangs. It was still too early to determine the pattern of this new growth, but by its very genesis it was pulling down the old order. On this basis, the "Easternizers" urged that Turkey should throw in her lot with the "East" to avoid destruction, perhaps taking the Russian Revolution as a model. The protagonists of this school, a small group of theoretical Marxists and idealistic intellectuals, had no practical conception of what Bolshevism would mean in Turkey. They were primarily concerned with liberation from the West. Many, if not almost all, envisaged a Turkey free of direct the Russian control as well.[2]

Since the end of December 1919, when Atatürk made it the unofficial headquarters of the nationalist movement, Ankara had become the center of political activity in Anatolia. As such, it attracted the inevitable quota of pressure groups and power seekers. Among these figured prominently "Easternizers" of the most fanatic stripe.

Shortly after the Grand National Assembly opened in April 1920, for example, Vakkas Ferit, a former District Governor whose university experience had led him to radical socialism, was already hard at work. In the words of an eyewitness:

Vakkas bey . . . went from table to table in the municipal gardens in front of the Assembly haranguing the deputies with fiery words in favor of communism. He suggested that it was the only way to salvation. . . . Vakkas gave such a philosophic explanation, with such sweet expressions and smiling face, that not only those at our table, but even those far away listened to him.[3]

This propaganda fell on receptive soil. By this time, the nationalists had already made overtures to the Soviets for material and moral support. As its first international act, the Ankara Assembly on April 26, 1920 had dispatched a request for Soviet aid. Patriotism thus seemed to dictate sympathy for the Bolshevik cause. In the enthusiasm of the moment, it became a fad among the Ankara nationalists from Atatürk on down to display trappings of communist appearance: Kemalists frequently called each other "Comrade," referred to their ministries as "People's Commissariats," and wore red-peaked kalpaks to indicate their affinity for the Bolsheviks.[4]

Out of this atmosphere the now semilegendary Green Army took form in the spring of 1920. Despite its name, this "Army" had little to do with military organization. Its functions rather were political. Atatürk had insisted that he believed its founders to be sincere "Easternizers" who hoped to harness the Islamic socialist current they saw flowing from Russia for the Turkish nationalist cause. To some extent Atatürk's claim seems valid: the movement was at least partially a genuine expression of the "Eastern Ideal." But in its central committee, beside convinced "Easternizers" like Minister of Finance Hakkı Behiç and Undersecretary of Interior Nâzım, sat extreme nationalists of the order of Muhiddin Baha Pars. Atatürk's disclaimer notwithstanding, however, the Green Army appears to have been formed with the connivance of the Ankara government, which saw in it a means to impress the Kremlin that the Turks were sincere in wanting a social revolution on the Russian model. Moreover, in order not to fuel Western fears that the Kemalists might in fact be Bolsheviks, the Green Army operated as a secret society, recruiting its members from the elite, not from the masses. Soon, in addition to its Ankara headquarters, the Green Army managed to set up a branch in Eskişehir. But, though its members traveled fairly extensively, it established no other formal subsidiaries.

The hybrid nature of the Green Army was strikingly evident in its statutes. On the one hand, it made proper noises about the creation of a radically new economic order based on state ownership of land and the means of production. Further accumulation of property of any sort was forbidden. Moreover, the Ankara headquarters was to be "in touch with Moscow and the headquarters of the Red Armies as well as with all countries having Green Army organizations." Yet, at the same time, the statutes warned that "especially those coming from Russia must be kept under intensive surveillance." The Green Army's organizers celebrated Islam as the basis for all their policies. They proclaimed that not only did their program not conflict with Islam, but would assure "the salvation of the age." In short, the Green Army stood for an amalgam of rather radical socialism with Islamic and nationist overtones.[5]

The Green Army thus formed a sort of all-encompassing umbrella in whose shadow many diverse groups were at work.

The most radical of these was that of Stalin's protégé, Sherif Manatov, who had come to Ankara toward the end of May 1920 as the representative of the Bashkir Republic. He was purportedly sent by Bashkir Vice-President Zeki Velidî Togan, who allegedly wanted to be rid of such an intensely radical communist. It seems logical to suppose that Manatov had been dispatched with the knowledge and approval of his former colleague Mustafa Subhi, who was then in the process of moving to Baku. But about this we have no evidence. In any event, Manatov was well chosen to operate in Turkey. A former student of psychiatry, he spent some time in Istanbul toward the start of the First World War. Here he became fluent in the Ottoman dialect. And once back in Turkey, he joined forces with Zinniatulla Navshirvanov, who soon after arrival from Istanbul had secured a post as Russian translator in the newly organized Directorate of Press and Information. The two wasted no time in undertaking an active program of open lectures on the virtues of the Bolshevik revolution and on the nature of communism. In fact, Manatov's was perhaps the first voice on Turkish soil to proclaim that Lenin had "invented a doctrine that differs from Marxism," a line that surprised the radical socialists of Istanbul when word of this activity filtered into their city. Moreover, through his easy access to Atatürk and other government leaders, he even attempted to convert the Anatolian leaders to adopt "the Soviet system."[6]

Manatov's exact relationship to the Green Army has never become clear. It is evident, however, that from the start he perceived the essential deceit of the Green Army's intentions. Thus, very likely following his initial instructions from Moscow, he set about cautiously and secretly gathering a band of reliable adherents to serve as a more orthodox communist instrument. This endeavor brought him into contact with Veterinary Major Hacıoğlu Salih, who was later to become the leader of the communist group in Ankara. About Salih's background we know relatively little, except that he was born about 1880 in Trabzon and graduated first in his class from the Istanbul military veterinary school in 1903. His interest in social problems may have dated, as it did for so many of his contemporaries, from his student days. At his trial in April-May 1921, he confessed to having been converted to radical socialism by Manatov's lectures. Be that as it may, these two, together with Navshirvanov and others, including several veterinary students and possibly also Tokat deputy (and first Undersecretary of Interior) Nâzım, now sought to work behind the scenes to manipulate such bodies as the Green Army and its loosely related partisan units, which were then engaged in blocking the Greek offensive in western Anatolia. Initially this activity was even subsidized from the secret funds of the Ministry of Interior; for at first neither Atatürk nor the Ankara government was evidently aware of Manatov's true intentions.[7]

If, as seems probable, it was this band of communists that was responsible for the so-called "Turkish Communist Party General Statutes" of June 1920, Manatov's intentions were radical in the extreme.* This program, said to have been printed on the official provincial press in Eskişehir, advanced a series of demands for the total transformation of Turkish society. Not only did these statutes envisage the introduction of a pyramidal system of "Soviets" to administer the country in the name of the proletariat, but they called for the abolition of private property, the nationalization of all commercial and industrial enterprises, the sequestration of excess personal property, and the imposition of heavy taxes during a transitional period ending with the abolition of money as a medium of exchange. In short, this program posed a categoric challenge to Kemalist rule, while paying only the slightest deference to the requirements of national defense.[8]

These were surprising demands. They were in fact the most radical ever to be advocated by any Turkish communist organization. So out of the temper of the times were they that they raise the question of whether the organization that advanced them was in any way an Anatolian party or whether it was merely the Anatolian outpost of, say, Subhi's party in Baku. For in its unreality, this document reflects the spirit

* See Appendix I for a full translation of these statutes.

of Russian wartime communism, not the realities of military operations against the Greek invaders. Significantly, too, this program openly confessed the Turkish party's absolute sub-servience to Baku. It specifically provided that the authority of this party should last merely until convocation of a "Baku Congress of the Third International." There is, moreover, reliable testimony to the continuing contact between Subhi and Manatov's group; and a steady stream of emissaries is known to have carried material to Anatolia to be circulated in the name of the "Turkish Communist Party." From all this, it seems probable that Manatov's band considered itself a branch of Subhi's Baku organization and was working essentially to prepare the way for Subhi's arrival in Anatolia.[9]

Manatov's work was no doubt facilitated by the presence of the first unofficial Soviet delegate, Verbov, who reached Ankara toward the start of the summer in 1920. He is said to have been an uneducated blacksmith, completely convinced of his new faith, and with an abiding love for humanity in the Russian Narodnik tradition. Verbov knew no language other than Russian except for a little bad French, but he was accompanied by a certain Neşir Vanoc, who probably served as translator. Halide Edib Adıvar, wife of the first Minister of Health and Social Assistance in the new Ankara government, records that Verbov frequently called at their house, bringing countless Soviet propaganda brochures in an attempt to convert them to communism.[10]

By mid-summer 1920, this activity was of course still in its early stages. Yet already Atatürk was beginning to have serious reservations about the wisdom of permitting free scope to such a loosely coordinated movement as the Green Army. Despite the fact that prominent members of the government, whose loyalty was relatively above suspicion, were among the Green Army's leaders, he apparently feared it was slipping under the control of individuals like those in Manatov's group, whose intentions he was by now beginning to suspect. Moreover, the Green Army was ever expanding its activity, seeking recruits on a scale that perhaps seemed dangerous. Thus in July 1920, Atatürk ordered the Green Army to cease operations and to disband.

Some of the more militant elements of the Green Army, however, did not want to obey this order. They immediately set about mobilizing their supporters in the Ankara Assembly to persuade Atatürk to permit their organization to continue.

The Green Army was not without influence in Parliament. Its 14 central committee members were all deputies. In addition, as early as the end of April 1920, its leaders had constituted the so-called "Populist Group" (Halk Zümresi) in the Assembly to represent their organization. Amorphous as its structure was, this grouping was probably the only effort toward coherent organization in Parliament at the time and soon commanded the allegiance of perhaps as many as 85 deputies. Along with Nâzım and Hakkı Behiç, its adherents numbered such prominent deputies as Mehmet Şükrü who published the pro-communist paper İkaz in Afyonkarahisar and later in Ankara, and Sheikh Servet Akdağ, who controlled a press in Konya that printed propaganda favorable to the communists. But even Atatürk's trusted editor of Anadoluda Yeni Gün (New Day in Anatolia), Yunus Nadi, was associated with this parliamentary faction and joined in interceding with Atatürk to rescind the ban on the Green Army.

So effective was this persuasion that Atatürk vacillated (or perhaps he feared that he lacked the force to see his desires carried out). Though he did not officially withdraw his order, he tacitly permitted the Green Army to continue. Moreover, bowing to the temper of the times, Atatürk now went so far as to allow Yunus Nadi to draw up the so-called "Populist Program" (Halkçılık Programı), a protest against imperialism and capitalism that the Assembly later published as a preface to its first organic statutes. But while Atatürk may have hoped through Yunus Nadi to channel this current into courses useful for the Kemalist regime, in fact the Populist Group became ever more a rallying point for those who were discontent with the government.[11]

Early in September 1920, the Populist Group performed the most dramatic political act of its life. Hakkı Behiç had served first as Minister of Finance, then since mid-July as Minister of Interior. In these posts he had furthered the cause of the Green Army, which had become for him something of an obsession. As the contradictions between the Ankara government and the Green Army intensified, however, Hakkı Behiç became more and more uncomfortable in his government role. At the beginning of September 1920, therefore, he resigned from the Interior Ministry. His replacement was selected at the session of Parliament on September 4, 1920. Seeing in this his golden opportunity, fellow Green Army leader Nâzım mustered the Populist Group for the occasion, and in the balloting received 98 of the 187 votes cast.

Nâzım's accession to the sensitive post of Minister of Interior presented Atatürk with a *fait accompli* he could not well ignore. Hakkı Behiç for all his conviction that the revolutionary East (which for him meant Russia) should be the model for Turkey's development, was at bottom loyal to the Kemalist movement. While he had perhaps outlived his usefulness as Minister of Interior, he still could be employed in other capacities as a reliable servant of the Ankara regime. Not so Nâzım. Since Nâzım had resigned as Undersecretary of Interior near the beginning of the summer, Atatürk had been following his activity. By now Atatürk had evidence which convinced him that Nâzım had offered his services to the Kremlin. The Ankara government had apparently learned that Nâzım and some comrades had sent a letter to Mustafa Subhi in Baku requesting funds. In these circumstances,

Atatürk, in an unusually high-handed act, forced Nâzım to resign his ministry as soon as he learned of the election. Subsequently, at a secret session of Parliament, Atatürk justified his actions so convincingly that on November 4, 1920, the Assembly even agreed to change the method of selection of cabinet ministers to prevent any possible recurrence.[12]

The Green Army movement, however, was rapidly moving beyond Atatürk's control. Contrary to his desires, its agitation and propaganda were increasing. Particularly in the Eskişehir region this movement found ready support. Already in June 1920 a "Muslim Bolshevik Committee" had reportedly been formed here. The Turkish Socialist Party's organ *İşçi* (Worker), moreover, seems to have continued its vigorous growth. In such a favorable atmosphere the Eskişehir branch of the Green Army organized by Behram Lûtfi (a teacher) and Mustafa Nuri (a journalist) flourished. Through it Manatov and his radical group were gaining significant influence over the leaders of the partisan bands that still formed the main military force of the nationalist cause.[13]

Eskişehir lay in the heart of the territory controlled by Ethem, the Circassian, who led one of the most powerful units of the nationalist irregulars. Ethem's partisan detachments, although notoriously badly disciplined and still largely bandit in character, rendered important services to the nationalists in the summer of 1920. In fact, Ankara had to depend heavily on these irregulars, as only the rudiments of a regular army existed on the Western front at that time. Ethem's bands, therefore, were used to destroy Anzavur and his caliphate army, whom the Sultan sent to attack Eskişehir; Atatürk was even obliged to summon them east of Ankara to Yozgat to quiet a serious local uprising. With every success the partisans became more powerful and Ethem came to act more and more independent of the Ankara regime.

Ethem himself had apparently been taken into the central

committee of the Green Army in June 1920, probably through the efforts of Diyarbakır deputy Hacı Şükrü. Entranced by the views of the "Easternizers," Ethem seems to have fallen rather far under the communist spell that Sherif Manatov was weaving around Eskişehir at that time. While, as a personal rival of Atatürk's, Ethem no doubt saw in the communist movement a source of support against the Kemalist leadership, he had a genuine if naive appreciation of communism. Even years later, in the memoirs attributed to him, he exuded pride that the Soviets appeared to consider him more trustworthy than they did the Kemalist leaders. Moreover, at the time, he praised the Soviet experiment in quite sympathetic terms:

Bolshevism will seize the world. If we meet it with the necessary receptivity, the nation will be fortunate in any event. Rest assured, Bolshevism will be very useful and fruitful for our future. Now Bolshevism is saving the country, and in future it will protect men's lives and happiness.[14]

Others of Ethem's entourage were even more intimately involved in the communist movement. One of Ethem's major units was led by Captain İsmail Hakkı, a figure whom Şevket Süreyya Aydemir has identified as a member of Subhi's party in Baku sent by the party to Anatolia to carry on "Bolshevik" activity. The 700-man force commanded by Hakkı, a former captain in the Ottoman Army, was popularly known as the "Bolshevik detachment," though apart from its commander its other members may not necessarily have considered themselves to be communists of any variety. Be that as it may, the name was symptomatic of the sympathy with which the partisans regarded the Russian experience as they understood it.[15]

Under Ethem's protection, Eskişehir became the center of press activity popularizing pro-communist views. Toward the

end of August 1920, Green Army organizer Mustafa Nuri
founded the newspaper *Arkadaş* (Friend), which apparently
followed a "populist" line. Soon Nuri was joined by Arif
Oruç, later the stormy petrel of the Turkish press world, who
returned to Eskişehir from service with the partisan units on
the Demirci front early in September. Oruç was probably a
rather radical socialist by this time. Through his experience
in the Green Army he seems to have come to regard "Bolshevism"—without any precise knowledge of what it represented—as a useful slogan to galvanize Turkey into defending
her rights and preparing for the birth of a new society.[16]

Oruç immediately saw need to give *Arkadaş* new direction.
At his initiative, the two now apparently changed its name to
Seyyarei Yeni Dünya (Partisans of the New World), symbol-
izing the adherence of Ethem's partisans to the "new world"
of Bolshevism. On its masthead this daily, which Oruç later
testified had a circulation of 3,000, boldly proclaimed itself
an "Islamic Bolshevik Newspaper." In fact, it was to carry
many articles devoted to providing the basic similarity between Muslim and communist doctrine. A Soviet observer
who visited Ankara shortly thereafter characterized its line
as a "primitive and ignorant, but relatively honest interpretation of communism." According to this source, *Seyyarei
Yeni Dünya* printed articles by members of the Comintern
as well as by Turkish communists. From the one issue that
is known to have been preserved, it is evident that the paper
was quite well informed about the course of events in Russia.[17]

Much about this venture still cannot be satisfactorily
explained. One of the more perplexing problems has been
to determine what relationship Sherif Manatov and his group
had to *Seyyarei Yeni Dünya*. Oruç in his court testimony
admitted to contact with Manatov, who evidently helped
shape his inchoate but strongly emotional attachment to
communist slogans. Mustafa Nuri may have had even more

intimate ties with Manatov's group. But whether Manatov could be considered in any way the guiding force behind this paper or whether he provided any material support for it cannot be told on the basis of available evidence. On the other hand, Ankara, for some presently inexplicable reason, did assist this paper. At least initially, the Kemalist government even provided paper for *Seyyarei Yeni Dünya,* a fact that the Director General of Press and Information proudly hailed in Parliament as a central achievement on September 28, 1920, several weeks after Western Front Commander Cebesoy had already warned of its hostility to the Ankara regime.[18]

Within a short time, however, the dangers of the communist movement could no longer be ignored.

On October 4, 1920, the first accredited Soviet diplomatic mission arrived in Ankara, headed by Counsellor I. Upmal-Angarskii. Already while in Erzurum in September, Upmal-Angarskii had openly indicated to Eastern Front Commander Karabekir that he desired the legalization of the Turkish Communist Party. Once in Ankara, the Soviets lost no time in setting to work. They called on Parliament, where they were welcomed as befitting a valuable ally and close collaborator. Contact was established with Nâzım and his unrepentent wing of the Green Army, who were apparently given a considerable sum of money for their activities. Among those in the Green Army with whom the Soviets forged an underground relationship were Ethem and Arif Oruç. Moreover, despite the objections of the Ankara government, the Soviet mission's contact with Oruç continued.[19]

These activities confirmed Atatürk's conviction that stronger measures were necessary to curb the dangerous tendencies of the Green Army and to bring the general communist current in Anatolia under his control. For by this time Atatürk had definitely concluded that Mustafa

Subhi's agents in Ankara and Eskişehir were working "to bring forth a social revolution in the country" for the benefit of Soviet Russia. To frustrate this design, Atatürk saw need to be prepared to "jail and banish" those who supported the communist movement. For this purpose, already as early as September 11, 1920, the Treason Act was broadened to embrace political as well as military subversion. Then, on October 4, 1920, the Law on Associations was amended giving the government the authority to prohibit organizations "opposing public law and state policy."[20]

But the main weapon Atatürk sought to use against communist subversion was far more original and daring: to set up his own "official" Turkish Communist Party. At the end of September 1920, therefore, Atatürk instructed Hakkı Behiç and other figures loyal to him to pull out of the Green Army organization altogether. And on October 18, 1920, they formed a so-called "communist" party directly under Atatürk's control. Through it he hoped to be able to channel the energies of those who were dedicated to radical social reform into the service of the nationalist revolution. Moreover, by establishing this pseudocommunist party it seemed possible to block the efforts of Soviet communists without casting the Ankara government clearly in the role of persecutor.

To avoid the possibility that this party might fall under the control of disloyal elements, Atatürk packed its leadership with his most trustworthy supporters. Its central committee included his top generals (Fevzi Çakmak, Ali Fuat Cebesoy, Kâzım Karabekir, Refet Bele, and İsmet İnönü) as well as some of the most prominent civilian leaders of the Kemalist regime (Yunus Nadi, Refik Koraltan, Dr. Adnan Adıvar, and Celâl Bayar). Further, in a circular sent to army commands in Anatolia on October 26, 1920, Party Secretary General Hakkı Behiç announced that the Green Army had been transformed into the new "Communist Party." In addition, he transmitted an order of the Minister of Interior to the effect that only those registered in this party and bearing official party identity documents would be allowed to carry on communist propaganda. A few days later, Atatürk followed this message with instructions that the communist movement should not be allowed to spread beyond the top military command.[21]

The Ankara government combined the creation of the "official" Communist Party with an energetic propaganda campaign seeking to publicize the differences between Turkish (i.e., legitimate) communism and Soviet (i.e., illegitimate) Bolshevism. This campaign had been foreshadowed as early as September 9, 1920, when the Kemalist mouthpiece *Hâkimiyeti Milliye* (National Sovereignty) had begun attacking the members of the Green Army as "charlatans" who had no idea of what communism was. By October, *Hâkimiyeti Milliye* was ready to carry the argument to its logical conclusion. On October 12, 1920, it set the tone of debate with a dramatic editorial entitled "The Two Communisms," followed in a few days with a companion piece called "Russian Bolshevism, Turkish Communism." "Anatolia today," proclaimed *Hâkimiyeti Milliye* in its first leading article, "is carrying on a great struggle for the sake of communist goals and is proceeding rapidly toward the gates of this new world with sure steps." Turkish tactics, however, were by no means to be copied blindly from Russian experience. For, as the paper pointed out, the historical development of the two countries had been quite different, necessitating an entirely different approach. The key difference, according to the editorialist, was that "Communism will be carried out [in Anatolia] without the need for the establishment of a harsh and bloody dictatorship in the form as in Russia." "There are two communisms . . . that go exactly parallel to each other toward the same goal, but which are different in form."

Yunus Nadi's paper, *Anadoluda Yeni Gün,* the official organ of the "official" Communist Party, followed up with a series of articles in the same vein. These are worth quoting at some length because they give the flavor of the argument Atatürk felt compelled to advance in his attempt to head off the growing communist movement.

At the present moment, the program of communist ideas is not only harmful, but even ruinous, for the country. When a soldier realizes that there does not have to be a fatherland, he will not go out to defend it; hearing that there does not have to be hatred of nations, he will not go out and fight the Greeks. . . . Besides that, our party activity, not being acquainted with the governmental organization of Soviet Russia, will not be able to create anything positive, and will destroy the old foundations of economic life and will bring the country to ruin. It is first of all necessary to become acquainted with Soviet Russia . . . and to liquidate all the military fronts. For what concerns the present moment, in the interests of the country *we must counteract all the agitators and propagandists who have come on their own initiative, without consent of our ruling organs.* [Only] Turks can introduce Bolshevism, and Bolshevism can be introduced [only] from above.

Our party [i.e. the "official" Turkish Communist Party] holds as ideals the program of the Russian Communist Party which is inapplicable as a whole even in Russia itself and which merely indicates the principal lines of direction of communism. But for the attainment of these ideals our party has composed a general practical program, containing tactical methods for agreeably applying the ideal program to the peculiarities and social conditions of our land.[22]

Other editorialists, such as Ali İhsan, whom *Anadoluda Yeni Gün* called the "Turkish Karl Marx," turned their attention to formulating the bases of a socialist program for

Anatolia, a program that turned out to resemble to a remarkable degree what Atatürk later carried out. According to
this scheme, private capital would be tolerated, but large
industry and capital accumulations would be gradually
nationalized. Another "official" party member, Mahmud
Esat Bozkurt, wrote in a feature article on October 20, 1920,
that he objected categorically and entirely to Bolshevism,
i.e., to Russian communism. He declared that Turkey must
work out its own destiny and must not copy another nation's
solution to its individual problems. He emphasized the
differences between Turkey and Russia, developing the idea
that Turkish communism was an implement to serve the
interests of Turkey by leading to the unification of the
nation. Indeed, Bozkurt unequivocally summed up Atatürk's
position on communism in the formula: "Communism is
not an ideal, but a means for the Turks. The ideal of the
Turks is the unity of the Turkish nation."[23]

The provincial press echoed this line, too. For example,
İkbal (Good Fortune) in Trabzon, while acknowledging
that "sooner or later Bolshevik principles will triumph all
over the world," cautioned that "in Turkey Bolshevism cannot be carried out immediately, even though Bolshevism is
the very best form of administration imaginable."[24]

But not only did the "official" Communist Party have a
role to play in combatting communist subversion at home;
Atatürk intended it to perform services abroad in cementing
Soviet-Turkish relations. Negotiations with the Kremlin
had broken down toward the end of August 1920 as a result
of disagreement over the Armenian question. The Turks,
who had called off their planned summer offensive against
Armenia at Soviet request, now no longer felt constrained
to remain inactive. Thus when the Armenians attacked in
September 1920, Karabekir was authorized not merely to
push them back, but to launch a general offensive as well.

Yet as the Turks soon extended their gains deep into territory held by the Armenians, it became all the more necessary
to reach accord with Moscow in order to avoid the possibility of clashes with Red Army forces in the area. For this
purpose, Ali Fuat Cebesoy, whom Atatürk had relieved as
Western Front Commander early in November 1920 for
failure to deal properly with Ethem, was designated Ambassador to Moscow.[25]

Along with Cebesoy's regular diplomatic mission, however,
the Ankara government decided to send four trusted members of the "official" Communist Party to impress the Kremlin with the sincerity of the Kemalists in making common
cause with them. Tevfik Rüştü Aras, the leader of this
delegation, was instructed to attempt to bolster the authen-
ticity of his party further by applying to the Comintern for
membership. Ostensibly this mission was to study the Soviet
system in order to provide Ankara with useful ideas that
could be transplanted into the Turkish environment. Heated
debate was touched off in the Assembly over the composition
of this delegation, however, when Nâzım insisted that its
members get a vote of confidence before their departure. All
agreed that there was much to be learned from analyzing
Soviet experience. But Nâzım and his supporters obviously
hoped to force selection of representatives favorable to them,
while the members of the "official" Communist Party ada-
mantly defended the government's choices from imputations
of insincerity. In the end, the government carried the day,
but its "Communist" representatives had little success with
Moscow, which rejected their request to join the Comintern
as not meeting the 21-point criteria set by the Second Congress of the Comintern in the summer of 1920.[26]

The formation of the "official" Communist Party sowed
considerable confusion in the communist movement in
Anatolia. For the politically naive, it was exceedingly hard

to see through the government's maneuver, particularly as the "official" communists loudly claimed allegiance to the Comintern. To add to this confusion, Atatürk took pains to prevent such figures as Nâzım and Sheikh Servet Akdağ from publishing their disclaimers of affiliation with the new creation. Moreover, the Ankara government apparently chose this period to carry out the arrest and expulsion of Sherif Manatov, whose efforts to promote the Moscow-oriented Communist Party had become glaringly obvious. Indeed, had it not been for the intercession of the Soviet mission, Manatov would likely have been given a stiff jail sentence. At the same time, Atatürk redoubled his efforts to inveigle the vain, but politically unsophisticated Ethem into the "official" party, encouraging him to believe that Ankara sincerely wished to further communist goals. And, by about the start of December 1920, Ethem, who was then in Ankara, apparently did consent to join the "official" Communist Party. He even agreed to order the transfer of *Seyyarei Yeni Dünya* to Ankara, where Atatürk assured him it would command more weight. For naive as it may seem today, Ethem probably viewed this move as useful in his grand design—which was no less than to replace Atatürk as leader of the nationalist regime. In any event, this paper, which remained ultimately loyal to Ethem, merely added to the confusion.[27]

The government's success in deflecting the communist movement convinced the die-hards in Manatov's group in particular that they had to form an officially recognized party if they hoped to carry on propaganda and preserve their organization independent of the Kemalist hierarchy. For this purpose, toward the end of November 1920, Zinniatulla Navshirvanov and Nâzım took the initiative in organizing the so-called "Peoples Communist Party of Turkey" (Türkiye Halk İştirakiyun Fırkası). Although this party seems to have continued underground relations with the Soviet mission in Ankara as well as with the émigré party in Baku, on 7 December 1920 the Ministry of Interior granted it official permission to operate. Perhaps it did so in order not to cause bad relations with the Soviets. To be sure, the Peoples Communist Party was dominated by leaders who were ultimately quite independent of the Baku organization; the Anatolian party, in fact, had a sharply different personality. It still recognized Islamic precepts in such areas as family life. Nor did it press for immediate revolution against the Kemalist regime. Yet, at bottom it offered a mechanism for the Moscow-oriented communists to continue their activity to some degree under the cloak of legality.[28]

One of the first major problems facing this new organization was to define its relationship with Ethem and his partisan bands.

Ethem's growing independence during the fall of 1920 had brought Atatürk to the conclusion that he must rapidly bring the irregulars to heel. İsmet İnönü had been appointed Western Front Commander in November 1920 with instructions to create a regular army incorporating the partisan formations as disciplined units. Ethem and his brothers waged dogged resistance to İnönü's efforts. Yet through most of December 1920 Atatürk still did not feel sufficiently strong to provoke a confrontation. Instead he sought to temporize. Hoping to soften the rebels' defiance, Atatürk sent repeated delegations of deputies to Ethem, who had returned to the head of his forces early in December. But, encouraged by Captain İsmail Hakkı of the "Bolshevik detachment" to revolt against the government, Ethem refused to back down. Thus, by December 26, 1920, the die was cast: İnönü publicly branded Ethem with treason. The following day, İnönü summoned all Circassian units to obey the orders of the Ankara government and launched military operations to destroy the partisan forces.

As an overt organization, operating with the permission of the Ankara government, the Peoples Communist Party recognized the danger of openly backing Ethem against Atatürk. Thus, although Ethem was probably a member of the Peoples Communist Party as well as of Atatürk's "official" party, the central committee decided to go on record as disassociating the party from Ethem's movement. This decision was communicated to the Kemalist government.[29]

Despite this rebuff, Ethem merely intensified his efforts to invoke communist sympathies for his cause. He had no other place to turn, and he undoubtedly felt that the Bolsheviks carried considerable weight in Ankara as a result of the important aid they were already providing. Hence *Seyyarei Yeni Dünya,* which up to this point had played a somewhat equivocal role in the controversy between Atatürk and Ethem, now openly sought to arouse communist support for the partisans. As soon as the government began military operations against Ethem, this paper issued a "call to the local railroad workers, appealing to them to strike" in order to hold up trains carrying troops to be used against Ethem. At the same time, Arif Oruç's nephew, Nizamettin Nazif Tepedelenlioğlu, summoned the Eskişehir workers and peasants to rise up and unite in the name of "Bolshevism" against the "dirty hands" (purposely ambiguous, but obviously referring to the Kemalists) who were holding them back from the glories of the new day. For not only did Ethem and his associates wish to create disturbances to hamper the government forces; but, according to Atatürk, as a means of assuring Soviet backing they "wanted to give the Bolsheviks the idea that it was possible to make a revolt" in Turkey.[30]

Ethem's tactics put the Soviet mission in an embarrassing

position. On the one hand, it was charged with cementing friendship with the Kemalists and with aiding them in their struggle against the Entente. At the same time, the Soviets found it difficult to disavow elements like Ethem who both vaunted their attachment to communism and also gave promise of being easy to manipulate. Moreover, the Soviet envoys could not be sure how the confrontation would come out between Ethem and Atatürk. Thus, although they apparently did not give material aid to Ethem—and indeed may rather have given private assurances of support to the Kemalists—the Bolshevik mission did not publicly disown the partisan rebels, but remained in some sort of contact until the very last moment. In fact, Nizamettin Nazif Tepedelenlioğlu took refuge in the Soviet Embassy to avoid arrest in connection with his appeal to the Eskişehir workers. Only after the failure of Ethem's revolt had become clear did he surrender to the Ankara authorities.[31]

As it turned out, Ethem's forces proved unable to resist the might of the regular army. Atatürk outmaneuvered him both politically and militarily. In Parliament his supporters faded away like a mirage. On the battlefield his troops deserted in droves rather than fight their fellow countrymen while Greek forces were advancing into Turkish heartland. Thus on January 5, 1921, Ethem's units were decisively whipped at Gediz. He and his brothers along with some of his chief supporters fled to the Greeks, who welcomed this opportunity to weaken the Turkish front.

With Ethem's flight, the partisan threat to the Kemalist regime was ended once and for all. Never again would communist-oriented forces present any serious military threat to the Ankara government. Henceforth, the armed forces of the young nationalist movement would be under the control of elements sharply hostile to the communists and wary of their influence. While the dispute over control of the Turkish military establishment had by no means been resolved, in future the contest would be between Atatürk and the "Westernizers." Neither contender had any interest in seeking communist support.

Ethem's defeat permitted some clarification of the political scene. While Atatürk took pains explicitly to absolve the leadership of the "official" Turkish Communist Party from any implication in Ethem's disloyalty, he moved rapidly against those pro-communist elements associated with Ethem. Even before Ethem's movement had been finally mopped up, the Ankara authorities moved to close *Seyyarei Yeni Dünya* for its inflamatory publications. On January 11, 1921, Hacıoğlu Salih was apprehended in a first wave of arrests for complicity in Ethem's revolt. But although Atatürk at the same time demanded the expulsion from the Assembly of Diyarbakır deputy Hacı Şükrü for his involvement in Ethem's rebellion, Parliament refused for the moment to sanction any action against its members. Only Ethem's brother Reşit, who had already fled to the Greeks, was expelled from membership and his name expunged from the parliamentary rolls.[32]

It was in these troubled days during and after Ethem's insurrection that Mustafa Subhi finally decided to exercise the permission Atatürk had granted him in the summer of 1920 to move his headquarters to Anatolia. Why he chose this moment cannot be told with any certainty. Perhaps he expected that Atatürk's regime was tottering and about to fall, thus offering a chance for an early takeover. In any event, he must have discovered that in the confused and fast-changing situation inside Turkey he could not effectively direct the communist movement from Baku. Be that as it may, Subhi set off toward the end of December 1920 for Kars, where he remained for a time with the Soviet plenipotentiary Mdivani and a retinue of trusted comrades. Both

Cebesoy, then on route to Moscow, and Eastern Front Commander Karabekir held long conversations with him at this time. Subhi apparently acquitted himself well in these talks, stressing his willingness to support the Ankara regime. The moderation of his words was belied by his activities, however. He could not resist actively disseminating communist propaganda; he was even unwise enough to try to set up communist cells in the Turkish army on the eastern front. As a result, two of his entourage were arrested in Kars for their propaganda activity. Moreover, unknown to Subhi his intentions were denounced to Karabekir by his supposedly faithful colleague Mehmet Emin.[33]

Local reaction to Subhi's group was by no means friendly. Hostile demonstrations, inspired undoubtedly by the local military commanders and the ultra-conservative Defense of the Holy Places Society, were organized against his entourage in Kars. After some weeks here, General Karabekir advised Subhi to proceed to Trabzon, declaring that otherwise the safety of the communists could no longer be guaranteed. But the communist delegation fared no better on its way to Trabzon. Wherever he went, Subhi found that counterpropaganda has been spread to the effect that the communists were coming to abolish private property and to tamper with the status of women.[34]

Trabzon itself was no safe refuge for Subhi and his companions. Though a key transshipment point for Soviet supplies, it had experienced weak and inept leadership from Ankara. Local notables, especially the leader of the boatman guild, Yahya (a staunch supporter of Enver Pasha), thus enjoyed relatively free rein. Ankara exercised control over Trabzon to a large degree by playing off local factions. Soviet officials, who had been stationed there since September 1920, had sought with indifferent success to fish in these troubled waters. Although the local press had seemed particularly well disposed toward Soviet Russia, even publishing an invitation to the Baku Congress issued by the Central Committee of Subhi's Communist Party, by December 1920 the mood of the populace had become hostile. The Soviet Consulate was subject to harassment; and when a delegation from the Soviet of Action and Propaganda passed through at this time, it had been forced to delay there for several weeks awaiting permission to proceed. During their stay, the members of this delegation even suffered indignities.[35]

When Subhi and his entourage arrived, they were greeted by an angry crowd. Nor were the Soviet officials resident there either able or courageous enough to afford Subhi's party any help. On January 28, 1921, Yahya and his followers induced or compelled Subhi and fourteen companions to board a boat. The offending communists were taken to an appropriate spot in the Black Sea and dumped overboard to drown.[36]

Just who was ultimately responsible for this act cannot be established with any certainty on present evidence. Ankara may have authorized it as a convenient way to be rid of a potentially dangerous competitor without having to accept responsibility for Subhi's disappearance. Local authorities, perhaps even including Eastern Front Commander Karabekir, may have taken it upon themselves to act on their own initiative. Most likely of all, however, is the possibility that Yahya, seeing in Mustafa Subhi a dangerous rival for his beloved Enver Pasha, simply took matters into his own hands. In fact, Yahya was later brought to trial for this offense and subsequently was killed under mysterious circumstances, presumably by Subhi's supporters.[37]

In Ankara, meanwhile, the Peoples Communist Party of Turkey managed a final gasp of activity. The apparent immunity of its parliamentary faction emboldened the party to undertake a new effort. In place of the defunct *Seyyarei*

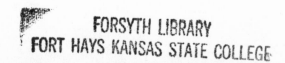

Yeni Dünya, therefore, on January 16, 1921, Nâzım and the journalist Abdülkadir began to publish a daily paper called *Emek* (Labor). In the six issues which followed, *Emek* showed that the line of the Peoples Communist Party had changed but little. This paper devoted considerable effort to proving the by now traditional refrain that the principles of communism did not contradict the Koran. It also attempted to refute the charge that communism itself had imperialistic aspects. But remarkably enough, *Emek* was not reluctant to attack Atatürk directly. In its last issue it uncompromisingly asserted:

Kemal [Atatürk] is the absolute ruler of Anatolia. Say he wins victory. Will the position of the peasantry be the better for this? Whatever victory Kemal wins it will not benefit the people of Anatolia. One man alone . . . can never deliver the country from need. . . . Only a social revolution can free the people of Anatolia from the yoke of capital. *Thus as soon as the war with the Greek imperialists is over, a civil war will begin in Anatolia.*[38]

Such an attack was more than the Ankara government could brook. Promptly it shut down *Emek,* arrested Zinniatulla Navshirvanov on January 27, 1921, in a roundup that probably also netted Abdülkadir, and requested the Assembly to permit trial of deputies who belonged to the Peoples Communist Party of Turkey. Faced with this prospect, Nâzım and Afyonkarahisar deputy Mehmet Şükrü publicly proclaimed in a letter to *Hâkimiyeti Milliye* that their party was withdrawing from activity in order not to muddy the waters "at this time when the nation needs unity." For in fact, at this moment the Ankara regime was preparing to send its representatives to London to take part in their first official diplomatic contact with the Western powers.[39]

This belated gesture of cooperation, however, could not save the Peoples Communist Party. The Assembly in due course granted the government's request to remove the parliamentary immunity of Nâzım and his colleagues. On April 12, 1921, he and the party's central committee were arrested. At their trial, which ended on May 9, 1921, the leaders of the Peoples Communist Party received heavy sentences. Nâzım, Zinniatulla Navshirvanov, and Hacıoğlu Salih were condemned to 15 years at hard labor, not for being communists, but rather for supposed implication in attempting to overthrow the government. Arif Oruç, whose involvement in Ethem's revolt was never firmly established and who seems to have recanted at least to a degree, was sentenced merely to enforced residence at a place of the government's choosing until the end of the struggle for independence. Others—Abdülkadir, Nizamettin Nazif Tepedelenlioğlu, Behram Lûtfi, and Mustafa Nuri—also received substantial jail terms. Deputies Mehmet Şükrü and Sheikh Servet Akdağ, on the other hand, were acquitted and were permitted to retain their parliamentary seats.[40]

At this time, too, the government took steps to discredit communist appeal in religious circles. The Minister of Religious Affairs now issued a "fetva" condemning this "dangerous and spurious movement which is incompatible with the Koran." He called all true believers to withdraw from the Peoples Communist Party; for not only were there some party sympathizers among the uneducated masses, but religious leaders (e.g., Sheikh Servet Akdağ) held important positions in the party. In these circumstances this effort to arouse religious opposition to communism was quite effective. Henceforth, the appeal of communism among conservative religious circles in Turkey decreased to the vanishing point. Never again would it be fashionable to believe that communism and Islam were either synonymous or compatible.[41]

These arrests brought communist activity in Turkey to a halt. But although Atatürk even published an interview with a Western correspondent in February 1921 denying that conditions in Turkey were favorable for communism, he was still unwilling to outlaw it per se. Nor was Ankara willing to admit to persecuting communists as such. When, for example, the Soviets protested these arrests as well as the murder of Mustafa Subhi, Ankara firmly denied that the issue of communism was in any way involved. Ambassador Cebesoy explained to Chicherin in June 1921 that these communists were not arrested merely because of their party affiliation, but because they

were constantly committing serious tactical errors, weakening the Turkish front by attempting a premature social revolution, which at the moment the Turkish people do not at all desire, and openly and directly opposing the laws and regulations of the Great National Assembly of Turkey. In view of such actions, I do not see how the action of the Turkish officials who apply the law against all troublemakers in Turkey can be misinterpreted.[42]

Moreover, Cebesoy was instructed to assure the Kremlin that Subhi's murderers would be brought to trial. While this may have been scant comfort to Moscow, particularly when Yahya was acquitted, the Soviets respected the realities of power. Hence aid to the Kemalists continued without a break.

For the Anatolian communist movement, however, these arrests and sentences were decisive. Though the government might sponsor debate on social reform—and even openly declare that Turkey should "move to the left"—never again would the Kemalists advocate "communism" in any form as the model for their behavior. It was now the etatism of Bismarck rather than the New Economic Policy of Lenin to which Celâl Bayar and his ilk harked for inspiration! Furthermore, the communists themselves had forever lost the sense of momentum they had enjoyed during these free-wheeling days. Communism would hereafter be important not as a contender for political power, but as an ideological influence working its leaven on Kemalist doctrine in more subtle form. The revolutionary stage of Turkish communism was over.[43]

CHAPTER V

Toward a Unified Party

The chief mistake that the utopians made was to think that it would be possible to establish and form a new sort of society, a new social system, in the absence of economic conditions necessary for the establishment of that society. . . . It is ridiculous to expect the capitalists to save the workers.

Sadrettin Celâl Antel, *Akşam*, March 5, 1921

The question of organization is the heart of the class question.

Şefik Hüsnü Deymer, *Aydınlık*, June 1, 1921

What is at stake is neither a religious heaven nor anything imaginary or supernatural.

Henri Barbusse, *Aydınlık*, October 1, 1921

Events were rapidly creating a new environment in Turkey. To be sure, the Greek menace, far from receding, continued to grow more acute. After being blocked temporarily in the two battles of İnönü at the start of 1921, the Greek advance toward Ankara resumed its seemingly inexorable course. Yet the Kemalist movement was coming of age. It had brought into being a regular government, which in January 1921 passed a Constitution Act, in effect displacing the Sultan. Moreover, Ankara was wresting an increasing measure of international recognition as well. Not only Moscow, but even the Entente powers had come to accept the need to treat with the Kemalists. The Italians, who had never had their hearts in carving out a sphere in southern Anatolia, finally pulled out their troops in July 1921. By this time, too, the French had sent Franklin-Bouillon to begin the long process of setting terms for their withdrawal. While the British were more stubborn, their envoys in the field had long warned of the impossibility of arranging any solution that did not take the Kemalists into consideration. The grudging invitation of Ankara representatives to the London Conference in February 1921 marked something of a turning point in Britain's attitude as well.

Istanbul felt the repercussions of these changing realities. Following the Allied military occupation in March 1920, Istanbul became a political backwater. Those active nationalist leaders who had not escaped to Anatolia were packed off to exile in Malta by the British. Many of the radical socialists, too, had departed. The others were forced underground. As a result, the Turkish intellectual community in Istanbul was effectively silenced. Yet the Sultan and his supporters—particularly after signing the humiliating Treaty of Sevres in August 1920—could in no wise fill this gap.

Under the patronage of the occupying powers, the Istanbul minority communities— especially the Greek, now came into their own. Even radical elements found new scope for activity. The occupation forces, while relatively vigilant in opposing sympathizers of the Anatolian nationalist movement or in rooting out communist agents among the flood of White Russian emigres, paid relatively little attention to labor activity, or indeed to social currents of any variety among the local communities in Istanbul.[1]

Sometime before the end of 1920, Serafim Maximos reappeared on the scene to launch a new venture among the minority communities in Istanbul. No doubt acting on instructions from the Kremlin, which paid considerable attention to his work, Maximos promptly undertook to form the so-called "International Union of Workers" (Union internationale du travaille), embracing principally Greek, Armenian, and Jewish workers of the maritime and construction trades. This union, whose membership probably came to number somewhere around 5,000, maintained close relations with Moscow. It joined the Red International of

Labor Unions shortly after the formation of that body in Moscow in mid-1921. As part of its effort to promote union activity, Maximos' organization published a weekly in Greek, *Neos Anthropos* (New Man), and conducted regular labor agitation, including a series of courses for workers.[2]

Not surprisingly, the Greek cast of the International Union of Workers limited its appeal in the Turkish community of Istanbul. Only a few hundred Turks proved willing to join. It was, of course, quite unrealistic to expect to bridge the gulf between Greek and Turk during these war years. Yet Moscow evinced disappointment at what it termed the "chauvinism" of workers in Istanbul that frustrated efforts to produce a truly international movement. And under this stimulus, perhaps originally in hopes of forging a united front of all nationalities, Maximos now established contact with Hüseyin Hilmi, whose Turkish Socialist Party was passing through a final burst of activity.[3]

Hilmi had taken full advantage of the temporary eclipse of the radicals on the departure of Ethem Nejat, Hilmioğlu İsmail Hakkı, and their colleagues in the spring of 1920. Thanks to the rivalry that then existed between the British and French elements of the occupation forces, Hilmi had been able to secure British support in a series of strikes against some of the major French enterprises in Istanbul. His remarkable success in winning concessions from management brought workers in droves to join the Turkish Socialist Party, swelling its membership to a peak that may have numbered not too far from the 7,000 claimed by Soviet sources. And, while these gains were to prove quite ephemeral (by mid-1922 the party had all but vanished), in the spring of 1921, Hilmi's organization demonstrated impressive vitality. It joined with Maximos' International Union of Workers and with the remnants of the Turkish Worker and Peasant Socialist Party in a city-wide May Day celebration of thousands of workers which completely shut down the municipal transportation system for the occasion.[4]

Hilmi, however, was not fated to enjoy uncontested predominance in the Turkish labor movement for long.

The Allied occupation had made it impossible for the Turkish Worker and Peasant Socialist Party to continue to operate legally in Istanbul. Even efforts to change the party's statutes to remove all traces of revolutionary taint or radical demands—if the allegations of modern Soviet writers to this effect can be trusted—were unavailing. In these circumstances, those leaders of the party's radical wing who had not fled to Anatolia now founded the nucleus of a secret communist group that was the direct ancestor of the present Turkish Communist Party. Şefik Hüsnü Deymer, with the assistance of Sadrettin Celâl Antel, organized this tiny band as far as can be told quite independently of Subhi's Baku party. By November 1920, this communist faction was engaged in organizing local committees in Istanbul and in carrying on underground agitation, though, to be sure, in the repressive atmosphere of Istanbul such activity could hardly have been extensive.[5]

With the fall of the Damat Ferit Cabinet in October 1920, however, the initial severity of the Allied occupation began to ease. It became possible once more to contemplate working legally through the Turkish Worker and Peasant Socialist Party, a course that offered far better prospects than relying entirely on small-scale and dangerous underground activity. Thus, as soon as the Tevfik Cabinet had been installed on October 24, 1920, Deymer and Antel lost no time in preparing to reactivate the Worker and Peasant party.

The French Communist Party exerted a major influence on this revival. Despite the vicissitudes of the occupation, the nucleus of the Turkish Worker and Peasant Socialist Party had maintained fairly regular contact with Paris, where Refik

Nevzat seems to have served as a window on the French movement. In addition, the Istanbul party sent a delegate,
H. Baydur, to Tours in December 1920 to observe the historic
French party congress take its decision to join the Comintern.
While in France, Baydur wrote for French communist organs
and solicited the recommendations of the French Communist
Party for the future development of the communist movement in Turkey. This intimate link was further reinforced
by the visit of prominent French Communist and Clarté
figure Magdeleine Marx Paz, who traveled to Istanbul in the
summer of 1921 to inspect and encourage her Turkish colleagues. She wrote articles in behalf of the Turkish Worker
and Peasant Socialist Party both for its revived journal and,
on her return, for *l'Humanité*.[6]

It was still difficult for the Turkish Worker and Peasant
Socialist Party to gain the acquiescence of the authorities in
Istanbul to return to overt operation. The party, indeed, had
to assume a guise that would not alarm the Allied forces in
particular. In this situation, its leaders, in line with guidance
from its French mentors, sought respectability by adopting
a form more nearly that of a branch of Barbusse's Clarté
movement than of an overt communist party. Hence, as it
gradually eased back into open activity in the beginning of
1921, the Turkish Worker and Peasant Socialist Party took
pains to present the face of a parlor debating society entirely
unconnected with Bolshevism or with events in Soviet Russia. Its members engaged in debate on "scientific socialism"
in such scholarly tones that even relatively moderate organs
like *Akşam* were willing to carry their articles.[7]

Nowhere was the resemblance to the Clarté movement
more pronounced than in the journal *Aydınlık* (Light) that
Şefik Hüsnü Deymer and Sadrettin Celâl Antel brought out
on June 1, 1921, in place of the defunct *Kurtuluş*. This new
periodical was frankly modeled on Barbusse's *Clarté*, for

which its name was an exact translation in Turkish. Soon *Aydınlık* even added to its cover the image of a woman looking expectantly to the dawn of a new day which was the symbol of the French journal. But the resemblance went far beyond mere superficials. Although the conviction that the working class would come to power in the near future underlay much of the work of the native Turkish contributors, not a mention of the Russian Revolution was offered. Nor did *Aydınlık* commend the works of Lenin and his followers to the attention of its readers. Instead, Antel, who served as *Aydınlık's* editor, set himself the "human obligation" to introduce his audience to the French humanist writings of Barbusse, Magdeleine Marx Paz, and their ilk, whose literature "shows us wide horizons shining with the brightness of the morning star." And it was in fact Barbusse's concept of the "Duty of the Enlightened," carried in *Aydınlık's* fourth issue, that dominated the thinking of this new organ.[8]

The *Aydınlık* group, however, was far from entirely homogeneous at this period. It ranged from doctrinaire liberals and more or less romantic admirers of communist slogans to "fellow-travelers" and true communicants of Moscow. Sadrettin Celâl Antel, who was now teaching philosophy at the Istanbul Girls Lycée and French at the Superior Normal School, represented along with Şefik Hüsnü Deymer the doctrinaire Marxist approach. Yet even they, however much they might consider themselves communists and look to Moscow for inspiration, still do not seem fully to have appreciated Leninism as distinct from classical Marxism. On the other hand, there were those like future Rector of Ankara University Şevket Aziz Kansu, not yet in his twenties, who contributed articles and poetry reflecting more the idealism of youth than any deep appreciation of communist theory. Others of the stripe of Nizamettin Âli Sav, a recent graduate of Heidelberg and Berlin universities in economics, and Ali

Cevdet seemed closer to the Marxist end of the political spectrum. Yet, to be sure, the views of all the *Aydınlık* contributors were still rather fluid. Some members drifted away from the group soon after publication began.

This was a period when the world-wide communist movement itself was engaged in doctrinal self-searching. The Third Congress of the Comitern, which convened in July 1921, marked an important swing in Soviet policy, a shift which had its repercussions on the Turkish communist movement as well. The Comintern had by now abandoned its hopes for early world revolution. Instead, this Congress set the goal of winning the allegiance of a majority of the working class before attempting any revolution. In this scheme of things the importance of the East in communist strategy mounted. More than ever it became obligatory for the communists to support anti-imperialist movements throughout the East, including of course the Kemalists. Yet in the aftermath of Subhi's murder and the suppression of the Peoples Communist Party in Ankara, this was not a particularly palatable message for the Turkish representatives present. Süleyman Nuri, a delegate from the remnants of Mustafa Subhi's Turkish Communist Party in Baku, complained bitterly at the persecution of communists by Atatürk and at the deceit of the Kemalists in forming the "official" Communist Party. Nonetheless, bowing to the Comintern's policy, he, too, agreed that the Turkish communists should cooperate in the struggle against the Entente.[9]

But despite the clear command of this Congress to support the Turkish nationalist movement, the line emanating from Moscow may have been somewhat ambiguous at this time. Relations with the Ankara government were passing through a period of considerable mistrust. The Soviets were naturally upset at Kemalist treatment of the Anatolian communists. Also disturbing to the Kremlin was the Ankara Parliament's delay until the end of July 1921 in ratifying the Treaty of Brotherhood signed in Moscow four months before. Moreover, in light of the seemingly inexorable Greek advance into Anatolia, the Kremlin, although continuing to send important shipments of guns and coin to the Turkish nationalists, was not yet fully convinced that Atatürk would succeed.

To hedge its bets, therefore, Moscow persisted in toying with Enver Pasha, who had ambitions of his own to head the Anatolian movement. Enver had taken refuge in the Soviet Union in 1920. Here, toward the end of the same year, he had formed a Peoples Soviet Party (Halk Şûralar Fırkası) as a revival of the Union and Progress party under Bolshevik patronage. The Peoples Soviet Party was a revolutionary organization, not specifically communist in outlook, but enough in the Bolshevik mold to single out imperialism and capitalism as its chief foes. To the Soviets its principal attraction undoubtedly lay in the prospect of manipulating Enver, who had promised to institute the most intimate relations once he should come to power. Thus, as the Greek offensive gained momentum in the spring of 1921, the Kremlin allowed Enver to redouble his efforts to extend his organization inside Anatolia. In conjunction with these plans, Enver came himself from Moscow to Batum at the end of July 1921. Here, under Soviet auspices, he convened a congress of the "Union and Progress (Peoples Soviet) Party" on September 5, 1921, calling on the Ankara government to cease persecuting his supporters and allow them freedom of political activity. Just at this point, however, the nationalist victory at the Sakaraya River stopped the Greek advance. Enver's organization inside Anatolia collapsed like a house of cards. Enver himself now turned his attention to Soviet Central Asia, where he was killed the following year leading a revolt against the Soviets.[10]

This constellation of events must have dictated considerable caution to the *Aydınlık* group in becoming publicly committed to the support of the Anatolian nationalist leadership. In any event, *Aydınlık* simply ignored the Kemalists all through 1921, complaining of the poverty of Turkish intellectual thought as though the Anatolian movement simply did not exist.

The question of tactics was particularly vexatious for the Turkish Worker and Peasant Socialist Party. On the one hand, it had to operate within the perhaps often lax, but always uncertain, constraints of the Allied occupation. The Istanbul authorities continually monitored its activities, censoring its publications with a heavy hand. At the same time, the party felt increasingly obliged to adapt to guidance from abroad, which, though at times inconsistent, generally urged it to bolder action. In addition to encouragement from Paris to broaden its intellectual appeal, the party received constant exhortation from the Comintern to increase its activity in the labor field.

In these circumstances, the Istanbul communist leaders judged it particularly unrewarding to continue any dalliance with Hüseyin Hilmi and his Turkish Socialist Party. Hilmi's involvement with the British authorities was becoming widely known, and his party had begun to take part in the work of the anti-communist Amsterdam International Federation of Trade Unions. Hence, the Turkish Worker and Peasant Socialist Party, as it gained momentum toward mid-1921, turned its attention to building its own labor organization, reviving the Turkish Worker Association, which had languished after the Allied occupation.

The Worker Association immediately set itself the task of uniting all Istanbul labor organizations in a confederation under its control. To this end, on August 5, 1921, the Association held its first congress. Here the assembled delegates issued a ringing appeal to the Turkish proletariat to join in a "united front against the coalesced forces of the bourgeoisie." But, while this gathering trumpeted slogans of "the grand inspirer of social revolution, Karl Marx," calling "proletarians of all countries" to join forces, the Association remained strongly infected with Turkish particularism. In fact, it soon proved almost as much a rival as an ally of Maximos' International Union of Workers, though by this time both were affiliated with the Red International of Labor Unions in Moscow.[11]

This activity, although evidently not very successful in winning the masses of workers for the Turkish Worker and Peasant Socialist Party, was obviously quite distasteful to the Allied occupying powers. Nor were their suspicions calmed when in December 1921 *Aydınlık* chimed in applauding the increasing activism of the workers in defending their rights and urging them to go "in the direction of conscious class struggle." Under this provocation, the Allied authorities felt obliged to act. After the December issue, *Aydınlık* was suspended, not to reappear for seven months. Heavy fines were imposed on Sadrettin Celâl Antel and Şefik Hüsnü Deymer. Nonetheless, underground agitation continued. The party is said at this time to have circulated among the workers of Istanbul an illegal publication called *Zincirli Gençlik* (Chained Youth).[12]

The union movement in Istanbul, too, entered a time of troubles. By the end of 1921 the British and French occupation forces, having composed their differences, had begun to crack down on labor organizations. Unions were no longer able to exact profit from strikes. On the contrary, workers even began to suffer persecution because of union membership. Already in November 1921 Serafim Maximos was arrested and held briefly, an event roundly condemned by a correspondent in *l'Humanité*. Under this government pressure, many deserted the labor movement. Hardest hit perhaps

was the Turkish Socialist Party. Despite efforts of labor leaders like Rasim Şakir of the streetcar union, in the space of a
few months Hilmi's party lost almost its entire membership.
Its *coup de grâce* came in mid-1922 with the defection of the
so-called "Independent Socialist Party," in which the communists claimed significant influence.[13]

Even the communist-led groups found it difficult to cooperate under these circumstances. The Turkish Worker
Association had sought to assert its leadership by assembling
an impressively large gathering of representatives of worker
bodies in July 1922. But although the special committee
headed by Kâzım, which this conference set up to supervise
the formation of a confederation of Istanbul labor organizations, did eventually agree on a Marxist program, the confederation remained only on paper. As it turned out, none of
the major Istanbul labor unions was willing to renounce its
own independence. So bitter was this feuding that a representative of the Turkish Worker Association complained in
Moscow that Maximos' International Union of Workers had
"sabotaged" the projected confederation, refusing to join on
grounds "that the working class was not yet prepared and
that it must first be educated."[14]

During this difficult period, the Kremlin undertook what
appears to have been the first serious purge of the Turkish
communist movement. People of rather varying outlooks and
inclinations were still associated with the party in Turkey.
In part, this was the legacy of the confusion originally generated by Atatürk's "official" Communist Party. Thus one of
the first tasks of the Executive Committee of the Comintern
after the Third Congress was to appoint a special committee
from the Balkan Communist Federation to attempt to re-
register those members of the communist movement in Turkey who met their criteria for loyalty and orthodoxy. Contemporary evidence of the effects of this purge is not avail-

able; but as testimony to the difficulty of this task, it was necessary to repeat this process several times in the ensuing few years. Even then the job remained incomplete. For only the rigors of becoming a truly underground party finally proved an adequate test of devotion.[15]

But while the communist movement in Istanbul was passing through these tribulations, the party in Anatolia was enjoying a final flowering.

Even after victory at the Sakarya in September 1921, the Kemalists still faced a critical stage in their struggle with the Greeks. Although Atatürk's forces had broken the Greek offensive here in weeks of furious fighting, the Turkish forces were too weak to follow up their advantage. In order to expel the Greeks and to gain final victory, it remained extremely important to continue the flow of Soviet money and arms that had been coming in ever-increasing quantities since the end of 1920. For this reason, once the immediate pressure of the Greek advance had been relieved in September 1921, Atatürk acquiesced to Soviet insistence on an amnesty for Nâzım and his associates in the Peoples Communist Party of Turkey. Not only did the government push through Parliament a special law to that effect on September 29, 1921; but as part of the preparations for the visit of Soviet General Frunze, Atatürk even permitted Arif Oruç to resume publishing his paper. This was now called simply *Yeni Dünya* (New World), the word "Seyyare" having been dropped as refering to Ethem's partisans.[16]

Ankara obviously considered Frunze's visit a key to receiving the increased aid necessary to bring the war to a speedy conclusion. In consequence, the Turks went to extraordinary lengths to reassure their guest of Turkey's loyalty to Soviet Russia and what it stood for. Atatürk, in fact, went so far as to declare publicly that the present Turkish regime was "the same form of rule as Soviet power in Russia." Moreover,

when Frunze departed, he took with him a signed treaty
pledging the solidarity of Turkey and the Ukraine in the
struggle against imperialism, as well as a letter to Lenin affirming that "the more important similarity between our
two countries is our struggle against capitalism and imperialism."[17]

Hard on Frunze's heels at the end of January 1922 came
the new Soviet Ambassador Aralov, bringing a retinue of 30
to swell the already large Soviet mission. To the satisfaction
of the Kemalists, Aralov conveyed the promise that the
Kremlin would step up its aid. In this connection, he also
invited the Anatolian regime to send up to 100 students to
Moscow for university study and offered the services of ten
teachers from Russia for a "University of the East" which
the Turkish press reported—quite prematurely—was being
established in Ankara. On the other hand, Aralov's mission
met firm opposition in its endeavors to induce Atatürk to
undertake sweeping social reforms among the peasantry.
Nor were the Kemalists more receptive to the offer of assistance in setting up a system of political commissars in their
military establishment. Here, Atatürk neatly turned the
tables, diverting the additional aid for his own propaganda
purposes instead.[18]

In these circumstances, the Ankara government even
permitted Nâzım and Hacıoğlu Salih in March 1922 to re-es-
tablish the Peoples Communist Party of Turkey. For its headquarters, the party used the *İkaz* printing press offices belong-
ing to Afyonkarahisar deputy Mehmet Şükrü. It was soon
actively campaigning to enlist members. Many of its former
adherents now drifted back into more or less intimate association with the party, though by no means all rejoined.
Zinniatulla Navshirvanov, Abdülkadir, and Nizamettin
Nazif Tepedelenlioğlu served as the backbone of the party,
although they may have been encouraged and assisted at

least to some degree by newcomers from Istanbul like Mehmet Vehbi Sarıdal and Nizamettin Âli Sav, who had belonged to the *Aydınlık* group. Because of communications difficulties, the Ankara communists apparently did not establish any close liaison with the Istanbul party, though irregular informal contact undoubtedly existed. Indeed, the Peoples Communist Party appeared as something of a rival of its Istanbul brothers for favor with the Kremlin, with whom the Ankara party was in far more direct contact.[19]

One of the first concerns of the Anatolian communists was to set up the weekly *Yeni Hayat* (New Life) as the official organ of the central committee of the Peoples Communist Party of Turkey. From the first issue of this publication on March 18, 1922, it was clear that prison had taught Nâzım and his associates some circumspection. No longer did they try to trade on the religious sensibilities of the masses. Instead, in keeping with the new tactics elaborated by the Comintern, they concentrated on economic issues as well as continuing the more traditional attacks against Western imperialism. Their style was simple, resembling little the literary heights of *Yeni Hayat*'s Istanbul counterpart, *Aydınlık*. Moreover, to make their points the editors of *Yeni Hayat* depended heavily on translations from Marxist and communist literature, not all of them particularly relevant to an Anatolian audience. In fact, the lack of original thought in *Yeni Hayat*, at least in its early issues, contrasted strikingly with the intellectual vigor of *Aydınlık*. It reflected the essential difference between the relatively unsophisticated activism of the Ankara communists and the essentially European salon socialist approach of the Istanbul faction.

In its third issue, *Yeni Hayat* carried the party's "Declaration to the Government of the Grand National Assembly,"* officially announcing its return to activity and explaining its

---

* See Appendix II for a full translation of this declaration.

purposes and philosophy. Unabashedly labeling itself Marxist, the Peoples Communist Party affirmed its attachment to the Third International. At the same time, the party proclaimed its support of the "National Pact" promulgated by the Kemalists. In fact, the Ankara communists pledged themselves to assist the government in every way in its struggle against imperialism, calling on "all communists and workers" in the world, especially those in the Entente countries, to rise up and force the "rabid" invaders to withdraw from Turkish soil. Internally, the party focused its main attention on the peasants rather than on the workers, of whom there were relatively few in rural Anatolia. It thus sought the creation of economic organizations designed to enable the impoverished peasantry to share in material advance. Only by so doing, the communists argued, would national independence be truly guaranteed against the attacks of imperialism. The party's declaration closed with an appeal to the government to reinstate Nâzım as Tokat deputy in the Assembly.

Not surprisingly, the Soviet mission played a considerable role in the life of the Peoples Communist Party of Turkey. In his memoirs, Ambassador Aralov admits to frequent contact with Nâzım and his associates. The Soviet Embassy gave a special reception attended by the party's leaders on the anniversary of the fall of the Paris Commune, the day of *Yeni Hayat*'s first issue. In 1922 Soviet officials took part with party members in a public celebration of May Day in Ankara. Here, not only was a telegram of congratulations sent to various Istanbul labor organizations, including the Turkish Worker and Peasant Socialist Party, but a 25–30 man delegation was dispatched to pay respects to the Soviet Embassy. Throughout this period, in fact, the Soviet diplomatic establishment shared with the Peoples Communist Party an active part in propagating the communist faith.[20]

Yet the relationship between party and Embassy was by no

means an easy one. According to Aralov's own account, some of the leaders of the Peoples Communist Party of Turkey insisted on overt Soviet backing in the struggle to deprive Atatürk of the right to name cabinet ministers in July 1922. Nâzım allegedly claimed to be able at this juncture to produce 120 votes in Parliament to install a "Russophile" cabinet. This demand was no doubt extremely embarrassing for the Soviets: not only were they by this point fully committed to the support of Atatürk's regime, but they were properly sceptical of Nâzım's ability to deliver the vote. In this situation, Aralov apparently saw no alternative to informing the Ankara government of Nâzım's intentions. Perhaps the Soviets feared that otherwise their relations with the Kemalists would be harmed. In any event, this was a risky maneuver. For, however little compunction the Soviets may have felt about sacrificing the impetuous Nâzım, they had no wish to destroy Hacıoğlu Salih and his wing of the party, which represented a valuable asset that the Kremlin was not at all ready to abandon.[21]

As it turned out, Atatürk did suffer a defeat in the Assembly. On July 8, 1922, Parliament voted to revert to the system of direct election of cabinet ministers that Nâzım had so effectively exploited two years before. And in these circumstances, on July 12, 1922, Rauf Orbay was elected Prime Minister.

But far from representing Nâzım's promised "Russophile" cabinet, Orbay and his colleagues ushered in a climate noticeably more hostile to communist interests. The new Prime Minister was a "Westernizer" and a staunch supporter of a liberal parliamentary system. He viewed the communists—and indeed the Soviets as well—with far greater suspicion than had his predecessors in office. Both the Soviet mission and the Peoples Communist Party began to encounter harassment by the government.

Despite this government hostility, which came to include

restrictions on the party's activity, the Anatolian communists continued to operate more or less openly. In mid-July, with the approval of the Ankara authorities, the central committee of the Peoples Communist Party announced plans to convene its first party congress on August 15, 1922. This congress was scheduled to approve the party's program, to determine its attitude toward the nationalist movement, to elect the various party officers (including its representatives to the Fourth Congress of the Comintern), and to report on Comintern activity and on the political situation in Anatolia. As the party's relations with the Orbay government deteriorated, however, permission for this gathering was withdrawn, particularly when the authorities learned that communists from Germany, France, and the Soviet Union had been invited. Nonetheless, the party persisted in preparing for its conclave; nor were the foreign delegates deterred from making their way to Ankara.[22]

The Comintern, perhaps to avoid posing a dramatic challenge to the Ankara regime, sent a low-level delegation headed by Sergei Zorin, a 32-year-old Russian propagandist. In what appears to have been the most impromptu fashion, he importuned Magdeleine Marx Paz and her husband, who were then on a visit to Moscow to join French renegade officer Jacques Sadoul and Ahmet Cevat Emre, to fill out the representation. Because of the dangers of attack by Entente naval forces, the Comintern group proceeded by submarine, accompanying the regular monthly courier to Ankara. Brushing aside the Turkish port authorities at İnebolu with assurances that they were merely a "study mission," the delegates finally reached their destination. Here they frankly revealed the purpose of their trip and sought—unsuccessfully, however—to induce leaders like Ali Fuat Cebesoy to intercede with the government to permit their congress to be held.[23]

Although the Ankara authorities refused to rescind their

ban, the party conclave nevertheless convened on schedule, but on the premises of the Soviet Embassy. The 30-odd delegates were a most mixed lot: in addition to the Comintern delegation, Soviet Ambassador Aralov represented Russia; Azerbaijanian Ambassador Abilov attended in the name of the Caucasus; at least two Germans (including one who was reputedly an expert on union movements) and an African Negro who spoke nine languages were on the scene. Among the representatives present from Anatolia besides the party leaders were at least two peasants and some arsenal and textile workers—if the testimony of the Germans who attended can be believed. Indeed, the communists vaunted an attendance of 80 percent of those invited, despite all obstacles posed by the Ankara government, including measures to prevent the participation of workers from state-owned factories. After an initial session, the congress postponed substantive debate until the first week of September.[24]

At the ensuing sessions the party devoted its main attention to working out its agricultural program in line with its earlier expressed views. Optimistically taking hope from the "example of the Russian Revolution," the party set itself the ultimate goal of turning the Turkish peasants into an active revolutionary element, though recognizing that at the moment the masses were "thoroughly enslaved by the religious ideas of Islam and by patriarchal customs." To the approval of at least some of its foreign representatives, the congress took the opportunity to reiterate that the party eschewed revolution for the duration of the struggle for independence. The convention closed by granting mandates to Hacıoğlu Salih, İsmail Hüsrev Tökin, Zinniatulla Navshirvanov, Nizamettin Nazif Tepedelenlioğlu, and two workers (Cemal and Galip) as delegates to the impending meeting of the Comintern in Moscow.[25]

With the decisive victory over the Greeks in September

1922, a fundamental change took place in relations with Soviet Russia. Support from this quarter began to loom less vital for the Kemalists. At the same time, the Kremlin was displaying the tactlessness of celebrating the Turkish victory by issuing a Comintern manifesto on September 25 proclaiming that "the Turkish government . . . certainly does not correspond to our ideals" and that eventually "the Turkish working class will have to fight against the government." This sentiment was echoed on Turkish soil as well. At a meeting convened on October 6, 1922, by the Peoples Communist Party in Mersin (then still under French administration), speakers warned that if Ankara continued its "reactionary policy" toward labor organizations, "the working class would be obliged to renounce support of the government."[26]

This agitation gravely compromised the claim of the local communists to special treatment. Already before the end of September 1922, the government had closed *Yeni Hayat* for its harsh editorial, "A Slap on the Back of the Neck of the Prime Minister." In the course of October and November 1922, the government carried out an extensive roundup of communists in Anatolia on the grounds that they were "plotting to overthrow the existing order." Nâzım and many of his colleagues were arrested. Only the delegates to the Fourth Congress of the Comintern apparently managed to escape apprehension.[27]

These arrests evoked strong reaction from the Kremlin and from those Turks who were beyond the reach of the Ankara regime. Hacıoğlu Salih published from Moscow a "Protest of the Peoples Communist Party of Turkey," bitterly denouncing the hostility shown by the Orbay government since its accession to power in July 1922. Ahmet Cevat Emre presented a resolution to the Red International of Labor Unions at its Second Congress in November 1922, calling workers of all nations to express their solidarity with the arrested comrades. *Pravda,* too, in a sharply worded leading editorial cautioned the Kemalists to "Make No Mistake," warning that, although the Entente's conduct at the Lausanne Conference signalled imminent hostilities, the Soviets could not be counted on for help if communist persecutions continued. The Comintern further underscored its disapproval by issuing an appeal in February 1923, directing the proletariat of all countries to deliver similar warnings to the Turkish government.[28]

It was in this atmosphere that the Fourth Congress of the Comintern convened in November 1922. This assemblage called for the strengthening of Soviet control over the international communist movement. Less room for individuality was to be left to the various local parties; the welfare of the Soviet state was to be given priority over national interests. Thus on the one hand, Turkish delegate Orhan (apparently a pseudonym) decried the recent arrests in Turkey, proclaiming that the Kemalists had not been truly revolutionary since accepting the British invitation to the London Conference in February 1921. He charged Ankara with following a policy of betrayal calculated to deceive both the Soviet leaders as well as the Turkish communists. Comintern leader Radek, however, who had only a few months before summoned the Kemalists to "union with Soviet Russia," took a larger view. While lamenting the arrests, he argued that the path to communism in Turkey was long, and cautioned that no early seizure of power should be contemplated. From his words it became unmistakably clear that Turkish communists must be ready to sacrifice themselves for the sake of larger Soviet interests.[29]

Part of this sacrifice was to allow the Peoples Communist Party of Turkey to die. Henceforth, those few party members who did not defect from the movement to join Atatürk were absorbed by the communist faction in the Turkish Worker and Peasant Socialist Party in Istanbul. Indeed, the Soviets may not have been entirely unhappy to see the Peoples Communist Party go. For the Comintern was then in the process of concluding that only one communist party should be permitted to exist in any one country. At the same time, the amalgamation of the Anatolian party with the Istanbul organization not only served the purpose of relieving tension in Soviet relations with Atatürk, but it allowed the creation of a unified party drawing on the intellectual resources of Istanbul and in touch with labor. Such a unified communist organization obviously offered a more promising base of operations for coping with the problems of a reunited Kemalist Turkey.

Though it did not put down deep roots of its own in Anatolian society, the Peoples Communist Party left a legacy that would haunt the communist movement in Turkey ever after. For, from his experiences with the Ankara party, Atatürk had come to be deeply suspicious of communist intentions. With communist desire for social change—as he then understood it—Atatürk evidently still had little quarrel. Certainly he was not yet ready to brand the communist diagnosis of social ills and prescription for their remedy as harmful per se. He did not see communism as dangerous in its theories. Rather it was the open disloyalty to his regime and the eagerness of the Anatolian communists for power that clouded Atatürk's view of the movement. Perhaps equally disturbing he found the connection with the Kremlin. For Moscow's intent to use the party as an arm of Soviet policy and its willingness to intercede on behalf of communists who ran afoul of the government could hardly have escaped Atatürk's notice. Quite naturally this suspicion and mistrust were to spill over to color his opinion of the Istanbul party as well.

CHAPTER VI

The Party and the Republic

Let's hope that the Turkish nation which has great competence in military affairs will in the economic realm be able to create a few Mustafa Kemals!
Vedat Nedim Tör, *Aydınlık*, August 1923

Rights are never given, but taken.
Haber, September 14, 1923

The worker is the master of masters!
Aydınlık, special workers supplement, January 1925

Damn feudalism along with its reactionaries, agas, sheikhs, caliphs, and sultans!
Orak Çekiç, March 5, 1925

The defeat of the Greeks on the battlefield brought to a close the military phase of the Turkish struggle for independence. Nationalist troops swiftly reoccupied the Aegean coast, forcing the Greeks to sign the Mudanya armistice in October 1922. Soon thereafter Allied forces withdrew from all Turkey save Istanbul, where the occupation dragged on until October 1923.

The end of military action permitted the confused jumble of political forces in Anatolia to shake down. The war had made strange bedfellows: conservative religious leaders worked side by side with militant social reformers. Democrats, monarchists, and communists all joined in the struggle against the invaders. Even personal rivalries were in large part put aside before the need for unity. And such basic problems as a decision on the nature of the regime were shelved with an artful formula to await the liberation of the Sultan. This patchwork obviously could not last once the pressures of war were withdrawn.

Continuing occupation of Istanbul created a crisis of authority that merely exacerbated these strains. Well before the Allied troops had evacuated the city, the Ankara government began to extend its authority to the former capital. On November 1, 1922, the Ankara Assembly decreed the abolition of the Sultanate. Later that month, upon the flight of the deposed Sultan Vahideddin, Parliament elected Abdülmecid to the religious office of Caliph which was temporarily permitted to continue. At the same time, the Ankara government declared that laws passed by the Kemalist legislature since 1920 were valid in Istanbul.

The communists in Istanbul were not slow to seek to exploit this confusion. Here, immediately after the expulsion of the Greeks from Anatolia, the International Union of Workers, in cooperation with the Turkish Worker Association, distributed leaflets in the Muslim quarters calling on workers to join in ousting the Entente occupation forces. This line accorded well with Kemalist desires. For once the armistice had been signed, the problem of securing Allied evacuation of Istanbul became one of Ankara's most pressing concerns. Atatürk, therefore, may have sought to stimulate agitation of this kind even by the communists. In fact, some Turkish observers believe that Kemalist agents played some part at this time in circulating an appeal signed by the "Turkish Communist Party General Headquarters and the Red Unions of Anatolia" urging the people to rise up and arrest Sultan Vahideddin.[1]

The Turkish Worker and Peasant Socialist Party, too, joined in this effervescence. *Aydınlık* had managed to reappear toward the end of July 1922. In view of the Allied censorship, however, it was at first obliged to exercise great caution. Nonetheless, the party leaders were able to applaud when the Turks ousted the Greeks from Anatolia. While *Aydınlık* could not resist claiming that the victory was partly due to the efforts of anti-war propaganda of Greek socialists on the workers and peasants in the Greek army, it did voice the hope that the victorious Turkish regime would henceforth work for the good of the worker and peasant class.[2]

To this audacity the Allied authorities in Istanbul reacted sharply. In October 1922, the International Union of Workers and its organ, *Neos Anthropos,* were closed. The Turkish Worker Association was forced to suspend activity and *Aydınlık,* too, was unable to appear that month. However, though some of the leaders of these organizations were apparently arrested at this time, they were soon released, for Allied power in Istanbul was rapidly waning. *Aydınlık* reappeared in November, and Allied censorship was lifted a few weeks later.

For the communists, the era of good feeling toward the Anatolian nationalists hardly outlasted military victory. With the destruction of the Peoples Communist Party of Turkey in Anatolia in October 1922, the attitude of the Turkish Worker and Peasant Socialist Party toward the Kemalist government began to harden. Şefik Hüsnü Deymer openly cautioned in *Aydınlık* that "the Anatolian revolution is very far from satisfying those who believe that nothing but a radical social revolution can save the nation." Even in his message of congratulation to the Grand National Assembly in Ankara on the abolition of the Sultanate, Deymer could not refrain from asserting that the true liberation of Turkey's workers and peasants could come only through "social revolution, relying on joint production and ownership." Yet, the Turkish Worker and Peasant Socialist Party assured the Kemalists that it would go "to the end" in support of the struggle against the "reactionary tendencies" of some Istanbul intellectual circles who wished to see the Sultanate restored.[3]

As occupation constraints eased, the labor movement in Istanbul began to stir. Moderate socialists of the Second International persuasion took the lead in attempting to organize the Istanbul workers. Of course, none of these various and competitive ventures was entirely satisfactory to the *Aydınlık* communists. They would have preferred to see the Turkish Worker Association revived. But, judging this impossible, they advised their supporters—not without considerable reservations—to cooperate with Istanbul deputy Numan, who was seeking to form a League of Worker Associations (Amele Dernekleri Birliği). Numan's projected confederation, however, found it almost impossible to pass beyond the planning stage. Numan himself lacked the necessary qualities of leadership, and he was never able to live down the suspicion that he was not a "true socialist." As it turned out, he proved quite unable to cope with the intrigues of the conservative socialists on the one hand and the Kemalists on the other.[4]

The Economic Congress which Atatürk convened in Izmir in February 1923 provided an issue that the Istanbul communists could not ignore. In honor of the occasion, *Aydınlık* devoted a whole issue to the labor movement, summoning the conferees to defend the interests of Turkey's workers and peasants against Western capital. Deymer, in the name of the Worker and Peasant party, advanced a comprehensive program of demands for the expropriation of large landlords, the formation of agricultural cooperatives, and the distribution of land to the landless. He also called for the improvement of working conditions in factories, the right to organize unions freely, and permission to maintain relations with international worker organizations. These points were echoed in a 39-point petition distributed at the Economic Congress by a group of delegates—apparently including Şefik Hüsnü Deymer himself—whose selection had been engineered by the party. But, although the Economic Congress, with its insistence on autarky, marked a giant step toward breaking the hold of foreign capital over the Turkish economy, it did little to satisfy the demands of the Turkish Worker and Peasant Socialist Party for reform in domestic industrial and agricultural conditions.[5]

This growing tendency for the communists to speak out did nothing to assuage the suspicions of the Kemalist authorities toward the movement in Turkey. Nor was the government's anxiety in any degree relieved when it learned that Hacıoğlu Salih, for whom an arrest warrant was outstanding from his days in Ankara, had returned to Turkey and was actively engaging in communist activity in Istanbul. Along with fellow delegate to the Comintern, Nizamettin Nazif Tepedelenlioğlu, Salih seems now to have taken a prominent position in the Turkish Worker and Peasant Socialist Party. Toward mid-March 1923, the police raided the party's headquarters, arrested Salih as a "fugitive" from justice, and packed him off rather unceremoniously to stand trial in Ankara.[6]

Even Salih's arrest, however, could not deflect the Turkish Worker and Peasant Socialist Party from undertaking a rather radical transformation.

In April 1923, the Assembly in Ankara announced its decision to hold elections in the summer. Ostensibly this move was necessitated by the obligation to select a body with a new mandate to ratify the peace terms then being worked out at Lausanne. In fact, Atatürk seized on elections as a means to eliminate the conservative opposition in Parliament. For now that the cement of national danger had been removed, the Assembly had become rent by a resurgence of opposition, much of it directed against his person.

With elections in the offing, the political pot in Istanbul rapidly came to a boil. Most of the Istanbul press, divining that their city stood little chance of regaining its political primacy without the Sultanate, adopted attitudes of varying hostility to Atatürk's regime. Many hoped for a return to constitutional monarchy. Almost all feared the prospect that Atatürk might emerge as a strongman on the order of Enver Pasha and other models of recent memory.

The Turkish Worker and Peasant Socialist Party was one of the few opposition elements that did not follow the more conservative path. Hence, to meet the demands of this new situation, the party saw need to shuck off its Clarté identity once and for all to enter the lists under more openly Bolshevik colors. No longer did it serve the party's interests to appear merely as a group of "parlor pinks." Henceforth, the Worker and Peasant Party was to emphasize its attachment to Moscow and the Comintern, appearing with many of the trappings of the international communist movement. And, indeed, through the Soviet Trade Delegation now resident in Istanbul, contact with the Kremlin was more direct and more constant than in the past.

In this context, Aydınlık saw need to change its tune fairly extensively. In honor of May Day, 1923, Aydınlık appeared with a strikingly new format. For the first time, it featured the slogan "Workers of the World Unite!" emblazoned on a red cover depicting workers holding a May Day banner. It carried a ringing appeal of the Turkish Worker and Peasant Socialist Party "to workers and peasants and people of modest means." Poems of the celebrated young poet Nâzım Hikmet, then still in Moscow,[7] were also given prominence beside articles by Deymer, Antel, Kansu, and others. To facilitate the study of radical socialist and communist theory Aydınlık offered an increasing array of pamphlets containing original analyses of communism as well as translations of the Marxist classics. Finally, the change in Aydınlık's direction was evident in the more popular, hortatory style of some of its articles, though it still was written in an idiom undoubtedly beyond the easy comprehension of workers, its ostensible audience.

The Istanbul communists, Muslim and non-Muslim alike, joined forces to attempt to use the by now traditional May Day celebration in Istanbul as an occasion to popularize their new line. In this venture they were not entirely successful, however. Kâzım from Van and the Greek communist Stavrides were apprehended by the police on the eve of the celebration for handing out circulars allegedly inciting the workers to revolt. And under the watchful eyes of the police, the May Day demonstration took place in quite orderly fashion and in a manner much to the liking of the Ankara authorities. Supporting Atatürk in his drive to regain control of Istanbul, the delegates sent telegrams to "the proletariats of the countries of the world" urging them "to intervene in favor of the evacuation of Constantinople at the very earliest possible moment so as to enable us to breathe freely again." In addition, the demonstrators acknowledged their gratitude to Atatürk, expressing the hope that he would "save them from economic slavery."[8]

Despite its growing militancy, the Turkish Worker and Peasant Socialist Party was by no means ready to launch a campaign of all-out opposition to the Kemalists. Recognizing that it was too weak to risk the challenge of the polls, the party threw its support to the Kemalists, who were effectively dominating the national election contests through the political machinery that was to form the base of the Republican Peoples Party. Deymer, in his *Aydınlık* article on the coming elections, thus explained at some length why the "socialist current" should "act hand in hand for a long time" with the Kemalists in opposing "black reaction." On this basis, he called his party's supporters to vote for those Kemalist candidates who sympathized with the "socialist revolution," progress, and the rights of workers.[9]

Nevertheless, the Ankara government was clearly taken aback by the new tone of the communist movement. Investigation into the abortive May Day activities of Kâzım and Stavrides led to the wholesale arrest of *Aydınlık*'s editors and communist leaders from all the Istanbul communities on charges of violating the Treason Act. At their trial, which began toward the end of May 1923, the several dozen defendants were accused of being in contact with foreign powers, seeking to extinguish Turkey's social and political order, inciting Turkish workers to revolt, organizing a secret Turkish Communist Youth League, and disseminating communist doctrine "which contains many principles opposed to the proposition of nation."[10]

The accused put up a spirited defense. Taking advantage of the sympathetic climate in press circles in Istanbul, Şefik Hüsnü Deymer printed a long apologia on May 27, 1923, in the progressive nationalist paper *İleri*. Here he explained that he and his associates had worked exclusively through *Aydınlık* and the Turkish Worker and Peasant Socialist Party, both legal organizations. He ridiculed the charge that the Communist Party sought to overthrow the government, pointing out that the party had but 150 members and that the Turkish workers "were not organized for social action." At the same time, Deymer, who denied the accusation of ever having visited Russia, vaunted his attachment to the Comintern, which he described as Turkey's sole staunch supporter during the struggle for independence. In court, however, the defendants based their case on a technicality: the Treason Act had not been properly promulgated in Istanbul. And in truth, this statute had not been announced by town criers as specified in its own provisions.[11]

Somewhat surprisingly the court accepted this defense. The accused were promptly released. But more than strict legalism may have been involved in securing this verdict.

For the Turkish press claimed that the government had proof that "Russian communists" had been involved in encouraging the *Aydınlık* circle. Indeed, according to these sources, it was to avoid the embarrassment of implicating officials of the Soviet Trade Delegation that the Ankara authorities agreed to free the Turkish communists on assurance that such subversive contact would not be continued.[12]

Be that as it may, although some of the former Peoples Communist Party leaders—including Nizmettin Nazif Tepedelenlioğlu, who had been arrested at the end of June 1923—were tried and sentenced in Ankara in July, the government did not thereafter press the issue against the Turkish communists in Istanbul. The communists from the minority communities, however, did not fare so well. The predominantly Greek International Construction and Carpenters Unions were closed once and for all. Gensberg and Serafim Maximos fled abroad, never to return.[13]

The Turkish communists, on the other hand, were encouraged by their release and now deepened their efforts in the labor movement. A wave of strikes broke out in the summer of 1923 offering the communists new chance for profit. The printers union in particular proved susceptibile to communist influence. And when the printers went on strike on September 7, 1923, the communist hand was clearly evident.

From the first, elements sponsored by the *Aydınlık* communists took control of the union. Mehmet, the chief of the Turkish Compositors Society, had quickly discredited himself by bowing to the threats of the publishers to withdraw recognition from the union if the strike continued. Thus, when Mehmet urged his companions to abandon their strike, the main body of strikers ignored him. Taking advantage of their opportunity, the recalcitrant printers, assisted by *Aydınlık,* now started a newspaper of their own, *Haber* (News). This was a finely printed full-size daily that appeared morning and evening to bring their side of the dispute to public attention and to counter the *Müşterek Gazetesi* (Joint Gazette) published by the newspaper owners. The strikers' organ called for the solidarity of the proletariat in familiar communist terms, seeking to drum up support for the printers in their struggle. But *Haber* did far more than give play to strike news. It also devoted great attention to attacking the League of Nations and to pursuing other issues equally extraneous to the dispute, but of priority interest to the Kremlin. In fact, according to a Soviet account, the strikers even demanded that Turkey establish more intimate relations with Soviet Russia.[14]

After two weeks of highly conspicuous controversy between owners and workers, the government intervened to force a settlement. Its solution was something of a compromise: the workers' demands for higher pay were largely satisfied, while the newspaper owners were allowed to raise the price of their papers.

The strike over, *Haber* was reportedly converted to a morning paper under the title *Vazife* (Duty). However, this venture, in which the *Aydınlık* communists continued to play a role, was forced within three months to suspend publication for lack of funds. There was still not sufficient audience among the intelligentsia nor even among the largely illiterate workers to support an undertaking of this size.[15]

Faced with this activity, the Kemalists themselves now entered the labor field.

Hüseyin Hilmi had been murdered in November 1922 under mysterious circumstances; and with him passed all traces of the Turkish Socialist Party. Rasim Şakir, director of the Aksaray depot of the streetcar company, succeeded him as the most popular labor leader in Istanbul. By the spring of 1923, he had banded together a sizeable group of unions to form the Istanbul General Worker Confederation

(İstanbul Umum Amele Birliği) . Something of a moderate, Şakir evidently gravitated into the Kemalist orbit during the election campaign of 1923, when he, like the communists, found himself unprepared to risk contesting the elections. Hence he, too, instructed his followers to vote for Atatürk's party. Late in the fall of that year, he expanded his Istanbul organization into a Confederation of Turkish Workers (Türkiye Amele Birliği) of 34 unions embracing—if Turkish labor sources can be believed—some 19,000 organized workers from Istanbul, 15,000 coal miners from Zonguldak, and 10,000 lead miners from the Balya-Karaaydın region. This Confederation espoused purely economic aims and was in no way connected with the communist movement. While the Ankara government did not officially recognize the Confederation, Şakir saw to the election of Dr. Refik İsmail (Secretary of the Kemalist Peoples Party in Istanbul) as Vice-President of his organization. For his part, Atatürk acknowledged the Confederation's loyalty and promised to cooperate in working out labor legislation. But after this rather meteoric start, Şakir's organization, like so many of its predecessors, proved astonishingly ephemeral. Its artificial combination of workers from diverse areas with many diverse interests had broken down completely by the middle of 1924. And the Kemalists, seeing no further profit from it, were content to let it disappear.[16] But during its short life, the Confederation effectively countered the influence of the communists and made sure that by far the largest portion of the labor movement remained out of their hands.

This was a period in which the destiny of the new Turkish state was shaped. Atatürk—thanks only in the most minute degree to the support of labor and the communists—won a crushing victory over his conservative opposition in the elections of 1923. Taking office, this time with the backing of his strong, well-organized, well-disciplined party, he began to put the capstone on the legislative and executive edifice he had so patiently constructed. In October 1923, Ankara was decreed the "seat of government of the Turkish state." But what was this state? Since the abolition of the Sultanate, it could no longer be called a monarchy. Yet for almost a year Atatürk had not seen it expedient to acknowledge publicly what was evident for the world to see: the Turkish state was in all but name a republic. This failing he soon rectified. On October 29, 1923, through a masterful scenario of political intrigue, he induced a none too willing Assembly to break irrevocably with the past and declare the Republic. This step he followed, after lengthy probing of military support, by the abolition of the Caliphate in March 1924. Henceforth, Turkey was to be a secular Republic.

Declaration of the Republic, like much of Atatürk's maneuvering, not only caught the communists off balance, but stole their thunder as well. In *Aydınlık* they had long urged such a move, perhaps not expecting to see their desires accomplished, certainly not this rapidly. Indeed, they had interpreted Fethi Okyar's accession to the Prime Ministry in August 1923 as signaling a retreat from reform. Thus the *Aydınlık* communists initially were unprepared to offer much of a new political program when Atatürk cut to the heart of the question of regime. Nor did they enjoy easy unanimity on how to view the new order in Turkey. Some of the Soviet advisers on the scene, like G. Astakhov, argued that Atatürk was a progressive who was leading Turkey in the right direction. Others seem to have viewed the Anatolian nationalists rather as budding fascists of the Mussolini variety.[17]

Under these circumstances, it was not surprising that *Aydınlık* let these basic changes in the regime pass without comment. Its November issue was devoted entirely to the anniversary of the Russian Revolution. Only in February

1924 did Şefik Hüsnü Deymer obliquely broach this subject for the first time with a single article pointing out the folly of considering legal and administrative reforms as social revolution. But it was not until May 1924 that *Aydınlık* directly confronted this issue, publishing an article entitled "What Does the Worker Class Think about the Republic?" In this and subsequent writings Deymer openly voiced dissatisfaction in the name of the workers, saying that mere proclamation of the Republic was not enough. For by this time, the controversy within the *Aydınlık* family over how to view the Kemalists seems to have been temporarily resolved. While the roots of this dispute were never entirely eradicated—and indeed would later contribute to a serious party split—for the time being the Istanbul communists joined under Deymer's lead to tax the government with representing no more than the bourgeoisie, ready not to save Turkey, but "to rob the nation as of old." To meet this situation, Deymer called the workers and peasants to organize as quickly as possible to defend their rights.[18]

These were days when new blood was flowing into the *Aydınlık* group. This publication was fast becoming the focal point for a nucleus of young men who were to play a major role in Turkey's intellectual development over the coming decades. Their dynamic approach and infusion of new ideas, some brought fresh from Moscow, would contribute to *Aydınlık's* rising circulation, which soon is said to have reached about 2,000, a figure which, if true, was a most impressive achievement for a theoretical journal of this sort.[19]

Prominent among the contributors who joined in the latter half of 1923 was Vedat Nedim Tör, a young economist who had graduated from the University of Berlin in 1922. Ever since his involvement in the *Kurtuluş* group in Germany in 1919, Tör had been deepening his interest in the application of communist doctrine. All during his stay in

Germany, Tör had kept in touch with his *Aydınlık* comrades, and at Şefik Hüsnü Deymer's suggestion had even been selected to represent the Istanbul party at the Fourth Congress of the Comintern in Moscow. Tör's approach was fundamentally economic: he was dedicated to building Turkey into an economically independent nation. For him, all political and social reform flowed from this concept. He was not much concerned with what Turkey could contribute to the international movement, but rather with what communist doctrine could do for Turkey. Indeed, the strong nationalist twist in his interpretation of communist theory was soon to bring him into conflict with the Comintern.[20]

Şevket Süreyya Aydemir also entered the *Aydınlık* circle at about the same time. At the close of the First World War, Aydemir had set off to Azerbaijan in quest of the Pan-Turanist ideal. Here he served as a village school teacher, experiencing the frustrations of trying to keep a fading dream alive. By the end of 1920, his disillusionment with Pan-Turanism had left him ready prey for the propaganda of Mustafa Subhi's Communist Party in Baku. Intoxicated with this new faith and its key to social problems, Aydemir joined the Communist Party and proceeded to Moscow late in the summer of 1921 along with Nâzım Hikmet and Vâlâ Nureddin Vâ-Nû to attend the newly established Communist University of the Toilers of the East. At this institution, Aydemir was exposed to a liberal education in communist theory and tactics. When he left after one school year, he was crammed with new-found lore which he hastened to disgorge on his return to Istanbul at the end of 1923. Lenin had become his hero. Indeed, Aydemir's first signed contribution to *Aydınlık* was a paean to his idol. Yet Aydemir, like Tör, viewed communism primarily as a route to salvation for Turkey, paying relatively little attention to its ramifications in the rest of the world. For all his enthusiasm toward his new faith, his Turkish orientation showed through. His nationalist proclivities emerged clearly in the book *Lenin ve Leninizm* (Lenin and Leninism), which he published jointly with Sadrettin Celâl Antel in 1924. Here he wrote: "It is now a historic duty of the day to make the country rich and progressive and a possessor of capital."[21]

But the problem of reconciling national aspirations with the internationalist requirements of communism was not confined merely to these newcomers. The whole *Aydınlık* circle was to a greater or lesser extent concerned with this issue. On the one hand, *Aydınlık*'s format reflected the new trend toward using the symbols of the world communist movement; its articles discussed the key issues of Marxist doctrine. But this journal did not openly label itself "communist" nor did the Turkish Worker and Peasants Socialist Party call itself a "Communist Party." Despite its dissatisfaction with the government and despite its inclination to play up the Russian Revolution, *Aydınlık* followed a relatively measured course. It sought in fact to appeal to the university youth and to imbue them with a desire to see radical social revolution. Yet *Aydınlık*'s editors took care not to give the government any imperious reason to react. It concentrated rather on issues connected with domestic economic and social reform which, of course, did not directly threaten the regime.

Aydınlık's stance, therefore, was not entirely satisfactory to the Comintern, which still hankered after a more blatantly "communist" position. In consequence, the Executive Committee of the Comintern formed a special committee to report on the Turkish situation; and at the Fifth Congress of the Comintern in June 1924, *Aydınlık* was singled out for considerable criticism. The Soviet delegate from the Ukraine, Manuilskii, berated *Aydınlık*—which he frankly labeled as the organ of the Communist Party in Istanbul—

for advocating class collaboration of the proletariat and the bourgeoisie. He was particularly critical of the tendency of the Istanbul communists to support the development of national capitalism as a weapon against foreign economic penetration. In Manuilskii's view, and here no doubt he was but echoing the views of the Comintern leadership, the error of the *Aydınlık* group was rooted in the "social patriotic ideology of the Second International." These criticisms, however, were flatly rejected by a Turkish delegate, Fapluk (an alias?), who insisted that the communists had collaborated with "revolutionary nationalism" exclusively, and this merely to oppose imperialism and such feudal survivals as the Caliphate. Moreover, while Fapluk admitted that a few Turkish communists had supported "State and Municipal Socialism within the framework of bourgeois democracy," he assured the Comintern that this deviation had already been corrected. Furthermore, Fapluk revealed that the party's case had been laid before the program commission, where the Turkish party expected to be vindicated.[22]

Fapluk, however, was somewhat premature in his assurances. For the Turkish communist movement still retained much of its own individuality. Even in as important a matter as the controversy over Leon Trotsky's deviationism, the Turks were remarkably slow in following the Comintern's lead. Trotsky and his supporters in the international movement had been utterly routed at the Fifth Congress of the Comintern. Yet as late as November 1924, some six months after the major European communist parties had already begun to condemn Trotsky with fulsome rhetoric, *Aydınlık* was still making favorable mention of his name in its anniversary issue on the Russian Revolution. Only at the first of the new year did *Aydınlık* finally join in the denunciation of its erstwhile idol, printing excerpts from an attack on Trotsky by Albert Treint, the Secretary General of the French Communist Party.

On matters of more parochial concern, however, the Turkish communists were quicker to react. While they continued to retain something of their own individuality, the *Aydınlık* writers soon undertook to clarify their views in a way more acceptable to the Kremlin. As early as September 1924, Deymer contributed an original analysis of national capitalism in Turkey which, though in all probability not entirely satisfactory to the Comintern, nonetheless marked a first step toward falling in line with Moscow's desires. The following month, Vedat Nedim Tör similarly began to redefine his concept of "Economic Salvation" for Turkey to accommodate "a national class struggle," which he now confessed was already under way. Moreover, while the *Aydınlık* group did not perhaps go as far in challenging the Kemalists as the Kremlin might have wished, nonetheless the tempo of agitation increased noticeably. In the process the Turkish Communist Party, as it later ruefully recognized, exposed almost all of its apparatus and began to operate in a manner far more like that of a normal political party than of a semiclandestine conspiratorial organization.[23]

In conformity with the Comintern's emphasis on establishing factory cells as the basis of communist activity, the Istanbul party turned its attention to the labor movement with renewed intensity. After the demise of the Kemalist-dominated Confederation of Turkish Workers, a new labor organization, the Workers Advancement Society (Amele Teali Cemiyeti), had come into being in the summer of 1924. While the loyal Kemalist, Dr. Refik İsmail, became head of this body, the communists apparently managed to gain a considerable voice in its governing council. The Workers Advancement Society devoted its primary attention not to labor agitation and strikes, but to an effort to secure favorable labor legislation from the Ankara Assembly. For, indeed, Parliament was then in the process of considering the comprehensive labor act promised at the Izmir Economic Congress. Hence, the Workers Advancement Society repeatedly memorialized Atatürk, distributed propaganda among workers, and finally in February 1925, held a series of meetings to prepare a counter-draft to the government's proposed labor bill. This draft was duly submitted to the Ankara authorities by a delegation elected by the assembled delegates, who claimed to represent some 30,000 organized workers, mostly from the railroad, transport, and port industries.[24]

To complement this activity, toward the beginning of August 1924, *Aydınlık* inaugurated a series of special worker supplements. These were pitched more on the level of sloganeering and carried briefer and more simplified articles than the parent publication. But the line was identical: "Organization means strength!" After the eighth issue in January 1925, however, these supplements were succeeded by the publication of *Orak Çekiç* (Hammer and Sickle) as the official party newspaper. It in turn devoted great emphasis to labor matters, publicizing in considerable detail the activities of the Worker Advancement Society and urging workers not to cooperate with "bourgeois parties and bourgeois politicians," a reference to both Atatürk's party and the newly formed Progressive Republican Party.[25]

All through this period, *Aydınlık* continued to attract new adherents.

Perhaps the most important of those to join at this time was the young poet, Nâzım Hikmet (who adopted the surname Ran in 1935, but changed this to Borzecki when he adopted Polish citizenship shortly before his death in 1963). Nâzım Hikmet was the scion of a prominent family that appears to have included the Polish renegade Mustafa Celalettin Pasha. In his early years, Nâzım Hikmet had been a disciple of Tevfik Fikret, Turkey's great modernist poet. By 1919, the eighteen-year old Nâzım Hikmet had already developed such individualistic views that he was dismissed from the Naval Cadet School in Istanbul. Thereupon, he passed to Anatolia, where he became easy prey for the radical socialists and anarchists—Spartakists—he met. Toward the end of that same year, he took a post as a school teacher in Bolu. Here he rapidly fell in with a certain Ziya Hilmi, a returnee from Germany who later proved to be an opium smuggler. Under Hilmi's tutelage, Nâzım Hikmet imbibed deeply of radical socialist doctrine and was soon converted to a rather personal and somewhat unorthodox communism. He undertook considerable poetic experimentation at this time, publishing poems in the Istanbul press and gaining a reputation which as early as July 1920 had even attracted the attention of Henri Barbusse in Paris. Toward the start of 1921, at Hilmi's urging Nâzım Hikmet set off for Russia to drink from the fountain of revolution. But his full conversion to communism seems to have taken place only after he finally reached Moscow and enrolled at the Communist University of the Toilers of the East. For some time before his return to Istanbul in December 1924, his poems had appeared with regularity in *Aydınlık*. They represented a new departure in Turkish poetic form, an attempt to meld sound and meaning in free blank verse. His poetry then as now became the rage of the young intelligentsia. Copies of his poems were passed from hand to hand among students in the lycées and at the university.[26]

Others who now became active in *Aydınlık* included Burhan Belge, who was later to make his mark as a journalist and politician. Belge, a man in his mid-twenties, had also studied in Germany. He reflected the concern with social problems characteristic of those who had seen Germany's social upheaval. More radical was Hikmet Kıvılcım, a medical student and Belge's junior by three years, who wrote in *Aydınlık*'s special worker supplements urging workers to unite. Kıvılcım seems to have been involved in organizational work in the labor movement as well.

But these new figures had little time to participate in the movement before the communist cause fell victim to quite unrelated developments on the political scene. After its experience in mid-1923, the *Aydınlık* group exercised considerable care not to challenge the regime so directly that it would feel bound to react. Even communist labor activity was conspicuous for its moderation and legalistic approach, though this did not prevent frequent arrest and interrogation of labor agitators. In fact, as the conservative opposition began to mass under the Progressive Republican Party at the end of 1924, the communists found themselves coming more and more to support the government. Thus, when the Kurdish revolt broke out toward the middle of February 1925, *Orak Çekiç* strongly assailed the rebels, branding the Kurdish uprising as a reactionary feudal movement. The paper did not even make the customary distinction between the leaders responsible for the rebellion and the misguided masses who would be potential allies of the communists if only properly enlightened. Nonetheless, despite this ungrudging support, the Ankara authorities did not hesitate to use the extraordinary powers granted in the famous "Law for the Maintenance of Order" of March 4, 1925. In the process of muzzling other shades of opposition, the newly installed government of İsmet İnönü closed both *Orak Çekiç* and *Aydınlık*.[27]

The Istanbul communists did not submit tamely. Instead, they apparently sought to challenge the government through the organ *Yoldaş* (Comrade), which İbrahim Hilmi set up in Bursa. Moreover, they continued their agitation among workers and in the university. Turkish communists even had the audacity to publish pamphlets celebrating May Day and to organize protest demonstrations against the closing of their main organs.[28]

To this the government reacted swiftly. Toward the beginning of May 1925, the police arrested those leading communists they were able to find. Only a few major figures like Şefik Hüsnü Deymer and Nâzım Hikmet managed to go underground; and after an abortive effort to continue their activities, they fled abroad.[29]

This time the communists were not able to plead any technicalities in their defense. The government charged them with violating the Penal Code by carrying on propaganda against the regime and by promoting the overthrow of the government. The Kemalists did not hesitate to accuse them of conspiring with a foreign power—the Soviet Union —though this point was not emphasized and there was still no effort to condemn communism as a doctrine. In appearance, then, the Turkish communists were sentenced for their acts, not for their beliefs. And the sentences announced on August 13, 1925, were extremely heavy: Deymer and Nâzım Hikmet were sentenced in absentia to 15 years; Şevket Süreyya Aydemir and Hikmet Kıvılcım received 10-year jail terms; many of the other defendants, including Sadrettin Celâl Antel and İbrahim Hilmi, were given 7 years in prison.[30]

These arrests and trials marked the end of the legal communist movement in Turkey. Although communism was not yet explicitly branded as subversive, the provisions of the Law for the Maintenance of Order gave the government an effective weapon with which to stifle dissent of all shades; and this law remained on the books for the next four years. Meanwhile, the Penal Code was entirely reformed in 1926 on the model of the Italian code. This new Code provided additional legal basis for acting against communist propaganda, though it did not yet contain the famous provisions of articles 141 and 142 introduced in 1936 to outlaw organizations advocating class struggle in any form. But with the readiness of the government to act against communists on whatever legislation was at hand, the Communist Party hereafter could exist only underground, where the government's vigilance tested the mettle of any hardy enough to join.

Epilogue

Efforts to violate the social order of the Turkish nation are doomed to defeat. The Turkish nation cannot accept the secret and dirty designs . . . of wretched, seditious fools . . . who want to work against themselves and against the supreme welfare of their country; and the Turkish nation is not a body that will tolerate them. . . . Those who want to divert it from its path are doomed to be crushed and annihilated. In this the peasants, workers, and especially our heroic army are wholeheartedly together. Let no one doubt this.

Mustafa Kemal Atatürk, statement to the people of Eskişehir, August 5, 1929

The struggle against the Kemalist Peoples Party is indistinguishable from the struggle against imperialism, which is again trying to bury the independence of the Turkish state. . . . The Turkish Communist Party advances a series of transitional political demands. Their aim is to lead the masses to a direct revolutionary struggle for their interests. . . . The Turkish Communist Party is carrying on a struggle for political and economic union with the USSR, inasmuch as only the closest cooperation between the USSR and the workers of Turkey can assure independence for Turkey and the free economic development of the country.

Program of Action of the Turkish Communist Party, İnkılâp Yolu, 1931

Turkey is in revolution. This revolution has not stopped. The movements we have experienced up to now, the revolts and the violence we have observed are only one stage of it. We have undergone a revolution. This revolution is not the goal of reform, but its means. If we stop at this stage of revolution, our revolution will be sterile. However, it is broadening and deepening. It has not yet said its last word.

Kadro, January 1932

The year 1925 marked the start of a period of social reform in Turkey. Heretofore the Kemalists had dealt primarily with their political problems. But over the next few years they would enact laws regulating various facets of social life in a manner almost as revolutionary as anything the communists had demanded. Dress, religion, law, language, and education all fell within the purview of Atatürk's reformist zeal. In short, the most sacred and sensitive areas of life were transformed by government fiat. Yet it was a mark of Atatürk's genius that this revolution could take place without completely abandoning parliamentary forms and without destroying utterly the social fabric. In Turkey, then, the new grew out of the old with a harmony that would be the envy of her neighbors and the amazement of the West.

Reform in form was followed by reform in content. While at first the new ways were adopted uncomprehendingly, Atatürk soon moved to develop understanding—at least among the elite—of the deeper implications of these reforms. He set about developing a consensus among the leading elements of society as to Turkey's course and aim. To this end, he added courses on the "Turkish Revolution" to the university curricula. He founded a Turkish Historical Society to celebrate the glories of the Turks as the central figure in history, the originator of all culture. He set up a Linguistic Society to reform the language in order to facilitate the transmission to the masses of the ideas of the elite.

Essentially Atatürk was building an elite united in its reformist attitude. This elite was to be the vanguard of society, the teacher in the grand school of the masses. And to enhance and ensure unity, Atatürk's party—the Republican Peoples Party—monopolized the political sphere. It brooked no rivals (save for a short but disastrous experiment in 1930). In fact, as the 1930s wore on, the Republican Peoples Party was to assume the form of a corporate state where party and government were fused at all levels. As part of this process, early in 1936 the Penal Code was finally amended to outlaw subversion of the "social or economic order" in Turkey, thus putting the legal capstone on the Kemalist structure of opposition to communism.[1]

It was against this backdrop that the further development of the communist movement took place in Turkey.

Atatürk's handling of the Communist Party was masterful and sure. He combined the carrot and stick in well measured proportions to limit to the utmost the threat from this direction. First he used the stick. The communists tried in 1925 received heavy jail sentences. Then they were isolated in prisons in the hinterland where conditions were particularly rigorous, especially for the urban intelligentsia, who formed the bulk of the party. On the other hand, once the full impact of prison life had registered, the communists were amnestied for one reason or another. (In 1926 they were released after the enactment of the new Penal Code.) But as soon as they returned to communist agitation, the government swooped down. In 1927 again many of those jailed in 1925 were taken into custody. This alternation between harshness and magnanimity—which became the pattern throughout the rest of the 1920s and the early 1930s—served effectively to weaken the will of those who experienced it.[2]

At the same time, Atatürk was applying another powerful lever to undermine the resolve of the communist stalwarts. He boldly offered the intellectual elite of the Communist Party the chance to enlist their energies in the Kemalist cause. Instead of casting them out as pariahs, tainted for life for their involvement with communism, Atatürk provided them opportunities to use their talents in government service and, indeed, to play an important role in the ideological development of Kemalism. His only condition was that they abandon the internationalist pretensions of communism and support his nationalist reform movement. Moreover, as Atatürk was in fact carrying out many of the social and even some of the economic planks espoused by the Turkish communists, his offer was doubly attractive.

Among the first to succumb was Sadrettin Celâl Antel.

Immediately on his release from prison in October 1926, Antel applied to the Ministry of Education for re-employment. This request was approved the following year and, Antel received a post as Civics Teacher and Instructor of Teaching Methods at the Istanbul Girls Normal School. Henceforth, Antel stuck to pedagogical affairs, and as a result was rewarded in the mid-1930s by being made Professor of Pedagogy at Istanbul University.[3]

Another major catch for the Kemalists was Ahmet Cevat Emre, who had spent most of the early 1920s abroad, serving as liaison between the émigré Turkish communists and the Comintern. Emre had been a Turkish language specialist whose Ottoman grammar book made considerable impact on linguistic circles during the closing days of the Young Turk period. Long a radical socialist, as early as 1909 he had been advocating social revolution as the sole way to progress. Even after joining Subhi's organization in Baku, however, Emre's main passion remained linguistic reform, a process he considered imperative for Turkish. Toward the end of 1927, after Emre had returned permanently to Turkey, he published a lengthy series of articles in *Vakıt* on the need for alphabet reform modeled on that just instituted in the Soviet Union. Almost immediately Atatürk extended Emre an invitation to participate in the Alphabet Commission then being formed to advise on the adoption of Latin characters. From this time forth, Emre played a leading role in linguistic reform, serving on the Executive Committee of the Turkish Linguistic Society and on the various commissions that directed the far-reaching revolution not only in the Turkish alphabet, but in its vocabulary and grammar as well. Moreover, he soon became a regular confidant of Atatürk's. In 1935, through Atatürk's personal intervention, Emre (who had joined the Republican Peoples Party) was elected to Parliament as deputy from Çanakkale.[4]

Toward the end of the 1920s Şevket Süreyya Aydemir too broke away from the Turkish Communist Party. In part he was rebelling against the more active control exercised by the Comintern since the Fifth Congress. He could no longer stomach what he castigated as its "childish interference and orders." Moreover, soon after his first release from prison, he was arrested a second time in 1927 for involvement in what the government claimed were attempts to incite a revolution. Following his acquital in court, therefore, Aydemir gave up his public relations post at the Soviet trading firm Arcos. Proceeding to Ankara, he fell in with his old friend Ahmet Cevat Emre, who had already begun establishing a position of favor with Atatürk. With Emre's help, Aydemir in 1928 received a post in the Ministry of Education dealing with professional education matters. At the same time, Aydemir found it possible to continue to develop and express his economic and social ideas that were soon to flower in the *Kadro* movement. Indeed, as early as January 1929, Aydemir was able to use the forum of the Turkish Hearth Society to lecture on his theory of permanent revolution and on the need for an elite cadre (in Turkish, *Kadro*) with which to carry it out.[5]

Another important figure to be weaned away from the communist movement in this period was Vedat Nedim Tör. Tör had become the Secretary General and ranking party official in Turkey after Deymer had fled to Vienna in the wake of the 1925 arrests. On release from jail in 1926, Tör appears to have established contact with Deymer in Vienna —allegedly through the Soviet mission in Istanbul, with whom Tör worked closely as an employee of the Arcos trading company. Nonetheless, Tör seems not to have been sufficiently radical to suit the "External Bureau of the Central Committee" of the Turkish Communist Party. This body at its conference in Vienna in 1926 had elaborated a rather extreme program calling for agitation against the Kemalists as well as for organizing factory-cells. As a result, the External Bureau decided in 1927 to send Deymer under an assumed identity to take charge of party activity inside Turkey. It was the resulting outburst of activity, including publication of a pamphlet titled *Bolşevik,* which led to the roundup in 1927 of 89 persons accused of attempting to create a dictatorship of the proletariat by revolutionary means. Tör, who was apparently the sole defendant to admit the existence of a communist organization, received notwithstanding a short sentence.[6]

These differences between Deymer and the External Bureau made Tör particularly vulnerable to Atatürk's tactics. Moreover, his close relationship with Aydemir must have also had a considerable effect in convincing Tör that he, too, should leave the formal communist movement to seek more effective ways to influence Kemalist thought. For Aydemir's propaganda activity in the Turkish Hearth Society in Ankara demonstrated vividly that it was possible to come to terms with Atatürk without abandoning the essence of the ideas earlier espoused by *Aydınlık.* Thus, toward the end of the 1920s Tör broke with the Communist Party and took advantage of the opportunity to join Aydemir and some of the lesser lights from the *Aydınlık* days who were preparing to launch a new movement through the periodical *Kadro.*

Meanwhile, the orthodox Turkish Communist Party was passing through a genuine time of troubles. The need to adapt to working underground was changing the essential nature of the party. No longer was it a haven for discontented intellectuals. It now required considerable courage and determination to participate in communist activity. Thus for the moment at least, almost no new blood was coming into the party. On the contrary, with the falling away of those who had formerly had a casual relationship with the party—

such as Burhan Belge and his ilk—and with the defection of some of the key party figures the Communist Party underwent a severe crisis. No one was above suspicion of deviationism. The test of party loyalty seems to have become primarily willingness to submit to the dictates of Moscow as transmitted by Şefik Hüsnü Deymer, who now strongly dominated the orthodox Soviet wing of the party.

In this situation the party conducted a series of purges that reduced still further its declining membership. Hacıoğlu Salih was dropped from the party in 1927 as a "Menshevik" and "Trotskyite." Just what the nature of his differences with Deymer may have been is hard to determine. Hacıoğlu Salih had always been both radical and independent of view. He may have been unwilling to bow to the party line as enunciated by Deymer less because he objected to the program than because he was unwilling to accept orders from Deymer as an individual. In any event, after his expulsion from the party, Hacıoğlu Salih seems to have made his way to the Soviet Union, where he eventually was killed during the purges of the 1930s. Even Nâzım Hikmet, whose interpretation of communism had always been rather personal, was expelled on similar charges around 1930. Again personality difficulties must have played a major role in his troubles with the party; and indeed, Nâzım Hikmet evidently managed to be readmitted to the party within a few years. Toward the end of his life, in the 1950s, he became one of the central figures in the communist movement.[7]

As a result of these internal schisms and as a consequence of the uncompromising opposition to the Kemalist regime proclaimed by the program of the Turkish Communist Party published in 1931, the communist movement in Turkey became reduced to a mere handful of faithful activists, supported by a few émigré leaders. The party came to be regarded as an agent of the Kremlin and little more than a transmission belt for Soviet propaganda. Especially after Atatürk spoke out on August 5, 1929, condemning "fools who lack fatherland or nation" who wanted to overturn the social order, the orthodox Moscow-oriented party found it impossible to regain momentum. In fact, by now the Communist Party had lost its earlier attraction for the Turkish elite, who almost unanimously turned their attentions elsewhere.

The misfortunes of the orthodox communist movement merely enhanced the prospects of the Kadroists. They now stepped forward to fill the intellectual void previously filled by the communist elite. In a real sense, the Kadroists—with few exceptions all former members of the *Aydınlık* group— had not deviated far from their earlier ideas expressed as Communist Party members. Their central idea remained that the elite in Tukey must awaken to its historic role as the revolutionary force in society. They urged this elite to evolve a comprehensive plan for state-directed development to overcome the inertia of the masses and the impediment of foreign capital. The Kadroists were powerfully influenced by the economic experiments then being introduced in the Soviet Union, especially the five-year cycle of planned economic development which they believed imperative for Turkey. They hoped that by formulating this economic program in a nationalist framework they could elaborate a revolutionary doctrine suitable not alone for Turkey but for other underdeveloped countries as well.[8]

Mardin deputy Yakup Kadri Karaosmanoğlu held the franchise for *Kadro,* which was apparently published with the semiofficial backing of the Ministry of Education. Atatürk himself approved of this intellectual experiment. Both he and other leading members of the government subscribed to it. Moreover, this journal had unquestioned influence on the policies of the government. The Republican Peoples

Party had the previous year enunciated a party plank calling for the creation of an etatist economy. For years to come, definition of this plank was to become one of the more contentious problems of Turkish political debate. And under the prodding of *Kadro,* Turkey's first five-year plan was introduced in 1934 in a halting and rather feeble effort toward centralized economic development. Though the concept of state economic planning would require many years to become established on the Turkish scene, *Kadro* can claim credit in no small measure for laying the base for this development.

The appearance of the vigorous intellectual movement generated by debate in *Kadro* naturally aroused its critics. It was not long before extreme nationalists in particular began to level their guns on the new publication. Even before the end of its first year, *Kadro* was being attacked by such figures as Ahmet Ağaoğlu in the columns of the influential *Cumhuriyet.* These critics assailed *Kadro* for going to extremes, though it was difficult to press this line of attack inasmuch as the doctrines *Kadro* espoused were ostensibly the tenets of the Republican Peoples Party, hence beyond question. Nonetheless, the storm against *Kadro* grew with time. Finally, at the end of 1934 the opposition won out. *Kadro* was closed after the first issue in 1935 by the expedient of posting its franchise holder, Karaosmanoğlu, abroad as ambassador.

After the mid-1930s, the Kemalist revolution began to show distinct signs of a hardening of the arteries. The young revolutionaries were aging. Vested interests had emerged. It was tempting to rest on the already impressive laurels won. Moreover, Atatürk was turning his flagging attention to foreign problems that appeared to hold the greatest threat to the regime: the clouds of the Second World War were gathering. Indeed, Atatürk's death and the exigencies of foreign danger would lead to a virtual moratorium on political activity until the end of the war. Thus the leavening process, which continued within the aging Republican regime, perforce went on underground. Though communist agitation— as evidenced by periodic discoveries of propaganda and arrests for organizational activity—continued, it would be only in the postwar upsurge of political ferment that the dormant seeds planted by the early communist movement could again sprout. And in this revival, many of the same figures and the same ideas again came to the surface.

Today the shape of communism and its challenges are admittedly much different than in the early days of the Kemalist Republic. The constellation of foreign power relationships has completely changed. Economic and social life has developed immensely. The political regime, though with occasional fits and starts, has blossomed impressively into a deeply rooted multi-party system. The process of this far-reaching development has unleashed divisive forces that have sundered in important degree the consensus of the elite forged in Atatürk's day. Turkey is now the scene of compulsive probing and groping for new approaches and new solutions to the ever-changing challenges of twentieth-century life. This dramatic revolution in attitudes has imparted new dimensions and new significance to the issue of communism. For, in the vastly more complicated situation of the present day, Turkey has not been able to solve the problem of incorporating its restless radicals into the system with the sure touch displayed by Atatürk a generation ago.

Turkish Communist Party General Statutes*

June, 1920

1. A Communist, i.e., Bolshevik, Party has been formed in Turkey to establish socialism and to make sure that world revolution which will assure prosperity and well-being to all humanity will take place immediately in Turkey.

2. The TCP [Turkish Communist Party] will struggle with all its might for the salvation of all oppressed nations and classes from the tyranny of capitalism and imperialism.

3. As regards form of administration, the Turkish Bolsheviks accept the principles of Russian Soviet organization.

4. The Turkish Bolsheviks will bring into being a true peoples republican government in the life of society by means of village, county, district, provincial, and central Soviets and will impose the dictatorship of these Soviets formed from the deprived poor until the institution of socialism.

5. The Turkish Bolsheviks will deprive the present bourgeois and oppressor classes of the right to vote in the elections for the Soviet governments.

6. In order to be successful in this struggle and in order to serve all humanity, the Turkish Bolsheviks have concluded a close union with the communist and socialist organizations in every country and will act together with them. They are also attached to the Third International.

7. The Turkish Bolsheviks reject war and militarism and all the inequalities and injustices caused therefrom. War and

---

* These statutes were translated from a copy provided by Mete Tunçay. The original is in the collection of the Türk Tarih Kurumu in Ankara.

fighting they consider legitimate only until the destruction of militarism and imperialism.

8. A temporary revolutionary army is being formed until the institution of socialism in the world as a result of social revolution.

9. The Turkish Bolsheviks would entirely nationalize, i.e., would recognize as the joint property of the nation, all sources of wealth and industry, such as land, banks, factories, businesses, buildings, railroads, ships, etc. On this basis private property is to be abolished. And production and general wealth are to be shared equally by the general public on condition that each [person] works according to his mental and physical capabilities.

10. Foreign trade and commerce are to be entirely in the hands of government monopoly. Internal free trade will be abolished immediately after cooperatives have been completely formed.

11. Articles of ornament and consumption that do not generate wealth and which are in excess of the quantity necessary for any individual are to be confiscated.

12. Those who are destitute, aged, maimed, and sick should share equally in the general wealth.

13. The Turkish communists would oblige every person attaining the age of puberty to work an average of 8 hours a day.

   a. Pregnant women should not work from 6 weeks prior to childbirth until 6 weeks after.

   b. As far as possible small children should be looked after by wet nurses and governesses, while those from 4 to 8 [years of age] should receive instruction in nurseries and kindergartens.

   c. The goal as regards general education presently consists of compulsory education for all children from 8 to 14 years of age without cost and where possible as boarders;

and [the goal] in future will be to extend this to those from 6 to 16 years of age.

d. Youths from 14 to 18 years of age and those who serve in mines and other difficult trades should work a maximum of 6 hours a day, and those in light occupations should work a maximum of 10 hours [a day].

e. Although higher education would not be mandatory, it should be free for everyone. Beyond this, special night schools for adults to learn to read and write in their spare time, general libraries, theaters, and museums should be set up.

14. The Turkish communists would separate government and religion. They recognize the total freedom of religion and do not violate the conscience of anyone. They proclaim freedom of conscience.

15. The Turkish communists recognize the free development of nations and would entrust to each nation the question of determining its own fate.

16. The Turkish Bolsheviks would abolish the old courts. Revolutionary tribunals would be set up only for a temporary period. Eventually it will be sufficient to have courts for civil compensation [only].

17. [The Turkish communists] would apply the death penalty as a legal recourse against the supporters of reaction only. In other matters the death penalty would be abolished.

18. The Turkish Bolsheviks would abolish normal political frontiers and customs formalities between Turkey and other nations that accept socialism.

19. The Turkish Bolsheviks consider the general debts charged against the nation and all treaties and stipulations to be null and void. And they would not recognize any sphere of influence on Turkish soil.

20. At the start of the revolution, indirect taxes are to be abolished. Other [taxes] would be collected as income taxes

[levied] according to the principle of geometrically increasing proportion. If need be, a new tax can be collected from the bourgeois class in the name of indemnity. Naturally all these measures would continue [only] until the day when money is abolished.

21. Doctors would be state officials and would be obliged to treat and care for the sick without charge. All hospitals and pharmacies would serve everyone gratis.

22. The Turkish Bolsheviks recognize poor human workers, such as the peasants, workers, laborers, government employees and servants who live solely by the labor of their hands and minds, [to be] the most sound supporters and elements of the party.

23. The Turkish Bolsheviks see it as their duty to act with complete openness and bravery in ideological debates to be held against the outmoded mentalities and superstition which must be destroyed in administrative and social organization. They abhor dissimulation and all administrative and political secret, concealed intrigue, and they absolutely will not hesitate to speak the truth openly to the people.

24. They consider it a maxim for themselves to defend and protect all members against persecution and attack made in any form on comrades who teach with the aim of serving the socialist Bolshevik party. . . .

25. The Turkish Communist Party will continue to enlighten and teach the people on these principles until receipt of the decisions of the Baku Congress of the "Third International" in Moscow.

GENERAL HEADQUARTERS OF THE TURKISH COMMUNIST PARTY

Ankara, 1920

The Declaration of the Peoples Communist Party of Turkey to the Government of the Grand National Assembly*

Recent events and circumstances in Turkey's economic and political life and the importance of its present historical situation impel our party, which has up to now temporarily suspended its activity, to return again to action with an open declaration of its aims and with a clarification of its point of view on the general situation of the country and on the internal and foreign policy of the government.

Our party, which stands on the platform of Marxism, will analyze its duties and organization in regard to the internal and external policy of the country with the aid of Marxist methods and, basing on these principles its estimate of the shape that events could take in future, will act as a guide to the previously determined general goal.

The "National Pact," which is the basic principle of the Turkish people and of the Turkish Grand National Assembly, is today our principle too. All proposals and decisions not in accord with this are rejected by our party.

The economic structure of Turkey and of the Near East can be characterized chiefly by the absence of large national industry. This special situation in our land points up the need to create and continue a general united front in the East against European and American imperialism. But [given] the present situation of Turkey's economic life, which in the

* Published in *Yeni Hayat*, April 1, 1922, no. 3, pp. 1–4.

main is based on small holdings and peasant producers, [Turkey has the choice of] coming to agreement with the West outside the National Pact and thus permitting the West to postpone its imminent death. Or [Turkey has the choice of] carrying out reform inside the country through bourgeois democratic methods, and of producing the economic innovations and organizations necessary to enable [Turkey] to resist imperialism in future and to confirm and continue the participation of the peasant majority in the burgeoning national revolution. To follow the first course would be for us to violate the much needed solidarity of the international oppressed masses, and for the government it would be to violate its own promise of independence that it gave to the nation. At the same time, it would violate and trouble our existing relations and treaties with the Russian Soviet Socialist Republic, which is a most fundamental and strong supporter of Turkey's freedom and independence and which has extended all sorts of aid both to all the East and to the government of the Turkish Grand National Assembly. Following the second course is the sole correct and saving solution as Mustafa Kemal Pasha [Atatürk] himself emphasized in his speech of March 1, 1922. The government must follow this course in any event. Although the peasant, who was declared in Mustafa Kemal's speech to be "the true master of the country," has been ground down by heavy taxes and brought to a miserable and exhausted economic position through the incompetence of the local government apparatus, as was many times written in *Hâkimiyeti Milliye,* and through the tyrannical pressures of large landowners, [the peasant] continued to struggle with fortitude at the battlefront and many times won honorable victories. This, too, showed that those exhausted peasants are still alert, work correctly, and are confirming once again their right to economic well-being by defending their own right to existence.

There are before the government many important questions about the postwar [situation]. One of the most important of these, if the national government is to survive in the future country, is the question of continuing the interest and favorable disposition of the peasants toward it. Therefore, as soon as the war is over there is firm need to produce a deep economic reform in land, tax, and administrative questions in the country. Otherwise, there is the chance that after the war the government machinery will be weakened by the outbreak of frequent disorders [brought about] by the demobilized soldiers and peasants.

Peasant sacrifice has been seen in Turkey's many national wars. After war is over, the peasants always demand in recompense for the sacrifices they made a bonus payment, the elimination of economic depression, and the reform of defects in government machinery. Everyone knows that during the last three years the amount of land cultivated and [number of] animals bred have experienced an important decrease. Taxes and custom duties have increased and exports declined. At the same time, the rise in price of the peasants' crops has been relatively insignificant. Therefore, by following present economic policy the peasant who devoted all his productive power to the battlefront will be deprived of the power of resistance. [Thus] he will be brought to defeat before imperialism, which is in any event stronger than he today. [Only] by changing internal economic policy will the peasant continue to be made useful for the defense of national independence. This is the outlook for the future. And these are the duties of internal policy. Besides this, there are many painful defects in our social life. We do not want to touch on these [in] practical [terms] at this important time.

In diagnosing the internal and economic situation of the country, we cannot fail to remember at least for a minute our foreign position. Even some internal questions which cannot be neglected must be subordinated to our foreign policy. As long as defense of the country's freedom and of its inviolability against attacks and aggression of bloodthirsty imperialism, continues in our foreign policy, our party, which is the defender of the rights of Turkey's peasants and workers, recognizes for itself a duty to support the government and aid in this policy. Let us make clear, too, the following points: We will invite peasants and workers to support the army and to continue their present forbearance and efforts to insure the victory of our heroic army. We will invite the communists and workers who are against the Greek invasion to [use] revolutionary means to dissolve the army of King Constantine, who is a puppet under the domination of the Allied powers, and of England in particular. And we will publish immediately a declaration to invite Greek communists to this duty through our party's special committee. These acts of ours are directed at reinforcing the military inclinations of our revolutionary soldiers, at rejecting propaganda of the Greek bourgeois generals regarding the "national character" of the battles against us, at assuring the unconditional surrender to our army of the Greek soldiers, and at matters concerning the internal situation of Greece. [In this last connection] we believe the government must be rather careful as regards the rights of the minorities in order to facilitate this matter.

In our opinion it is a duty to insure that, with the exception of those against whom there is firm evidence of attempt to oppose the interests of the revolutionary country, all citizens enjoy legal equality. We regard the Greek officers, generals, and bourgeoisie as the real source of these [antirevolutionary] beliefs of the Greek government, and all our pressure must be directed against them alone.

[Our] policy will be shaped [partly] in the form of defense of the poor and the peasant and partly in the form of pressure on those who are the main ones responsible. [It] will expose the nature of the tricks that the government of Greece wants to play in the name of "National Defense Policy."

Let us repeat: We will aid the government of the Turkish Grand National Assembly in every way in the struggle against imperialism. At the same time, we demand also the acceptance of the principles we proposed above. Here let us declare that it is necessary always to receive with caution all capitalist companies and enterprises coming from America, Belgium, and France. They want by exploiting our economic weaknesses to make us accept very onerous conditions and in this way to open on our rich and fertile soil a field of competition with British capital [that rests] on the rich soil of Arabia, Iraq, and Egypt. The result of such a capitalist struggle entering our country will be [to cause] the struggle of two fraternal peoples, the Turks and the Arabs, at the instigation of two aggressive capitalist groups.

We have entered the period of national revolutions in the East, and especially in the Near East. Hence, in the struggles against the Western aggressors and their men by the peoples and societies of Iraq, Syria, the Hejaz, Egypt, and elsewhere in the countries of the Islamic East which have always been brothers and friendly to us, our foreign policy must be based on the principle of [extending] all sorts of aid to these brothers who are fighting for freedom and independence.

We believe we must take as a basis for our Eastern policy the formation of a conscious united front for the struggle and defense of all the East against world imperialism, and that we must convene a congress of all Islamic nations to put strongly into practice this consciousness, setting up a general alliance of Eastern peoples and arranging meetings such as conferences of particular Eastern countries. The results of such congresses and conferences naturally will be very beneficial for the world of humanity and will facilitate the legitimate actions of the Eastern world. In addition, they will form an effective and positive answer to the failure to invite us to the Genoa Conference, at which the world imperialists live in a dreamland—where even the American government argues against our participation in the conference at a time when they are sending their men to [our land] to get economic privileges.

Now and henceforth for the East in general the time has come to rise in order to create a tight unity with the workers of the world who have been struggling for four years to destroy European and American capitalism and to destroy tyrannical imperialists by uniting by the millions all the oppressed in the name of the interests of the peasants of the East. The solidarity and unity of the East must be as much economic as it is political and military.

In sum, our party's point of view on these questions is the point of view of all communist parties of the world and of the communist Third International, to which we belong and which unites all those around it. These principles are the means of assuring the perfection of the Turkish administrative machinery and its complete freedom, the increase in the East of the revolutionary influence of the Turkish Grand National Assembly government, the reinforcement of our relations and treaties with Soviet governments, and the question of meeting the very just demands of our peasants. On these minimum demands that the times propose to us, we are ready to come to agreement on a practical and real basis with elements adopting the words of Mustafa Kemal Pasha [to the effect that] "the peasants are the true masters of our country" and with socialist and populist groups in the country and in the Assembly. We have a profound conviction that European workers and laborers will force acceptance of this invitation of ours and of the Third International, and that by carrying out our proposals they will very soon force England and other invader states to withdraw from aid to the Greek government. The Greek workers, and the Greek army that is composed of them, will ultimately turn the arms in their hands on the generals of the King and will turn against these rabid generals who do not shrink from committing crimes and infamy in order to preserve the interests of European capitalists in Anatolia.

Our party's present policy is merely to unite and concentrate all forces of salvation of the East in order to deepen the national revolution and to continue the struggle against aggression.

Since the day our party officially began activity by securing government approval for its program on December 7, 1920 (1336), there have been those who unfortunately wanted to violate and trouble our relations with the government. In this connection we emphasize that no decision has been taken up to now to return Tokat deputy comrade Nâzım, who is a member of our party and one of the most sincere fellow travelers of Eastern revolution, to his still vacant seat in Parliament. Moreover, our party in all its activity and acts is pure and free from personal ambitions and the defect of personal passion. We are going into action not to oppose those who are against us, but with the aim of assuring the salvation of the East on the bases shown above by inviting the cooperation of those who support these concepts.

GENERAL HEADQUARTERS OF THE PEOPLES
COMMUNIST PARTY OF TURKEY

Notes

CHAPTER I

1. See A. Biliotti and Ahmed Sedad, *Législation ottomane depuis le rétablissement de la Constitution* (Paris, 1912), pp. 54–55, 275–78. Cf. A. D. Novichev, "Zarozhdenie rabochego i sotsialisticheskogo dvizheniia v Turtsii," in Leningrad University, *Uchenye zapiski Leningradskogo Universiteta*, 1962, no. 304, pp. 9–10.

2. V. I. Lenin attended the meeting of the International Socialist Bureau (hereafter cited as ISB) in October 1908 when the Armenian "subsection" was formed. See V. I. Lenin, *Collected Works*, v. 15 (Moscow, 1963), pp. 241–42.

3. Stefan Velikov, "Sur le mouvement ouvrier et socialiste en Turquie après la révolution jeune-turque de 1908," *Études Balkaniques* (Sofia), 1964, no. 1, pp. 31–32, 35–36; Dančo Zografski, *Za rabotničkoto dviženje vo makedonija do Balkanskata vojna* (Skoplje, 1950), pp. 224–25; Giannes Kordatos, *Historia tou Hellenikou ergatikou kinematos* (Athens, 1956), pp. 238–39; Novichev, pp. 15–16. Cf. Joshua Starr, "The Socialist Federation of Saloniki," *Jewish Social Studies*, Oct. 1945, v. 7, no. 4, pp. 325–26, who was somewhat confused in his understanding of the chronology of events.

4. Starr, pp. 325–27; Kordatos, pp. 240–46; Velikov, pp. 36–38; Martin Hartmann, *Der Islamische Orient Berichte und Forschungen*, v. 3: *Unpolitische Briefe aus der Türkei* (Leipzig, 1910), pp. 19–20, 34–35, 187–89, 248; Halis Okan, "Uslovija, pojava i razvitie na rabotničeskoto i sotsialističeskoto dviženie v Turtsija," *Istoričeski pregled*, 1960, no. 4, pp. 94–96; L. S. Stavrianos, *Balkan Federation* (Hamden, 1964), pp. 185–86. Cf. Mete Tunçay, *Türkiye'de Sol Akımlar: 1908–1925* (Ankara, 1967), p. 34/n. 43.

5. Starr, pp. 326–27. See also, ISB, *Huitième Congrès socialiste international tenu à Copenhague du 28 août au 3 septembre 1910. Compte rendu analytique*, v. 8, (Gand, 1911), p. 457.

6. Niyazi Berkes, *The Development of Secularism in Turkey* (Montreal, 1964), pp. 344–45, 348, notes this influence. On Rasim Haşmet see A. Cerrahoğlu, *Türkiye'de Sosyalizm*, v. 2 (Istanbul, 1966), pp. 74–76. Z. F. Fındıkoğlu, *Ziya Gökalp, sa vie et sa sociologie* (Paris, 1936), p. 17/n. 1, asserts on the basis of Hartmann's work that the German socialist leader A. Bebel influenced the thinking of the Turkists. In fact, however, Hartmann, p. 20, merely records the acquaintanceship of the Salonika Jewish socialists with Bebel's writings.

7. The name "Mehmet Mecit" remains open to some question. See Tunçay, p. 57/n. 118. Velikov (p. 39), citing Bulgarian journals, calls him Mehmet

Meždet; Hartmann (p. 248) records the name as Mehmed Mešed, indicating that the publication *Irgat* was identical with *O Ergatis*.

8. On the Istanbul Socialist Center, see Kordatos, pp. 170–74; ISB, *Bulletin périodique*, 1912, no. 8, pp. 68–69; Velikov, pp. 39–40, 47; Ov. Petrosian, *Bibliografiia armianskoi periodicheskoi pechati (1900–1956)* (Erevan, 1957), p. 164. Velikov refers to the Socialist Center as the "Social Democratic Party," but it is clear from the membership he lists that the two are identical. The N. Janos cited in his work is a variant spelling of N. Giannios.

On *İşçiler Gazetesi* see Hartmann, p. 195, who reports in Sept. 1909 that 32 issues had already appeared. Cf. Tunçay, p. 21/n. 6.

9. *Sabah*, Aug. 6 (Aug. 19, New Style), Aug. 21 (Sept. 3, N.S.), 1325 (1909); *Tanin*, April 26 (May 9, N.S.), May 22 (June 4, N.S.) 1326 (1910).

10. On Hilmi, see Tunçay, pp. 25 ff.; Tarik Z. Tunaya, *Türkiyede Siyasî Partiler* (Istanbul, 1952), pp. 303 ff.; V. A. Gurko-Kriazhin, "Rabochee i sotsialisticheskoe dvizhenie v Turtsii," in Mikhail Pavlovich [Velt'man] el als., *Turtsiia v bor'be za nezavisimost'* (Moscow, 1925), pp. 138–39; Mustafa Kemal [Atatürk], *Put' novoi Turtsii*, v. 2 (Moscow, 1932), pp. 373–75; Bezmi Nusret Kaygusuz, *Bir Roman Gibi* (Izmir, 1955), pp. 25–26; Münir Süleyman Çapanoğlu, *Türkiyede Sosyalizm Hareketleri ve Sosyalist Hilmi* (Istanbul, 1964), pp. 48–55, 68–69. On Baha Tevfik, see also Hilmi Ziya Ülken, *Türkiye'de Çağdaş Düşünce Tarihi* (Konya, 1966), v. 1, pp. 365–87.

11. For Jaurès' letter, see *İştirak*, March 20 (April 2, N.S.), 1326 (1910). The text is given in Tunaya, p. 311; Novichev, p. 19, gives a full Russian translation. Cf. Tunçay, p. 36.

12. "Sosyalistliğin Âtisi," *İştirak*, Feb. 27 (March 12, N.S.), 1325 (1910). This quotation also appears in Tunaya, p. 306/n. 13.

13. For a discussion of the proper date for the founding of the Ottoman Socialist Party, see Tunçay, pp. 29–30/n. 30. He concludes that existing confusion can largely be eliminated by considering references to August to mean Old Style, hence that the party was formed during the first week of Sept. 1910 N.S.

14. Tunaya, pp. 307–308, 312–14. Cf. Tunçay, pp. 38–40.

15. See "Sosyalistliğin Âtisi," *İştirak*, Feb. 27, 1325 (March 12, 1910, N.S.), March 6, 1326 (March 19, 1910, N.S.). Çapanoğlu, p. 54, attributes this article to Baha Tevfik. Hilmi's only signed article in *İştirak* ("Şûrayı Ümmet'e Cevap") was devoted to Islam. See also Tunçay, p. 31.

16. On Parvus' activity see Z. A. B. Zeman & W. B. Scharlau, *The Merchant of Revolution* (London, 1965), pp. 125–44; Niyazi Berkes, pp. 271, 335–37, 427.

17. Khaim T. Eidus, *Ocherki rabochego dvizheniia v stranakh Vostoka* (Moscow, 1922), p. 75, claims Parvus took part in a May Day demonstration in Istanbul along with Rumanian socialist leader Christo Rakovskii.

18. Velikov, p. 47. Cf. Tunçay, pp. 27–28. Çapanoğlu, pp. 53–54, claims Pertev Tevfik's *Muahede* also supported the party. Tunçay, after investigating *Muahede*, concluded that it had nothing in common with socialism, though he admits that Tevfik may have sympathized with Hilmi.

19. ISB, *Bulletin périodique*, 1912, no. 8, p. 45; Starr, p. 327; Stavrianos, pp. 184, 186; Zografski, pp. 236–37; Kordatos, pp. 249–51.

20. For the program of the Paris branch see Tunaya, pp. 312–14.

21. For Subhi's role in *İfham* and the National Constitutional Party see Ahmet Bedevi Kuran, *Osmanlı İmparatorluğunda İnkılâp Hareketleri ve Millî Mücadele* (Istanbul, 1956), pp. 548–50; *28–29 Kânunusani 1921 Karadeniz Kıyalarında Parçalanan Mustafa Subhi ve Yoldaşlarının İkinci Yıldönümleri* (Moscow, 1923), p. 4 (hereafter cited as *28–29 Kânunusani*).

22. ISB, *Bulletin périodique*, 1912, no. 8, p. 69; no. 9, pp. 5–7. See also G. H. D. Cole, *The Second International, 1889–1914: A History of Socialist Thought* (London, 1956), v. 3, part II, p. 607.

23. ISB, *Stockholm* (Stockholm, 1918), pp. 365–67; Velt'man et als., pp. 135–36; Avram Galanti, *Türkler ve Yahudiler* (Istanbul, 1947), p. 91; Tunçay, p. 47; Zinniatulla Navshirvanov, "Sotsialisticheskoe dvizhenie v Turtsii," *Novyi Vostok*, 1922, no. 2, p. 620.

CHAPTER II

1. M. Zekeriya [Sertel], "Avrupada Kızıl Tehlike," *Zaman*, Aug. 22, 1918.

2. See Tunçay, p. 104.

3. On the "Spartakists" see Vâlâ Nureddin Vâ-Nû, *Bu Dünyadan Nâzım Geçti* (Istanbul, 1965), pp. 62–98, 109. Cf. Tunçay, pp. 145–46/n. 7.

4. "The 'Bolshevist' Plot," *The Orient News*, May 2, 1923; France, Ministère des affaires étrangères, *Bulletin périodique de la presse turque*, Sept. 12–13, 1923, no. 29, p. 14, "Le Communisme en Turquie"; A. M. Shamsutdinov, "Pervyi s'ezd Kommunisticheskoi Partii Turtsii," in Akademiia Nauk SSSR, *Kratkie soobshcheniia instituta narodov Azii*, v. 30 (Moscow, 1961), p. 227. R.P. Kornienko, *Rabochee dvizhenie v Turtsii 1918–1963 gg.* (Moscow, 1965), p. 16, claims that the first meeting of this organization took place on Oct. 30, 1918, and that many of its members were returnees from Russia.

5. For Subhi's speech to the First Congress of the Comintern, see Institut Marksa-Engel'sa-Lenina pri TsK VKP (b), *Pervyi kongress Kommunisticheskogo Internatsionala Mart 1919 g.* (Moscow, 1933), pp. 244–46.

6. Şevket Süreyya Aydemir described Navshirvanov's character in a personal letter dated Jan. 19, 1967. Cf. Samih Nafiz Tansu, *İki Devrin Perde Arkası* (Istanbul, 1964), pp. 537, 553; *28–29 Kânunusani*, p. 73.

7. On Antel see Hasan Âli Yücel, *Dâvam* (Ankara, 1947), p. 22; Ülken, v. 1, p. 282, v. 2, pp. 759–60.

8. Tunaya, pp. 465–67, gives the Turkish Socialist Party's program. Fethi Tevetoğlu, "Türkiye'de Sosyalist ve Komünist Faaliyetler," *Türk Kültürü,* Sept. 1966, no. 47, p. 1011, reports that the Turkish Socialist Party decided to send Dr. Refik Nevzat and Hasan Sadi Birkök as delegates to the International Workers and Socialist Conference at Berne on Feb. 3, 1919. Other delegates were sent to the socialist conference convened by the Second International in Amsterdam, August 5–10, 1919. See also Tunçay, p. 54.

9. Cf. Tunçay, pp. 49–51. *İdrak* particularly supported the wave of strikes that gripped Istanbul in mid-1919; indeed, the two-week strike of streetcar workers at the end of May 1919 was apparently directed by the leaders of the Turkish Socialist Party.

10. This proclamation was published in both Turkish and German. *Kurtuluş* (Berlin), May 1919, no. 1–2, pp. 24–28. Cf. Tunçay, p. 145.

11. Osman Nebioğlu, *Türkiyede Kim Kimdir* (Istanbul, 1961–62), pp. 510, 568, 601; English translation: *Who's Who in Turkey* (JPRS, Washington, 1963), pp. 697, 786, 835.

12. Tunaya, pp. 438–39; Tevetoğlu, pp. 999–1005. The painter Nâmık İsmail was its nominal head. See Tunçay, p. 150 & n. 17.

13. *28–29 Kânunusani* pp. 71–75; Tunçay, pp. 111–12/n. 134; *Tonguç'a Kitap* (Istanbul, 1961), p. 264 Kornienko, p. 21, however, claims that Ethem Nejat headed the nucleus of the "true" Turkish Communist Party formed at this time. According to Kornienko, this communist group, based in the Golden Horn area of Istanbul, was in touch with Mustafa Subhi in Russia and distributed his paper *Yeni Dünya.* Kornienko alleges that this group was also in contact with Bulgarian, Hungarian, and French communists and carried on agitation among the Entente forces in Istanbul. Unfortunately Kornienko does not give sufficient information to permit meaningful identification of this group. He may here be referring to agitation carried on primarily in the Russian refugee community in Istanbul by Soviet agents, some of whom were later rounded up by the British. See Constantinople Embassy Dispatch no. 67, Feb. 25, 1921 [in the National Archives], "Memorandum of Bolshevik Activities at Constantinople," which reports the arrest of Dorofeeff and others who were carrying on activities under the guise of the International Red Cross in touch with such foreign places as London, Prague, and Vienna. On the basis of available evidence, it seems doubtful that any formal communist party was established in 1919, though men like Ethem Nejat may already have considered themselves communists.

14. Constantinople Embassy Dispatch no. 148, Jan. 31, 1928 [in the National Archives]; Tunçay, pp. 147–48/n. 11, 150. Şevket Süreyya Aydemir, in a personal letter dated Feb. 28, 1966, describes Deymer as a very emotional person

who hid his passions. Aydemir adds that Deymer "was not a man for the masses; he was a committee man." Cf. İlhan Darendelioğlu, *Türkiyede Komünist Hareketleri* (Istanbul, 1962), pp. 52–54.

15. Şefik Hüsnü [Deymer], "Yarınki Proletarya," *Kurtuluş*, Oct. 20, 1919, no. 2, pp. 18, 21. On Barbusse see David Caute, *Communism and the French Intellectuals. 1914–1960* (London, 1964), pp. 65–67, 77–78.

16. See especially R[efik] N[evzat], "Sosyalizm ve Fransız Muharrirleri," *Kurtuluş*, Feb. 19, 1920, no. 5, pp. 82–83; Romain Rolland, Henri Barbusse, Georges Duhamel, "Beynelmilel Mütefekkirlerin Birinci Konferans İçin," *Kurtuluş*, Feb. 19, 1920, pp. 81–82.

17. See, for example, Ethem Nejat, "Proletarya Kimlerdir," *Kurtuluş*, Sept. 20, 1919, and his "Serseriler-Terbiye-Sermaye," *Kurtuluş*, Feb. 19, 1920.

18. Tunçay, pp. 154–55, quoting from *Tarik*, Oct. 24–25, 1919.

19. Tunaya, p. 439; Tunçay, pp. 149–50.

20. Ali Fuat Cebesoy, *Moskova Hâtıraları* (Istanbul, 1955), p. 60; Kâzım Karabekir, *İstiklâl Harbimiz* (Istanbul, 1960), pp. 509, 618–19, 628–30.

21. See Tunaya, pp. 441–44, for the National Turk Party's program. Adıvar was later approached by Atatürk to head his "official" Communist Party.

22. *Zhizn' Natsional'nostei*, June 15, 1920, no. 18 (75), p. 3.

CHAPTER III

1. Mehmed Moustafa Soubhy [Mehmed Mustafa Subhi], "L'organisation du crédit agricole en Turquie," in Institut International d'Agriculture, *Bulletin du bureau des institutions économiques et sociales*, Oct.–Nov. 1910, no. 2, pp. 59–76; English translation: International Institute of Agriculture, *Bulletin of the Bureau of Economic and Social Intelligence*, Oct.–Nov. 1910, v. 1, no. 2, pp. 59–76.

For Subhi's early life, see Ali Yazıcı, "Mustafa Subhi Yoldaşın Tercümei Hali ve Siyasî Şahsiyeti," *28–29 Kânunusani*, pp. 3–7.

Some sources aver that Subhi was of Albanian origin. Ahmet Kemal Varınca, who knew Subhi at the lycée in Erzurum, says he was there known as an Albanian. See his "Mustafa Suphi'nin Macerası," *Meydan*, Feb. 1, 1966, cited in Tunçay, p. 100/n. 97. Reha Oğuzkan, *Kızıl Faaliyet* (Istanbul, 1943), p. 2, attributes to I. Raguza, *Staline* (Paris, 1938), p. 190, a report to the effect that Zinoviev assured Stalin that Subhi was Albanian. Oğuzkan, however, completely misquotes his original source on this point, for Raguza makes no mention of Subhi's ethnic origin. Tunçay rejects Varınca's allegation for lack of corroborating evidence. This matter requires further study.

W., "Les relations russo-turques depuis l'avènement du bolchevisme," *Revue du Monde Musulman*, Dec. 1922, no. 52, p. 207, calls Subhi the son of Ali Rıza, governor of Janina province.

2. Kuran, pp. 548–50. On Subhi's activities at this time, see also *28–29 Kânunusani*, pp. 4–9, 54–65 & *passim; Bol'shaia Sovetskaia Entsiklopediia* (Second edition), v. 41, p. 184; Tunçay, pp. 100–104; Sultan-Galiev, "Mustafa Subhi i ego rabota," *Zhizn' Natsional'nostei*, 1921, no. 14 (112) ; E. Ludshuveit, "Konferentsiia levykh turetskikh sotsialistov v Moskve letom 1918 goda," in Akademiia nauk armianskoi SSR, Sektor vostokovedeniia, *Vostokovedcheskii sbornik*, v. 2 (Erevan, 1964), pp. 174–92.

Subhi translated Bouglé's book, *Qu'est-ce que la sociologie?*, into Turkish under the title, *İlmi İçtimaî Nedir?* In 1912 he published his treatise on the Tripolitan War, *Vazifei Temdin* (The Duty of Civilization) .

3. Cf. Cebesoy, pp. 41–42.

4. On Sherif Manatov and the Muslim Bureau, see Fethi Tevetoğlu, "Hafî Türkiye Komünist Partisi ve Türkiye Halk İştirâkiyûn Fırkası," *Türk Kültürü*, Feb. 1967, no. 52, pp. 255–58. Tevetoğlu quotes also from Dr. Samih Çoruhlu [Akdes Nimet Kurat], "İstiklâl Savaşında Komünizm Faaliyeti," *Yeni İstanbul*, July 4, 9, 10, 1966, on Manatov's background.

Cf. Richard Pipes, *The Formation of the Soviet Union* (Cambridge, 1964) , pp. 157–61; Gotthard Jäschke, "Der Weg zur russisch-türkischen Freundschaft," *Die Welt des Islams*, 1934, v. 16, p. 30. For Manatov's first meeting with Subhi, see *28–29 Kânunusani*, pp. 9–11.

5. Ludshuveit, pp. 179–80, 185–91. The first issue of *Yeni Dünya* appeared on April 27, 1918.

Subhi was apparently more an activist than a theoretician. Ludshuveit pillories Subhi for "ideological immaturity" which led him to advocate a "mechanical transfer of Russian example and experience" onto the far different Turkish scene. Ludshuveit adds that Subhi's approach caused disagreements with those who wished to see *Yeni Dünya* become principally a theoretical journal of socialist thought.

6. Tunçay, p. 103/n. 105; *28–29 Kânunusani*, p. 54.

7. Ludshuveit, p. 185.

8. "S'ezd turetskikh levykh sotsialistov," *Izvestiia*, July 26, 1918, p. 6.

9. *Ibid.;* "Konferentsiia levykh turetskikh sotsialistov," *Izvestiia*, July 25, 1918, pp. 4–5. Subhi was apparently carrying on a struggle against right-wing socialists in the Turkish movement. The Executive Committee of Turkish Socialist-Communists issued a statement on Aug. 17, 1918, announcing that it was breaking off relations with "socialist conciliators" and would unswervingly seek to carry out the true legacy of Marx. See Ervand Kazarovich Sarkisian, *Velikaia Oktiabr'skaia sotsialisticheskaia revoliutsiia i natsional'no-osvoboditel'naia bor'ba v Turtsii* (Erevan, 1958) , p. 46.

10. Institut Marksa-Engel'sa-Lenina pri TsK VKP (b) , *Pervyi kongress Kommunisticheskogo Internatsionala Mart 1919 g.*, p. 245.

11. *28–29 Kânunusani*, p. 57.

12. On Soviet-Turkish relations, see Gotthard Jäschke, "Le rôle du communisme dans les relations russo-turques," *Orient*, 1963, no. 26, pp. 31–44; Tevfik Bıyıklıoğlu, *Atatürk Anadolu'da (1919–1921)*, v. 1 (Ankara, 1959), pp. 18–22, 64–72. On Enver Pasha, see Dankwart Rustow, "Enwer Pasha," *Encyclopaedia of Islam* (Leyden, 1962–63), v. 2, pp. 698–702.

13. Karabekir, *passim;* Tansu, pp. 338–42.

14. Karabekir, pp. 519–20, 609–12. The Operations Branch was composed of Staff Capt. Mustafa, Baha Sait, Süleyman, Yakup, and three unnamed "Russian Bolsheviks." The Publications Branch was headed by Dr. Fuat Sabit, and the Propaganda Branch by former Zor District Governor Salih Zeki. Cf. Mehmet-Zade Mirza-Bala, *Millî Azerbaycan Hareketi* (Berlin, 1938), p. 188, who reports Capt. İhsan, Lt. Bahaeddin, and Lt. Vehbi served in this party.

15. See Subhi's report on organizational activities to the First Congress of the Turkish Communist Party in Baku in Sept. 1920 in *28–29 Kânunusani*, pp. 54–65. Subhi claimed a run of press of 4,000 copies for *Yeni Dünya*, 2,000 of which he said were distributed in Turkey. While these claims appear exaggerated, some copies probably did circulate in Anatolia, at least as far as the Eastern Front Commander in Erzurum. Will Kord-Ruwisch, "Die Arbeiterpresse in der Türkei," *Zeitungswissenschaft*, 1926, no. 4, p. 54, reports that 12 issues of *Yeni Dünya* were published in all. Cf. Cebesoy, p. 37.

16. Cebesoy, pp. 37–38, 125–26. This unit should not be confused with the "Bolshevik detachment" in Ethem, the Circassian's forces. See Chapter IV, p. 77.

17. Cebesoy, pp. 35–39; Karabekir, pp. 821, 832; T.B.M.M., *Zabıt Ceridesi*, Devre I, v. 3, p. 299. Cf. *Die Welt des Islams*, v. 20, 1938, p. 124.

18. Gotthard Jäschke in "Kommunismus und Islam im türkischen Befreiungskriege," *Die Welt des Islams*, 1938, v. 20, p. 111, and Tunaya, p. 531, accept Yunus Nadi's claim in *Cumhuriyet*, July 28, 1931, that the declaration issued July 14, 1920, was printed in Eskişehir and was the work of a secret communist party organized by Sherif Manatov and Arif Oruç (to whom Jäschke and Tunaya also add Salih Zeki in apparent confusion with Veterinary Major Hacıoğlu Salih). In fact, however, Arif Oruç in *Yarın*, July 29, 1931, convincingly demonstrates that this declaration was issued by Mustafa Subhi's Communist Party in Baku. (See Chapter IV, note 9.) Oruç explained that the declaration was brought to Eskişehir and Ankara by Süleyman Sami, adding that it was only on September 6, 1920, that he, Oruç, finally reached Eskişehir from the Demirci front. Testimony at the trial of Nâzım and his associates in April–May 1921 is consistent with Oruç's account. See the serial article " 'Yeşilordu' Cemiyeti" in *Yakın Tarihimiz*, 1962, v. 1, pp. 69–72, 101–104, 133–35, 172–74, 215–16, 233–35, 281–83, 297–98; also Feridun Kandemir, *Atatürk'ün Kurduğu Türkiye Komünist Partisi ve Sonrası* (Istanbul, n.d.),

p. 172. Salih Zeki apparently returned to Baku, without proceeding beyond Trabzon. See Karabekir, pp. 832–33.

19. For excerpts of Atatürk's correspondance with Subhi (date unknown), see V. A. Gurko-Krizahin, *Blizhnii Vostok i derzhavy* (Moscow, 1925), p. 104; and his "Politicheskie gruppirovki Turtsii," *Novyi Vostok*, 1922, no. 3, p. 55. Cf. Ali Fuat Cebesoy, *Milli Mücadele Hâtıraları* (Istanbul, 1953), p. 475; Tunçay, pp. 116–17/n. 145.

For Atatürk's public reaction, see T.B.M.M., *Zabıt Ceridesi*, Devre I, v. 3, p. 189 (session of Aug. 14, 1920).

On Dursunoğlu, see the article by Çoruhlu in *Yeni İstanbul*, July 11, 1966, quoted in Tunçay, p. 115/n. 143.

20. The appeal for aid, sent by the Ankara Parliament just three days after its opening, reached Moscow early in June 1920 after a number of vicissitudes en route. The Soviets immediately responded on June 3, 1920, accepting the proposal to initiate formal relations and inviting a Turkish delegation to Moscow. The Turkish Foreign Minister with a small retinue arrived in Moscow on July 19, 1920, where on Aug. 24 he initialled a draft agreement with the Soviet government. This instrument was never ratified because of disagreement over Armenia, a problem that vexed Soviet-Turkish relations for the ensuing year.

21. The Communist International, *The Second Congress of the Communist International* (1921), pp. 147–48 (session of July 28, 1920).

22. The Communist International, *Pervyi s'ezd narodov Vostoka* (Petrograd, 1920), pp. 116–17, 137–51. The Baku Congress set up a Soviet of Action and Propaganda in the East to which İsmail Hakkı and Süleyman Nuri were elected as Communists, and former Secretary General of the Committee of Union and Progress Bahaeddin Şakir was elected from the "non-party faction." Şakir was murdered the following year in Berlin along with former triumvir Talât.

23. For the Congress of the Turkish Communist Party in Baku, see *28–29 Kânunusani*, pp. 52–66; A. M. Shamsutdinov, pp. 232–36; Şevket Süreyya Aydemir, *Suyu Arayan Adam* (Istanbul, 1965), pp. 149–234; *Kommunist* (Baku), Sept. 10–21, 1920; Tunçay, pp. 114–15.

24. Stasova apparently played a major role in dealing with the Turkish communists. For example, it was to her that Ethem Nejat brought the request from communists of "Anatolia and Eskişehir" for aid from the Baku party. Stasova finally agreed to send first 150,000 liras in gold, then 100,000 more, and finally a third installment of 150,000. At least the first shipment was apparently sent with the Soviet mission which arrived in Ankara on Oct. 4, 1920. See *Yakın Tarihimiz*, v. 1, p. 133.

25. Cf. Karabekir, p. 834. Ahmet Cevat Emre, who had left Istanbul toward the end of 1919, now emerged as a prominent member of the Foreign Bureau.

According to Çoruhlu in *Yeni İstanbul*, July 11, 1966, the central committee of the Turkish Communist Party in Baku included: Mustafa Subhi, Ethem Nejat, Mehmet Emin, Nazmi, Hilmioğlu İsmail Hakkı, İsmail Hakkı (from Kayseri), and Süleyman Nuri. Hüseyin Said, Asım Necati, and Selim Mehmetoğlu were alternate members; and Süleyman Sami, Lütfü Necdet, and İsmail Çitoğlu were candidate members. See Tunçay, p. 116/n. 144.

CHAPTER IV

1. So prevalent was the popular identification of Islam and communism that some religious circles, such as the Advancement of Islam Society (Tealii İslam Cemiyeti), issued declarations warning against this notion. See *Peyami Sabah*, Feb. 17, 1920; Tunaya, p. 463. Even the provincial press on occasion cautioned its readers that Islam could not be reconciled with Bolshevism. See *Açıksöz* (Kastamonu), Feb. 22, 1920 [quoted in Nurettin Peker, *1918–1923 İstiklâl Savaşının Vesika ve Resimleri* (Istanbul, 1955), p. 143]. Cf. G. Astakhov, *Ot sultanata k demokraticheskoi Turtsii* (Moscow, 1926), pp. 33–34; Kandemir, pp. 189–90; T.B.M.M., Devre I, v. 4, p. 183 (session of Sept. 18, 1920). To be sure, many in Anatolia had only the sketchiest idea at best about the Bolshevik revolution. See "V Turtsii letom 1920," *Zhizn' Natsional'nostei*, 1920, no. 38 (94). For the views of extreme nationalists, see T.B.M.M., Devre I, v. 6, pp. 12–16 (session of Nov. 22, 1920) and v. 17, pp. 57–58 (speech of Hamdullah Subhi Tanrıöver, session of Feb. 20, 1922).

2. Halide Edib [Adıvar], *The Turkish Ordeal* (New York, 1928), p. 171, gave the classic statement of the "Eastern Ideal." "It was an amorphous collection of ideas arising from thwarted desires for some more congenial state of affairs which would be appropriate to the East. These ideas were of course very much influenced by the Russian Revolution."

3. Damar Arıkoğlu, *Hâtıralarım* (Istanbul, 1961), p. 152. See also *Yakın Tarihimiz*, v. 1, pp. 216, 281, 298; Kandemir, p. 18.

Vakkas Ferit soon became an important member of the Green Army, working closely with Hakki Behiç, and traveling widely in Anatolia to carry on his propaganda.

4. Bıyıklıoğlu, p. 68; Arıkoğlu, p. 152; T.B.M.M., Devre I, v. 6, pp. 12–16.

5. For the Green Army's statutes see *Yakın Tarihimiz*, v. 1, pp. 103, 234–35; Kandemir, pp. 148–51, 155–57. Excerpts are also in Alimov & Godes, *Ocherki po istorii Vostoka v epokhu imperializma* (Moscow, 1934), pp. 72–73. P. Kitaigorodskii, "Oktiabr'skaia revoliutsiia i natsional'no-revoliutsionnoe dvizhenie Turtsii," *Krasnyi Internatsional Profsoiuzov*, 1927, no. 10 (81), pp. 407–11, characterized this program as crude but "clearly populist, peasant-worker" in orientation.

6. H. Baydour [Baydur], "Chronique internationale: En Turquie," *La revue communiste*, Dec. 1920, no. 10, p. 374. Baydur, speaking for the Istanbul communists, criticized Manatov for not basing his activity on the "organized masses of peasants and workers," adding that "the young Sherif Manatov knows nothing of Marx, nor of the worker movement; he claims that Lenin, about whom he speaks continually, has invented a doctrine that differs from Marxism."

Manatov's acquaintanceship with Lenin apparently dated from the days of the First World War when Manatov met Lenin in Switzerland. After the Bolsheviks came to power, Manatov constantly insisted on this basis to be on intimate terms with Lenin. See Tevetoğlu, "Hafî Türkiye Komünist Partisi ve Türkiye Halk İştirâkiyûn Fırkası," pp. 257–58.

On Navshirvanov, see Tansu, pp. 537, 553, who reports also that Navshirvanov's wife and sister-in-law formed a group called "Activity among Women and to Enlighten Women," which attempted to spread "leftist ideas" among the women of Anatolia. Cf. V. Kasparova, "The Women's Movement: The Women's Movement in the Near East: Turkey," *International Press Correspondence*, April 10, 1924, no. 24, pp. 222–23.

7. *Yakın Tarihimiz*, v. 1, p. 281; Tansu, p. 552. Cf. Tunçay, p. 138/n. 188.

8. Türkiye Komünist Partisi, *Türkiye Komünist Partisi Umumi Nizamnamesi* (Ankara, June 1920). This document, though ostensibly published in Ankara, is probably identical with the Communist Party program which Tansu, p. 543, indicates was published in Eskişehir. Tunçay, pp. 92–94, accepts this identification as almost certainly valid, noting that Western Front Commander Cebesoy had begun investigating the publication of such a Communist Party program some time before mid-September 1920. See Cebesoy, *Millî Mücadele Hâtıraları*, pp. 471–72.

Şevket Süreyya Aydemir, *Tek Adam*, v. 2 (Istanbul, 1964), p. 374, on the other hand, claims that these statutes belonged to the "official" Communist Party established by Atatürk. Aydemir, however, seems clearly mistaken. By content these statutes obviously clash with the tenets of Atatürk's pseudocommunist party. Moreover, in June 1920 Atatürk's "communist" party had not yet been formed.

For materials that Manatov's group may have been instrumental in publishing elsewhere in Anatolia, see T.B.M.M., Devre I, v. 4, p. 347 (session of Sept. 28, 1920). Tansu, p. 549, quotes Atatürk's testimony at Nâzım's trial to the effect that Manatov was arrested as a result of a declaration printed at Eskişehir. There is not sufficient evidence to be able to tell whether the declaration in question was the program discussed above or another document.

9. This reference to a "Baku Congress" is puzzling. It is doubtful that plans for the convocation of the Congress of the Peoples of the East were very far along before the end of June 1920. On the other hand, Mustafa

Subhi may have decided fairly early in June to convene a party congress later that year in Baku. Whichever congress the statutes intended, news of these events in Russia and Baku may have been brought to Manatov by the unofficial Soviet delegate, Verbov, who reached Ankara at about this time.

Evidence that other important party documents were sent from Baku to Manatov's group is more concrete. Arif Oruç testified later that Süleyman Sami had delivered three party documents to his Anatolian colleagues. One of these documents Oruç identified as the "July Declaration." See above, Chapter III, n. 18.

10. On Verbov (or Verlov as he is sometimes called), see Halide Edib Adıvar, *Türkün Ateşle İmtihanı* (Istanbul, 1962), pp. 151–53; Turkey, T. C. Dışişleri Bakanlığı, *Dışişleri Bakanlığı Yıllığı 1964–65* (Hamid Aral, ed.), p. 488; Kandemir, p. 190.

11. Yunus Nadi began work on this program in Aug. 1920. For the text and subsequent Assembly debate of the Populist Program, see T.B.M.M., Devre I, v. 5, pp. 363–70 (session of Nov. 18, 1920). In the course of debate, the spokesman of the special parliamentary committee set up to consider the organic statutes openly acknowledged that Soviet experience had influenced its authors.

Soviet sources—Atatürk, *Put' novoi Turtsii*, v. 4, pp. 298–99; V. A. Gurko-Kriazhin, "Politicheskie gruppirovki Turtsii," *Novyi Vostok*, 1923, no. 3, pp. 54–55; and Velt'man et als., pp. 84–86—give a summary of what they call the Populist Group's "program." This is considerably different in degree of detail and in the range of topics covered from the Populist Program as ratified by Parliament. The document from which the Soviet writers have drawn their summary shows the Populist Group to have been quite close to the Green Army in outlook, for its program contained a mixture of radical socialist and traditional Islamic notions. In view of the similarity of name, it is possible that the program quoted by Soviet authors was the original draft that Nadi presented to the special parliamentary committee, and that during its deliberations the committee refined and condensed the statement to the form eventually adopted by the Assembly.

12. Evidence that Nâzım had requested funds from the Baku party was presented at his trial in April–May 1921. The government accused Nâzım of having received two million liras in gold from the Soviet delegation. See below, n. 19.

Atatürk pointed to the dangers of Nâzım's election as a reason for ending the cumbersome system whereby Parliament elected all cabinet members by separate secret ballot. Atatürk also cited Nâzım's election as part of the rationale for forming a political party of his own in order to prevent such men from attaining high position. See [Atatürk], *A Speech Delivered by Ghazi Mustapha Kemal* (Leipzig, 1929), pp. 427–29. Although Nâzım's foreign connections were exposed at this time, he was not further penalized and continued to attend Parliament as before.

Çerkes Ethem'in Hâtıraları (Istanbul, 1962), pp. 103–106, reports Ethem's claim that Atatürk sought Ethem's assistance in persuading Nâzım to resign.

13. *Pravda*, July 20, 1920, reports on the basis of the Istanbul press that a "Muslim Bolshevik Committee" in Eskişehir had issued a proclamation in the latter part of June celebrating "its solidarity with Bolshevik principles." This may have been the work of Ethem Nejat who appears to have passed through Eskişehir at about this time and allegedly organized a group of communists. (See Chapter III, note 24.) Mustafa Nuri may be identical with the person of the same name who wrote for *İştirak* in 1910. Cf. Tunçay, p. 35/n. 44 quoting *Yeni İstanbul*, May 15, 1966.

14. Velt'man et als., p. 94, quote of a statement to *Seyyarei Yeni Dünya*. Ethem, in the memoirs attributed to him, denied any knowledge of the Green Army. Evidence to the contrary, however, is overwhelming. *Çerkes Ethem'in Hâtıraları*, pp. 58–61, 109–10.

15. *Çerkes Ethem'in Hâtıraları*, pp. 130, 163–64; Tunçay, pp. 80–81/n. 44.

16. *Yarın*, July 29, 1931; *Çerkes Ethem'in Hâtıraları*, pp. 109–10; Tunçay, p. 87; A. D. Novichev, *Krest'ianstvo Turtsii v noveishee vremia* (Moscow, 1959), p. 35. Novichev also reports that the paper *İşçi ve Köylü* appeared irregularly in Eskişehir at this time as an organ of the Populist Group.

17. M. V. Frunze, *Sobranie sochinenii* (Moscow, 1929), v. 1, p. 622. The sole issue of *Seyyarei Yeni Dünya* available in the Millî Kütüphane in Ankara (that of Oct. 11, 1920) reports a speech of Trotsky's and the formation of a Soviet regime in Bukhara. For Oruç's own version of the founding of *Seyyarei Yeni Dünya*, see Kandemir, pp. 176–81.

18. T.B.M.M., Devre I, v. 4, p. 345; Cebesoy, *Millî Mücadele Hâtıraları*, pp. 471–72.

19. At his trial in April–May 1921, Nâzım denied having received two million liras in gold from the Soviets. However, he argued that receipt of money in itself would not have been a crime inasmuch as the statutes of the Peoples Communist Party he formed soon after the arrival of the Soviet mission in Ankara permitted the acceptance of "gifts from higher headquarters." These statutes, Nâzım pointed out, had been approved by the Ankara government. See *Yakın Tarihimiz*, v. 1, p. 172.

For Soviet relations with Ethem and Oruç, see Bıyıklıoğlu, p. 68. It is impossible to clarify the nature of Oruç's relations with the Soviets on the basis of present evidence. Oruç originally made contact with them through Manatov. Like Ethem, Oruç probably never became a member of the Moscow-controlled (i.e. Subhi's Baku) Communist Party. Indeed, Oruç was probably more manipulated by the Soviets than a true communicant of Moscow.

20. Cebesoy, *Millî Mücadele Hâtıraları*, pp. 472–75. For the Law on Associations, see *Takvimi Vekayi*, Oct. 4, 1920, no. 3972.

21. Cebesoy, *Millî Mücadele Hâtıraları*, pp. 508–12.

Jäschke in *Die Welt des Islams*, v. 20, 1938, p. 112, claims that the "official"

Turkish Communist Party was established by Tevfik Rüştü Aras as early as May 1920. He cites no convincing evidence for this assertion, however, and may have been misled by the fact that Aras represented this party in a delegation sent to Moscow in the winter of 1920–21. In any event, this claim runs directly counter to the information developed during the trials in April–May 1921 as well as conflicting with Aras' own statement to *Yön*, Oct. 30, 1964, no. 83, p. 5.

Aydemir, *Tek Adam*, v. 2, p. 375, also states he believes preparations for the "official" party began well before Oct. 1920, because the statutes he attributes to this party were dated June 20, 1920. As indicated in note 8 above, these statutes were probably printed in Eskişehir by Manatov's band; in any event, their content is not consistent with the position of Atatürk's "official" Communist Party.

Sarkisian, *Velikaia Oktiabr'skaia sotsialisticheskaia revoliutsiia*, p. 67, claims that the Kemalist government assigned 15,000 liras for the organization of the "official" Communist Party and for carrying on agitation and propaganda.

22. Velt'man et als., pp. 95–96, 98, emphasis added. The latter paragraph of this quotation, at least, was drawn from the "Manifesto" of the "official" Communist Party, which was published in *Anadoluda Yeni Gün*, Nov. 18, 1920. See Kornienko, pp. 29–30.

23. Velt'man et als., pp. 98–102.

24. See "V Turtsii," *Pravda*, Oct. 14, 1920.

25. Atatürk, *A Speech*, p. 436, revealed that he had empowered Cebesoy to take the obstreperous Ethem to Moscow in any capacity Cebesoy wished, merely to remove Ethem from the scene. This proposal, however, came to nought.

26. T.B.M.M., Devre I, v. 6, pp. 11–16 (session of Nov. 22, 1920). In the course of debate, one speaker questioned the propriety of sending "communists" of any sort. To this, extreme nationalist Muhittin Baha Pars, a leading member of the "official" Communist Party, replied that Bolshevism was the "scientific basis for saving the country, for saving the nation, and for saving humanity."

27. *Çerkes Ethem'in Hâtıraları*, p. 108; Frunze, p. 622; *Yakın Tarihimiz*, v. 1, p. 102.

Oruç, who continued as editor of the paper, joined the "official" Communist Party at this time as well. See Kandemir, p. 178. After its move, the paper changed its slogan to "the Turkish Bolshevik Newspaper."

A. D. Novichev, "Antikrest'ianskaia politika Kemalistov v 1919–1922 godakh," *Voprosy Istorii*, 1951, no. 9, p. 67, claims that Atatürk seized Oruç's paper and made it into the organ of the "official" Communist Party.

On Manatov's expulsion, see Tansu, p. 549; *28–29 Kânunusani*, p. 11; Tunçay, p. 95.

28. *Yakın Tarihimiz*, v. 1, pp. 102–103, 174, 215; Kandemir, p. 182. Cf. Tunçay, pp. 96–98. At the Communist trials in April–May 1921, the government produced a declaration probably written—if, as seems likely, it is indeed genuine—somewhat before Ethem's revolt was fairly under way, signed by Ethem as Secretary General (presumably of the Green Army) and Hacıoğlu Salih for the Green Army. This document announced the impending formation of the Peoples Communist Party. See Kandemir, pp. 128–29. In *Yakın Tarihimiz*, v. 1, p. 297, the name of the party to be formed is given as the "Turkish Peoples Communist Bolshevik Party" (Türkiye Halk İştirakiyun Bolşevik Partisi). This may represent an early intent, later rejected, to include the term "Bolshevik" in the name of the party.

29. *Yakın Tarihimiz*, v. 1, p. 283.

30. *Cumhuriyet*, July 27, 1931, published the text of the appeal "To Eskişehir Workers." Frunze, p. 622, reports the efforts to induce the railroad workers to strike. On Jan. 8, 1921, Atatürk gave his analysis of Ethem's revolt to Parliament. T.B.M.M., Devre I, v. 7, p. 227. According to Atatürk, *A Speech*, p. 453, Hayri from *Seyyarei Yeni Dünya*, Arif Oruç's nephew Nizamettin Nazif Tepedelenlioğlu, and others set off from Ankara on Dec. 21, 1920, to attempt to bribe the troops sent by Atatürk against Ethem. One of the members of the group, however, informed Atatürk of the purpose of their trip.

31. Kandemir, p. 182. Atatürk told Parliament on Jan. 8, 1921 (T.B.M.M., Devre I, v. 7, p. 227) that "the Bolsheviks, too, understood how unprincipled and unorthodox these men [i.e. Ethem and his associates] were." However, Soviet sources show that to the end the Soviets themselves remained in dispute over Ethem's movement. See Velt'man et als., pp. 92, 94; Inal Butaev, "Ocherki vostokovedeniia," *Zhizn' Natsional'nostei*, March 22, 1922, no. 4 (10) , pp. 5–6. Frunze, pp. 339, 622, complained that after Ethem was drawn into the "official" Communist Party he played a "provocative role" against the interests of the Soviet communists. Cf. B. Ferdi, "Evoliutsiia Kemalizma . . . ," *Sputnik Kommunista*, 1927, no. 10 (43) , p. 31.

32. In the Assembly on Jan. 3, 1921, Atatürk publicly absolved the "official" Communist Party and its leader Hakkı Behiç specifically of any implication in Ethem's treason. See T.B.M.M., Devre I, v. 7, p. 160. At this time, too, Atatürk answered rumors that a person carrying a secret document from the "official" Communist Party had been arrested for having written a letter encouraging Ethem to revolt.

Seyyarei Yeni Dünya's printing offices were destroyed on Jan. 2, 1921. On the arrests, see *Yakın Tarihimiz*, v. 1, p. 298; *28–29 Kânunusani*, p. 13. Cf. T.B.M.M., Devre I, v. 7, pp. 228–30 (session of Jan. 8, 1921) . Hacı Şükrü was subsequently tried and acquitted on these charges.

33. Tunçay, pp. 119, 113/n. 137. Other accounts indicate that the two

members of Subhi's entourage, Süleyman Sami and Mehmet Emin, were left behind because they were sick. See *Yeni İstanbul*, July 14, 1966.

34. Velt'man et als., pp. 105–106; Karabekir, pp. 909–10.

35. Karabekir, pp. 956–64; U.S.S.R., Narodnyi komissariat po inostrannym delam, *Biulleten'*, Jan. 12, 1921, no. 57, p. 10, and Feb. 13, 1921, no. 65, p. 30; *Kommunist* (Baku), Sept. 21, 1920.

36. Along with Mustafa Subhi, 14 others were killed: Ethem Nejat, Hilmioğlu İsmail Hakkı, Kâzım Ali, Hakkı the artilleryman, Şefik, and 9 whose names are unknown. See Tunçay, p. 121/n. 153; *28–29 Kânunusani*, p. 16.

Velt'man et al., p. 107, states that within two months Capt. Nedim Agâh was similarly murdered at Trabzon.

37. Karabekir, pp. 1147–48; Sami Sabit Karaman, *İstiklâl Mücadelesi ve Enver Paşa—Trabzon ve Kars Hâtıraları: 1921–1922* (Izmit, 1949), p. 19; *28–29 Kânunusani*, pp. 16–17. Tunçay, p. 122/n. 153, quotes Ahmet Kemal Varınca to the effect that Ankara was not aware of Subhi's murder until after the event.

The Soviets did not openly acknowledge Subhi's murder for several months, possibly in order not to ruffle relations with Ankara. For on March 16, 1921, negotiations finally produced a Soviet-Turkish treaty. When thereafter they did protest energetically about this murder as well as about the persecution of communists in Turkey, Ambassador Cebesoy replied disclaiming any responsibility. See *The Nation*, Sept. 7, 1921, v. 113, p. 273.

38. S. Velt'man, "Novaia Turtsiia v otrazheniiakh anatoliskoi pressi," *Novyi Vostok*, 1922, no. 2, p. 643, emphasis added. *Emek* alleged that its article about Atatürk was reprinted from the "Turkish communist" newspaper *Ziya* published for Turks in Bulgaria by the Bulgarian Communist Party. On *Ziya*, which reputedly had a circulation of 1,800, see Joseph Rothschild, *The Communist Party of Bulgaria* (New York, 1959), p. 107/n. 84.

Thanks to this active Turkish community, for the ensuing two years Bulgaria served as an important center of influence on the communist movement inside Turkey. Among the material emanating from this source were works such as Faruk Asrî, *Komünizm: Mesleki İştirakiyunu Tetkik* (Filibe, 1922), which was a partial summary of Charles Rappoport's *Précis du Communisme*. See Tunçay, p. 164/n. 42.

39. *Hâkimiyeti Milliye*, Feb. 2, 1921; Tunçay, p. 126/n. 161.

40. *Yakın Tarihimiz*, v. 1, p. 298; Kandemir, p. 183; S. Velt'man, p. 643.

41. S. Velt'man, p. 643.

42. *The Nation*, Sept. 7, 1921, v. 113, p. 273.

43. For the new line of communism and "the left", see "Sağdan Sola Doğru" in *Hâkimiyeti Milliye*, March 6, 7, 8, 1921; "Sol ve Sağ Nedir?" in *Anadoluda Yeni Gün*, March 8, 9, 1921. On Celâl Bayar's views of "state socialism," see Tunçay, p. 129/n. 171.

CHAPTER V

1. For example, Maurice Pernot, *La Question turque* (Paris, 1923), p. 12, reported the arrest on June 29, 1920, of many suspected communists, apparently from among the White Russian émigré community in Istanbul, and their summary deportation to Sevastopol. Magdeleine Marx Paz, "L'Humanité en Orient," *l'Humanité*, Nov. 4, 1921, reported the deportation of 500 Russians suspected of sympathy for the Soviets.

2. The International Union of Workers was organized along industrial lines allegedly following the model of the American Industrial Workers of the World. Maximos' organization was composed primarily of three component unions: the International Building Workers Union with some 2,000 members (of which about 500 were said to be Turks) ; the International Sailors Union with some 1,500 members (including about 300 Turks) ; and the International Carpenters Union with 250 members. See Tunçay, p. 155/n. 26. Tunaya, p. 465, and Çapanoğlu, p. 73, report that Maximos at this time was head of "Pan Ergatikon," an organization they describe as the Istanbul branch of the Greek Communist Party. See also, Eidus, pp. 73, 78–79; Velt'man et als., p. 138; D. Kuz'min, "Rabochee dvizhenie v Turtsii," *Novyi Vostok*, 1922, no. 2, p. 159; Kornienko, p. 35.

3. Tunaya, p. 465, and Çapanoğlu, p. 73. Eidus, p. 80, gives Moscow's assessment in 1922 of what had to be done to overcome this "chauvinism."

4. As early as Feb. 1921, however, the Soviets were well aware of Hilmi's relations with the English and were calling him an "English agent." See U.S.S.R., *Biulleten'*, March 5, 1921, no. 67, p. 43, quoting *Die Rote Fahne*, Feb. 8, 1921. Thereafter Soviet writers regularly claimed that Hilmi was simply bought by the English and blindly followed their instructions. On the other hand, Çapanoğlu, pp. 65–66, 73–74, although accepting the allegation that Hilmi was eventually put on the British payroll and may have worked for the British intelligence service, convincingly demonstrates that Hilmi exploited the British far more than they did him.

On the May Day demonstration, see Çapanoğlu, pp. 78–79, 82–83; Tunçay, p. 55; Kornienko, p. 36.

5. H. Baydur, pp. 373–77; Kornienko, pp. 23, 36; E. F. Ludshuveit, "Posleoktiabr'skii revoliutsionnyi pod'em v Turtsii," in Moscow University, *Vestnik moskovskogo universiteta*, 1949, no. 7, p. 48. Tunçay, p. 152/n. 20; and Tevetoğlu, *Türk Kültürü*, Sept. 1966, p. 1001/n. 36, report the claim that the Turkish Communist Party was formed by the joining of the *Aydınlık* group (Deymer and Antel) with Maximos' International Union of Workers and the left wing of the Henchak Society. Tunçay is somewhat sceptical of the Henchak involvement, though he admits it is possible.

Though in fact, these three groups may have cooperated, it is evident that each maintained its separate identity. Hence it is probably more correct to consider the Turkish ethnic group organized by Deymer and Antel alone as the ancestor of the present Turkish Communist Party. Tunçay, p. 95/n. 81, notes that a document bearing the date Nov. 21, 1920, was circulated by "the Central Committee of the Turkish Communist Party" concerning membership in a local ward administrative committee. Tunçay believes this was circulated either by Manatov's group or Subhi's Baku party. Judging from the evidence in Baydur's article, however, it seems questionable that either of these bodies was active in Istanbul at this period.

6. Baydur wrote of his experiences at the Socialist Party Congress. See his "Le mouvement ouvrier en Turquie," l'Humanité, Jan. 4, 1921, p. 3. Baydur was particularly exercised at the reference by French Communist Jean Longuet to Enver Pasha's statement that no proletariat existed in Turkey. He also warned his French audience not to confuse the nationalist movement in Anatolia with the proletarian movement, pointing out that Atatürk was leading a clearly bourgeois government which cooperated with Soviet Russia for purely political reasons.

Madame Paz, who was then still using her maiden name of Magdeleine Marx, contributed several articles to the second issue of Aydınlık in July 1921. Back in France, she described her impressions in a lengthy series of articles for l'Humanité, titled "L'Humanité en Orient" (Nov. 3, 4, 6, 7, 8, 10, 17, 24, 26, 29, 30, Dec. 3, 8, 10, 1921).

7. See, for example, Sadrettin Celâl [Antel], "Hayalperest Sosyalistler," Akşam, March 5, 1921.

8. Sadrettin Celâl [Antel], "Cihan Harbi ve Edebiyat," Aydınlık, Aug. 1921, no. 2, pp. 41–44. A paragraph of this article was deleted by the censor. See also Henri Barbusse, "Müteffekrînin Vazifesi," Aydınlık, Oct. 1, 1921, no. 4, pp. 90–91 (translated by Deymer). On the relationship of Aydınlık to the Clarté movement, see Kord-Ruwisch, p. 55; Vladimir Brett, Henri Barbusse; sa marche vers la clarté, son mouvement Clarté (Prague, 1963), p. 317. Magdeleine Marx [Paz], "L'Humanité en Orient," l'Humanité, Nov. 30, 1921, p. 2, reports that "the magazine Clarté . . . has just been founded and edited in Turkish by a very active group." A. D. Novichev, "Vliianie velikoi oktiabr'skoi sotsialisticheskoi revoliutsii na sud'bu Turtsii," in Leningrad University, Uchenye zapiski Leningradskogo Universiteta, 1962, no. 304, pp. 100–101, states that "a group of artists, writers, and journalists created in Istanbul a branch of the international organization of progressive Western European writers [called] 'Clarté.'"

9. Communist International, Biulleten' III kongressa, Moscow, July 20, 1921, no. 23, p. 485.

10. On Enver Pasha, see Dankwart A. Rustow, pp. 698–702; Cebesoy, Moskova Hâtıraları, pp. 161–62; 187–88; Aydemir, Tek Adam, v. 2, p. 383;

Sabahattin Selek, *Anadolu İhtilâli*, v. 2 (Istanbul, 1965), pp. 280–82. Irandust, *Dvizhushchie sily kemalistskoi revoliutsii* (Moscow-Leningrad, 1928), p. 99, claims Enver "thought he could deceive the broad masses as well as the Soviet republic."

11. Magdeleine Marx [Paz], "L'Humanité en Orient," *l'Humanité*, Nov. 30, 1921. According to Madame Paz, the manifesto issued by this congress protested "against the principles on which capitalist society is based . . . which permit the exploitation of man by man, and nations by nations." Cf. İlhan Darendelioğlu, *Türkiyede Komünist Hareketleri* (Istanbul, 1962), v. 1, p. 20.

The rivalry between the Turkish and Greek labor organizations eventually grew to considerable proportions, leading to an open exchange of recriminations. See below, n. 14.

12. "Mürettipler Grevi Münasebetiyle," *Aydınlık*, Dec. 1, 1921, no. 6, p. 172; Kord-Ruwisch, p. 55. Kord-Ruwisch, through an apparent error in transcription, calls this illegal publication *Zincirbend Gençlik*, claiming that "despite all controls, it enjoyed broad circulation among the workers of Istanbul."

13. "L'état de siège à Constantinople," *l'Humanité*, Dec. 19, 1921, p. 3; Al'mukhamedov, "Kommunisticheskoe dvizhenie v Turtsii," *Kommunisticheskii Internatsional*, 1923, no. 25, column 7069. Eidus, p. 73.

14. Orhan, "Situation in Turkey," *International Press Correspondence*, Jan. 1923, no. 116, p. 972. On the July 21, 1922, conference, see Tunçay, p. 161; Ş[efik] H[üsnü] [Deymer], "İşçi Teşkilatlarını Tevhit Konferansı," *Aydınlık*, Aug. 20, 1922, no. 8, pp. 218–19. Turkish Worker and Peasant Socialist Party member Ali Cevdet gave a long speech at this meeting urging workers to unite. See his "Türkiyenin İktisadi ve İçtimai Vaziyeti," *Aydınlık*, Aug. 20, 1922, no. 8, pp. 210–13; Sept. 20, 1922, no. 9, pp. 227–29. Kâzım who headed the program committee is probably identical with Kâzım from Van. See Tuncay p. 156/n. 29.

The rivalry between the Turkish and Greek labor organizations reached the point where supporters of the Turkish Worker Association accused the International Union of Workers of seeking to lure workers into their union in an underhanded manner, i.e., of attempting to steal members from the Turkish Worker Association. See Şefik Hüsnü [Deymer]. "Memleketimizde Amele Sınıfının Vaziyeti," *Aydınlık*, Feb. 10, 1923, no. 13, p. 323. For their part, the leaders of the International Union of Workers cast aspersions on the inability of the Turkish Worker Association to "raise the intellectual level of" its members. See "Pis'mo 'Mezhdunarodnogo Soiuza Rabochikh,'" *Krasnyi Internatsional Profsoiuzov*, 1922, no. 11 (22), p. 1051. Tunçay, p. 155 & n. 26, estimates that the Turkish Worker Association had 500 members; Eidus, p. 79, claimed 1,000.

15. Jane Degras (ed.), *The Communist International*, v. 1 (London, 1956), pp. 326–27. The Executive Committee of the Comintern announced on

March 4, 1922, that the Balkan Communist Federation would "concern itself with the organization of the communist movement in Turkey."

16. Frunze, p. 622. In response to Soviet representations, Ankara had assured the Kremlin that it would "liberate all imprisoned Turkish communists and hand over to justice those guilty of the murder of the Turkish communist Mustafa Subhi." See Ivan Maiskii, *Vneshnaia politika RSFSR 1917–1922* (Moscow, 1923) , p. 165.

Excerpts from the Dec. 14, 1921 issue of *Yeni Dünya* were quoted in P. P. Moiseev & Iu. Rozaliev, *K istorii sovetsko-turetskikh otnoshenii* (Moscow, 1958) , p. 25. *Yeni Dünya* is said to have continued until March 1922.

17. Türk İnkılâp Tarihi Enstitüsü (ed.) , *Atatürk'ün Söylev ve Demeçleri*, v. 2 (Ankara, 1952) , pp. 26–29; "Documents," *International Affairs* (Moscow) , Nov. 1963, pp. 116–17. For the Frunze visit, see A. N. Kheifits, "Rol' missii M. V. Frunze v ukreplenii druzhestvennykh sovetsko-turetskikh otnoshenii," *Voprosy istorii*, 1962, no. 5, pp. 90–104; Frunze, *passim*. While Atatürk was most conciliatory, Hikmet Bayur, acting head of the Ministry of Foreign Affairs, complained to Frunze that the Soviets were carrying on "communist" propaganda in Turkey.

18. On Aralov's mission, see his *Vospominaniia sovetskogo diplomata 1922–1923 gg.* (Moscow, 1960) , *passim;* abridged English translation: "Diplomats Look Back: In the Turkey of Atatürk," *International Affairs* (Moscow) , 1960, no. 8, pp. 81–87; no. 10, pp. 97–103; no. 11, pp. 96–102.

For the University of the East, see *Anadoluda Yeni Gün*, March 16, 1922; *Vostok*, 1922, no. 1, p. 124.

19. Hoover Institution Library has a handbill printed in Ankara on the *İkaz* press with a handwritten notation that it was circulated in April 1922. This leaflet announced that the Peoples Communist Party of Turkey was reregistering members.

20. Aralov, "Diplomats Look Back," *International Affairs*, 1960, no. 11, pp. 100–101; "Amelenin Bayramı," *Hâkimiyeti Milliye*, May 3, 1922. The May Day telegram was signed by Istanbul deputy Numan as "Representative of the Turkish Workers League" (Türkiye İşçiler Birliği Murahhası). Cf. Tunçay, p. 134/n. 179.

21. *International Affairs*, 1960, no. 11, pp. 100–101. For a more contemporary account, see G. Astakhov, "Sdvigi v Angarskom Medjlise i ikh smysl," *Izvestiia*, Aug. 17, 1922.

22. The agenda of the Peoples Communist Party congress was published in the newspaper *Bolu*, July 18, 1922. For the full text, see Tunçay, p. 137/n. 185. Aydemir, *Tek Adam*, v. 2, p. 373, gave excerpts from this agenda.

23. Magdeleine Marx [Paz], *La Perfide* (Paris, 1925) , *passim*, gives a vivid description of her trip to Ankara. She refers to her French traveling companions by aliases and uses the initials "A. F." in describing her fruitless attempts

to win over Ali Fuat Cebesoy. The primitiveness of Anatolia clearly horrified her, and she was evidently much disconcerted by the suspicion which her mission encountered. She was obviously not impressed with Ahmet Cevat Emre and seems to have had little sympathy for the people of Anatolia, whether communists or not. Cf. *l'Humanité*, Oct. 13, 1922, for Sadoul's report on the congress.

24. Lenoid & A. Friedrich, *Angora: Freiheitskrieg der Türkei* (Berlin, 1923) , p. 56; *Oriente Moderno*, 1922–23, v. 2, no. 4, p. 220; Tunçay, p. 137/n. 186; *Le Bosphore* (Istanbul) , Aug. 24, 1922; Füruzan Hüsrev Tökin, *Türk Tarihinde Siyasî Partiler* (Istanbul, 1965) , p. 67. Cf. Ahmet Cevat [Emre], "Kommunisticheskoe dvizhenie v Turtsii," *Pravda*, Oct. 26, 1922.

25. Leonid & A. Friedrich, pp. 56–68. The quote is from p. 59.

Şevket Süreyya Aydemir, in a personal letter of Feb. 28, 1966, to the author recorded his recollections of the composition of the delegation to the Comintern Congress. Cemal and Galip may have been refused admission by the Comintern. See below note 29.

26. Degras, pp. 368–70, 380–89, 454; L. D—ii, "Pervaia konferentsiia predstavitelei fabrik i zavodov Kilikii," *Krasnyi Internatsional Profsoiuzov*, 1922, no. 12, pp. 1145–46.

27. See Tökin, p. 67. Tunçay, p. 136/n. 184, reports the rumor that the offending editorial was written by Nizamettin Nazif Tepedelenlioğlu.

Tunaya, p. 531, and following him others, claim that on July 21, 1922, the Orbay government banned communist propaganda. No law or decree to this effect was issued by the government at this time, however; and it appears that no such official action was in fact taken on this date.

Present evidence does not permit confident establishment of the date of *Yeni Hayat*'s closing. Kornienko, p. 40, quotes from the issue of Aug. 8, 1922, a declaration "which affirmed the loyalty of the Peoples Communist Party to the government for the duration of the war." Kord-Ruwisch, p. 54, reports that a total of 26 issues of *Yeni Hayat* were published. (He adds that it had a circulation of 1,000.) If so, *Yeni Hayat* evidently survived until mid-September 1922.

28. Gotthard Jäschke, *Die Welt des Islams*, v. 20, 1938, pp. 135–36, published the "Protest of the Peoples Communist Party of Turkey against the Government of the Turkish Grand National Assembly" signed by Hacıoğlu Salih as Secretary General of the party. Jäschke or his original source, *Kızıl Şark*, Nov. 7, 1922, no. 1, p. 40, appears to have incorrectly described Hacıoğlu Salih as "Chairman of the Delegation to the *Third* Congress of the Comintern." Salih, however, was in jail in Turkey from Jan. 1921 until the end of Sept. 1921, hence never attended the Third Congress of the Comintern. Cf. Em. Iaroslavskii, "Ne proschitaites', gospoda Kemalisty!" *Pravda*, Feb. 4, 1923.

29. Communist International, *Fourth Congress of the Communist International* (London, n.d.) , pp. 219–22, 235–39. The Fourth Congress specifically

recognized two separate communist parties in Turkey: one, the Peoples Communist Party of Turkey in Ankara (which claimed a membership of 300), sent 6 delegates—see above n. 25—of whom 2 were refused admission; the other, the Turkish Worker and Peasant Socialist Party (whose membership was then unknown even by the Comintern), sent 3 delegates. *Ibid.*, p. 291. The Istanbul party's delegates were Vedat Nedim Tör (who came from Berlin where he had been studying), Sadrettin Celâl Antel, and Celâl the bearded. See Tunçay, pp. 138–39/n. 188.

CHAPTER VI

1. Tunçay, pp. 157–58/n. 31, gives the text of this appeal "To Istanbul Workers Irrespective of Religion and Sect!" This declaration called the workers to a general strike against the Sultan's government. It also praised the "brotherhood of the masses of Turkish and Greek workers" and summoned the Allied troops in Istanbul to rise against their commanders.

2. See *Aydınlık*, Sept. 20, 1922, especially "Victoires d'anatolie," p. 243. (*Aydınlık's* table of contents was given in both French and Turkish at this period. The text was all in Turkish.)

3. Şefik Hüsnü [Deymer], "Discussion autour des idées révolutionaires," *Aydınlık*, Nov. 1, 1922, no. 10, p. 265. For the congratulatory telegram Deymer sent to the Ankara Assembly, see *Aydınlık*, Dec. 10, 1922, no. 11, p. 295. This telegram and its reply are reproduced in full in Tunaya, p. 439.

4. On Numan, see "İstanbul İşçiler Arasında," *Aydınlık*, Jan. 6, 1923, no. 12, pp. 317–18; France, *Bulletin périodique de la presse turque*, May 20–21, 1923, no. 26, p. 8. "Turkish Communist Union," *The Orient News*, May 15, 1923, p. 2, reported that the police discovered communist influence in this organization toward the end of April 1923 and arrested its members.

5. The Feb. 1923 issue of *Aydınlık* was devoted entirely to the labor movement. For Deymer's program, see *Aydınlık*, Feb. 10, 1923, no. 13, pp. 333–36. For the 39-point petition, see B. Potskhveriia & Iu. Rozaliev, "Trebovaniia rabochei gruppy na Izmirskom ekonomicheskom kongresse 1923 g.," in Akademiia nauk SSSR, *Kratkie soobshcheniia instituta vostokovedeniia*, 1956, v. 22, pp. 82–87. P. Kitaigorodskii, "Rabochee dvizhenie v Turtsii," *Kommunisticheskii Internatsional*, 1925, no. 11 (48), p. 169, claims that Şefik Hüsnü Deymer was elected a delegate to the Congress. Cf. Kornienko, pp. 44–46.

6. "En Turquie: Le Coup de 'complot,' " *La vie ouvière*, March 23, 1923. Salih was arrested on March 13, 1923, transported to Ankara, and arraigned on March 17. Cf. Christo Kabaktschieff, Letter from Constantinople," *International Press Correspondence*, June 28, 1923, no. 47 (27), pp. 459–60.

7. Şevket Süreyya Aydemir, in a letter to the author on Jan. 19, 1967, explained that Nâzım Hikmet could have been in touch with his Istanbul colleagues by mail. Apparently there was no postal censorship at this time.

8. "The 'Bolshevist' Plot," *The Orient News*, May 2, 1923, p. 1.

9. Şefik Hüsnü [Deymer], "İntihabat ve Yoksul ve Orta Halli Sınıflar," *Aydınlık*, May 1923, no. 15, pp. 383–85. See also, Türkiye İşçi ve Çiftçi Sosyalist Partisi, "Türkiye İşçi ve Köylü ve Orta Halli Halk Kütlelerine," *Aydınlık*, May 1923, no. 15, pp. 405–406. Cf. Kornienko, p. 48.

10. On the trial, see *Tanin*, June 4, 1923; France, *Bulletin périodique de la presse turque*, Sept. 12–13, 1923, no. 29, pp. 13–14; Kornienko, p. 49; Eric Verney, "Under Kemalist Rule," *International Press Correspondence*, July 5, 1923, no. 28, pp. 480–81; H[enri] P[aulmier], "Le 'complot' de Constantinople se termine par un non-lieu," *La vie ouvrière*, June 29, 1923, p. 3. G. Astakhov, *Ot sultanata*, pp. 79–82, describes the proceedings as they appeared to a Soviet observer in Turkey at this time.

11. France, *Bulletin périodique de la presse turque*, Sept. 12–13, 1923, no. 29, p. 14.

Some leading editorialists in Istanbul, while expressing more or less aversion to communism, defended the *Aydınlık* group. For example, Yakup Kadri Karaosmanoğlu observed that "all the defendants in the present trial were not perpetrators of disorder and dangerous agitators. Certain of them were pure theoreticians who professed an ideal commanded by the love of humanity." Moreover, Karaosmanoğlu added that "it is impossible not to recognize that the *Workers of Europe* in some places and at certain moments are not in the right." Arguing that Turkey was completely unlike Europe, having not a single "capitalist worthy of the name," he concluded, however, that "it is then folly to provoke in our land" a class struggle.

Writing in *Akşam*, Falih Rıfkı Atay explained that from personal acquaintance with the accused he knew them to be "incapable of engaging" in anything designed to "sow disorder." Atay "concluded from 'the investigation that he himself had made' that the affair was exaggerated."

The Istanbul authorities immediately took steps to promulgate the Treason Act according to the strict requirements of the law. See "Proclaiming the Law of Treason," *The Orient News*, June 20, 1923, p. 2.

12. "Turkey," *Current History*, Aug. 1923, v. 18, pp. 895–96; A. de la Jonquière, "Angora et Moscou," *l'Asie française*, Sept.–Oct. 1924, no. 24, pp. 337–38. Cf. "Russian Communist Propaganda in Constantinople," *The Orient News*, June 10, 1923, p. 2.

13. "Arrest of a Turkish Communist Editor," *The Orient News*, June 28, 1923, p. 2; Henri Paulmier, "On arrête toujours en Turquie," *La vie ouvrière*, July 6, 1923; Verney, p. 481; "Turkey," *Current History*, Aug. 1923, v. 18, p. 896; France, *Bulletin périodique de la presse turque*, Sept. 12–13, 1923, no. 29, p. 14.

182   THE ORIGINS OF COMMUNISM IN TURKEY

The Ankara trials were said to have involved 30 persons, including an
ex-deputy (former Tokat deputy Nâzım?) as well as "several lawyers and
journalists," accused of trying to overthrow the Turkish government and
establish communism in Turkey.

14. See *Haber*, Sept. 14, 1923, evening edition; *The Orient News*, Sept.
11, 12, 22, 1923; Kord-Ruwisch, p. 55; G. Astakhov, "Rabochee dvizhenie
v novoi Turtsii," *Krasnyi Internatsional Profsoiuzov*, 1924, no. 2–3 (37–38),
p. 233. Kitaigorodskii, "Rabochee dvizhenie v Turtsii," p. 171, claimed that
in the strike of the workers of the Eastern Railways—which he also alleged
was led by communists—the strikers likewise demanded that closer ties be
established with the USSR.

Kornienko, p. 61, states that the printers also published *Adıl* (Justice)
to popularize their views.

15. Kord-Ruwisch, p. 55; Lütfü Erişçi, *Türkiyede İşçi Sınıfının Tarihi*
(Istanbul, 1951), p. 19.

16. France, *Bulletin périodique de la presse turque*, June 24–25, 1923, no.
27, p. 7: "Le parti ouvrier," reported that Rasim Şakir had demanded that
his union be allowed to designate at least five candidates who were workers
to run on the Kemalist slate. See also Çapanoğlu, pp. 64, 72; Kitaigorodskii,
"Rabochee dvizhenie v Turtsii," pp. 166–71; Kemal Sülker, *Türkiyede
Sendikacılık* (Istanbul, 1955), pp. 26–27; "İstanbul İşçiler Arasında," *Aydınlık*,
Jan. 6, 1923, no. 12, p. 317; Erişçi, p. 18; Tunçay, pp. 164, 175. "Turtsiia:
S'ezd rabochego obshchestva 'Amele-Teali,'" *Mezhdunarodnoe rabochee
dvizhenie*, 1926, no. 44 (85), p. 14.

Cf. "L'Assassinat du chef du parti socialiste, Hilmi Bey," *Le Bosphore*,
Nov. 18, 1922, p. 2.

17. On the views of the *Aydınlık* group immediately before the declaration
of the Republic, see Şefik Hüsnü [Deymer], "Yeni Millet Meclisinden Halk
Ne Bekliyor?" *Aydınlık*, Aug. 1923, no. 17, pp. 434–37; and his "İnkılâp
Esasatının Tadili," *Aydınlık*, Oct. 1923, no. 18, pp. 458–60. Cf. Tunçay, p. 171.
See also Astakhov, *Ot sultanata*, pp. 63–71: "Revoliutsionnaia ideologiia
Kemalizma v protsesse kristallizatsii," a chapter written in the latter half
of 1923. While Astakhov noted that there were differences of opinion among
Kemalists over the question of reform, he accepted the claim put forth in
Hâkimiyeti Milliye that the Turkish revolution was intended to benefit "the
popular masses, the hungry, the naked, and the barefoot." He was clearly
impressed by Atatürk's moves to free the economy from dependence on Europe
and to crush the reactionary opposition in Istanbul. Astakhov approvingly
recited speeches of Ahmet Ağaoğlu "extolling Marxism, Lenin and Trotsky,"
and an article by Ziya Gökalp in *Hâkimiyeti Milliye* making a class analysis
of Anatolia. In general, Astakhov approved of *Hâkimiyeti Milliye*'s line at
this time, particularly its identification of "the working class, led by Marx
and Engels," as the new revolutionary factor in the world. He concluded that

"in the interpretation of European history, the editorialists of the Ankara papers far outstrip the polished publications of *The Times* and *Le Matin.*"

18. Şefik Hüsnü [Deymer], "Turk Burjuvazisinin Aile Kavgaları," *Aydınlık,* June 1924, no. 22, pp. 562–65. See also his "Amele Sınıfı Cumhuriyet Hakkında Ne Düşünüyor?" *Aydınlık,* May 1924, no. 21.

19. Kord-Ruwisch, p. 55.

20. Starting in Aug. 1923, Tör published a series of articles in *Aydınlık* on Turkish agriculture, economic independence, and unemployment. Here he first developed the ideas that were later to flower in the *Kadro* movement.

21. Aydemir described his experiences in his autobiographical *Suyu Arayan Adam.* See especially pp. 230–390, 430. Cf. his "Lenin ve Leninizm," *Aydınlık,* Feb. 1924, no. 20.

22. Demetrio Boersner, *The Bolsheviks and the National and Colonial Question 1917–1928* (Geneva, 1957), p. 140; Communist International, *Fifth Congress of the Communist International* (London, n.d.), pp. 188–89, 193, 209–10.

The Comintern claimed that membership in the Turkish Communist Party had doubled from the 300 members shown at the time of the preceding Congress, while the number of "decisive" and "consultative" votes allotted the Turkish party had been cut to a total of 3. Degras, v. 2, p. 94, reports that the Communist Party in Turkey had been dissolved after the Fourth Congress of the Comintern, then re-established and finally dissolved again. If this reorganization represented more than bureaucratic procedure in Moscow, it may have had some bearing on the irregularity with which *Aydınlık* appeared during this period. The problem of party organizational difficulties at this time requires elucidation.

23. Deymer's articles betray a growing suspicion of Kemalist economic policy. See his "Devlet İnhisarına Niçin Taraftarız?" *Aydınlık,* Sept. 1924, no. 25, pp. 642–44; "Türk Köylüsünün Kurtuluşu," *Aydınlık,* Jan. 1, 1925, no. 29, pp. 775–77; and "Türkiyede İktisadi Mesele—1," *Aydınlık,* Feb. 1925, no. 30, pp. 811–13.

Following the Comintern criticism, Tör appeared somewhat defensive about his views. See his two-part article " 'İktisadi Kurtuluş'tan Ne Anlıyoruz?" which began in *Aydınlık,* Oct. 1924, no. 26; and his "Sınıf Menfaatları ve Politika," *Aydınlık,* Dec. 1924, no. 28.

See also A. Shami, "Vostok pered kongressom Kominterna," part I: "Turtsiia," *Za partiiu,* 1928, no. 7 (11), p. 21.

24. "Turtsiia: S'ezd rabochego obshchestva 'Amele-Teali,'" p. 14; Kitaigorodskii, "Rabochee dvizhenie v Turtsii," p. 173; Sülker, p. 27; *Le Tanine,* Jan. 22, Feb. 15, 21, 1925; *Orak Çekiç,* Feb. 26, 1925, no. 6. Cf. Tunçay, pp. 189–90.

25. *Orak Çekiç,* Feb. 12, 1925, no. 4, p. 2. Cf. Tunçay, pp. 187–91.

Orak Çekiç appeared weekly starting on Jan. 21, 1925. It may have been originally intended to call this paper *Emekçi*, as the last known "extraordinary worker issue" of *Aydınlık*, Jan. 1925, no. 8, reported the imminent appearance of a weekly worker newspaper by this name. No paper called "Emekçi" is known to have been published at this time.

26. On Nâzım Hikmet, see Vâ-Nû, *passim*, especially pp. 148–52, 206–208; Halide Edib [Adıvar], *Conflict of East and West in Turkey* (Lahore, 1935), pp. 222–24; Akper Babaev, *Nazym Khikmet* (Moscow, 1957), pp. 14–37; *Bol'shaia Sovetskaia Entsiklopediia*, second edition (1957), v. 46, p. 136; first edition (1935), p. 538.

On his relations with Barbusse, see Brett, p. 317, who indicates that Barbusse dedicated an article to Nâzım Hikmet in *Clarté*, July 31, 1920, p. 3.

For Nâzım Hikmet's somewhat rigid interpretation of communism at this point, see especially his "Türkiyede Amele Sınıfı ve Amele Meselesi," *Aydınlık*, Sept. 1924, no. 25, pp. 661–63.

27. See *Orak Çekiç*, Feb. 26, 1925, no. 6, and March 5, 1925, no. 7; Tunçay, pp. 189–91. For the Soviet version of the suppression of the communist movement in Istanbul, see B. Ferdi, "Kommunisticheskoe dvizhenie v Turtsii," *Kommunisticheskii Internatsional*, Oct. 22, 1926, no. 6 (64), pp. 44–48.

28. *Le Tanine*, May 9, 11, 1925; Makhail Pavlovich [Velt'man], *Revoliutsionnyi Vostok*, part I: *SSSR i Vostok* (Moscow-Leningrad, 1927), p. 302; Kitaigordskii, "Rabochee dvizhenie v Turtsii," pp. 173–74. Shami, p. 22, claims that *Yoldaş* attained a circulation of 1,000.

29. Babaev, pp. 41–42; Kitaigorodskii, Rabochee dvizhenie v Turtsii," p. 174; Tunçay, pp. 189–90; *Akşam*, July 22, 1925.

30. *Vakıt*, Aug. 1, 1925, published the indictment. See also the statement of Minister of Interior Şükrü Sökmensuer on communism, Jan, 29, 1947, in *Ayın Tarihi*, Jan. 1947, no. 158, pp. 10–11.

EPILOGUE

1. Law no. 3038, June 11, 1936, amended Articles 141 and 142 of the Penal Code to provide 5–12 years at hard labor for efforts forcibly to overturn the social order or to promote class struggle.

2. Aydemir described his jail experience in his *Suyu Arayan Adam*, p. 427: "Now the automaton who returned to Istanbul from Moscow was dead. Anatolian reality . . . gripped me in these four walls of prison." The rigors of jail in Anatolia are also recounted in S. Üstüngel, *Savaş Yolu* (Sofia, 1950); Russian translation: "V tiur'me i na 'vole,'" *Novyi Mir*, 1951, no. 9, pp. 82–133.

3. Antel was temporarily suspended from his teaching post at Istanbul University in 1944 in connection with a university demonstration. He was subsequently acquitted in court and was returned to his position. See Yücel,

pp. 22–23, and his *Hasan-Âli Yücel'in Açtığı Davalar ve Neticeleri* (Ankara, 1950), p. 65.

4. Emre's autobiographical *İki Neslin Tarihi* (Istanbul, 1960) avoids all mention of his activities in the communist movement. Subsequently in *Tarih Dünyası*, Dec. 1, 1964–Feb. 1, 1965, v. 1, pp. 88–93, 146–51, 278–85, Emre described this period in his "1920 Moskovasında Türk Komünistleri." Nizamettin Nazif Tepedelenlioğlu answered these articles. See his "Ahmet Cevat Emre'nin Moskova Hâtıraları Dolayısıyla—Cevap Veriyor," *Tarih Dünyası*, March 1–June 15, 1965 v. 1, pp. 478–81, v. 2, 72–74, 167–68, 176, 255–59.

Emre was the author of the famous letter protesting the murder of Subhi and his companions published by Mikhail Velt'man in his *Revoliutsionnaia Turtsii* (Moscow, 1921), pp. 119–21.

Şevket Süreyya Aydemir in a letter of Feb. 28, 1966, explained that it was Emre who brought him (as well as Nâzım Hikmet and Vâ-Nû) to Moscow. According to Aydemir, Emre "never mixed in the party movements in Turkey. He was not a man of the street or of the masses." Aydemir admits that Emre worked in the "central organization of the Comintern" and served as "a teacher in the Eastern Languages Institute in Moscow."

5. Aydemir, *Suyu Arayan Adam*, p. 461.

6. Constantinople Embassy Dispatches no. 61, Nov. 23, 1927, and no. 148, Jan. 31, 1928, report on these arrests and trials. See also *Cumhuriyet*, Nov. 20, 21, 22, 27, 1927; İlhan Darendelioğlu, v. 1, pp. 47–53; Institut Marksa-Engel'sa-Lenina, *Programmnye dokumenty Kommunisticheskikh Partii Vostoka* (Moscow, 1934), pp. 147–58; *Ayın Tarihi*, Jan. 1947, pp. 11–25.

7. Hacıoğlu Salih had also been arrested in 1927. Darendelioğlu, v. 1, pp. 47, 57, also reports that Hacıoğlu Salih was a member of the Central Committee of the Turkish Communist Party prior to his expulsion.

Mete Tunçay, in a letter to the author, explained his view that Salih and Nâzım Hikmet, though differing in many respects as regards doctrine, may have been the real revolutionaries in the party; while Deymer and the orthodox party leadership appeared rather more Menshevik in outlook. However this may be, it was at this time, too, that the Turkish Communist Party lost such other members as architect Semih, Dr. Süleyman Neşati, and Nuri Haydar, all of whom eventually accepted government posts.

Cf. Fethi Tevetoğlu, "Hafî Türkiye Komünist Partisi ve Türkiye Halk İştirâkiyûn Fırkası," *Türk Kültürü*, Feb. 1967, no. 52, p. 267; Aclan Sayılgan, *İnkâr Fırtınası* (Istanbul, 1963), pp. 164–65.

8. *Kadro*, Jan. 1932, no. 1, explained the philosophy of this periodical. See especially pp. 1, 6–9.

Select Bibliography

I. OFFICIAL PUBLICATIONS AND DOCUMENTS

Communist International. *Biulleten' III kongressa.* Moscow, July 1921, no. 23.

————. *Fifth Congress of the Communist International.* London, n.d.

————. *Fourth Congress of the Communist International.* London, n.d.

————. *Pervyi s'ezd narodov Vostoka.* Petrograd, 1920.

————. *The Second Congress of the Communist International.* America, 1921.

France. Ministère des affaires étrangères. *Bulletin périodique de la presse turque.* 1919–1935.

Institut Marksa-Engel'sa-Lenina pri TsK VKP (b). *Pervyi kongress Kommunisticheskogo Internatsionala Mart 1919 g.* Moscow, 1933.

————. *Programmnye dokumenty kommunisticheskikh partii Vostoka.* Moscow, 1934.

International Socialist Bureau. *Bulletin périodique,* no. 1–13, 1910–1913.

————. *Huitième Congrès socialiste international tenu à Copenhague du 28 août au 3 septembre 1910. Compte rendu analytique.* v. 8. Gand, 1911.

————. *Stockholm.* Stockholm, 1918.

Turkey. Agence d'Anatolie. *Bulletin.* 1920–1921.

Turkey. *Takvimi Vekayi.* Oct. 4, 1920, no. 3972.

Turkey. T.B.M.M. *Albüm.* Dönem: I. April 23, 1945.

Turkey. T.B.M.M. *Zabıt Ceridesi.* Devre I (1920–1923). vv. 1–29.

Turkey. T.C. Dışişleri Bakanlığı. *Dışişleri Bakanlığı Yıllığı. 1964–1965* (Hamıd Aral, ed.).

Turkey. T.C. İçişleri Bakanlığı. Emniyet Genel Müdürlüğü.

Türkiye'de Siyasî Dernekler. v. 2. Ankara, 1950.

Türkiye Halk İştirakiyun Fırkası. *Halk İştirakiyun Fırkasından.* Ankara, n.d. [Handbill with handwritten notation that it was circulated in April 1922.]

Türkiye Komünist Partisi. *Umumi Nizamnamesi.* Ankara, June 1920.

U.S. Department of State. *Papers Relating to the Foreign Relations of the United States,* 1919. v. 2. Washington, 1934.

U.S. National Archives. Constantinople Embassy Dispatches. 1921–1928.

U.S.S.R. Ministerstvo inostrannykh del SSSR. *Dokumenty vneshnei politiki SSSR.* vv. 2–4. Moscow, 1958–1960.

U.S.S.R. Narodnyi komissariat po inostrannym delam. *Biulleten'.* 1920–1922.

II. BOOKS

Halide Ebid [Adıvar]. *Conflict of East and West in Turkey.* Lahore, 1935.

———. *The Turkish Ordeal.* New York, 1928. Turkish edition: *Türkün Ateşle İmtihanı.* Istanbul, 1962.

Abid Alimov and M. Godes. *Ocherki po istorii Vostoka v epokhu imperializma.* Moscow, 1934.

Semen Ivanovich Aralov. *Vospominaniia sovetskogo diplomata 1922–1923 gg.* Moscow, 1960.

Damar Arıkoğlu. *Hâtıralarım.* Istanbul, 1961.

Mehmet Arif. *Anadolu İnkılâbı: Mücahedatı Milliye Hâtıratı (1335–1339).* Istanbul, 1340 (1924 New Style).

G. Astakhov. *Ot sultanata k demokraticheskoi Turtsii.* Moscow, 1926.

Mustafa Kemal [Atatürk]. *Put' novoi Turtsii.* vv. 1–4. Moscow, 1929–1934.

———. *A Speech Delivered by Ghazi Mustapha Kemal.* Leipzig, 1929.

Şevket Süreyya Aydemir. *Suyu Arayan Adam.* 2d ed. Istanbul, 1965.

———. *Tek Adam.* vv. 2–3. Istanbul, 1964–1965.

Akper Babaev. *Nazym Khikmet.* Moscow, 1957.

Niyazi Berkes. *The Development of Secularism in Turkey.* Montreal, 1964.

Adrien Biliotti and Ahmet Sedad. *Législation ottomane depuis le rétablissement de la Constitution.* v. 1. Paris, 1912.

Tevfik Bıyıklıoğlu. *Atatürk Anadolu'da (1919–1921).* v. 1. Ankara, 1959.

Demetrio Boersner. *The Bolsheviks and the National and Colonial Question (1917–1928).* Geneva, 1957.

Vladimir Brett. *Henri Barbusse; sa marche vers la clarté, son mouvement Clarté.* Prague, 1963.

Münir Süleyman Çapanoğlu. *Türkiyede Sosyalizm Hareketleri ve Sosyalist Hilmi.* Istanbul, 1964.

Edward H. Carr. *A History of Soviet Russia: The Bolshevik Revolution, 1917–1923.* vv. 1 and 3. London, 1950–1953.

David Caute. *Communism and the French Intellectuals. 1914–1960.* London, 1964.

Ali Fuat Cebesoy. *Millî Mücadele Hâtıraları.* Istanbul, 1953.

———. *Moskova Hâtıraları.* Istanbul, 1955.

Çerkes Ethem'in Hâtıraları. Istanbul, 1962.

A. Cerrahoğlu. *İslâmiyet ve Osmanlı Sosyalistleri; İslâmiyet ve Yöncü Sosyalistler.* Istanbul, 1964.

———. *Türkiye'de Sosyalizm.* vv. 1–2. Istanbul, 1965–1966.

G. H. D. Cole. *The Second International, 1889–1914: A History of Socialist Thought.* v. 3, part II. London, 1956.

Boris Moiseevich Dantsig. *Turtsiia.* Moscow, 1949.

İlhan Darendelioğlu. *Türkiyede Komünist Hareketleri.* vv. 1–2. Istanbul, 1962–1963.

Jane Degras (ed.). *The Communist International.* v. 1. London, 1956.

Khaim T. Eidus. *Ocherki rabochego dvizheniia v stranakh Vostoka.* Moscow, 1922.

E. T. Eliçin. *Türk İnkılâbı Yahut Şark ve Garp.* Istanbul, 1940.

Ahmet Cevat Emre. *İki Neslin Tarihi.* Istanbul, 1960.

Haşim Nahid Er-Bil. *Komünist Beyannamesi'ne karşı Milliyetçi Beyannamesi.* Istanbul, 1950.

Lütfü Erişçi. *Türkiyede İşçi Sınfının Tarihi.* Istanbul, 1951.

Xenia Joukoff Eudin and Robert C. North. *Soviet Russia and the East, 1920–1927: A Documentary Survey.* Stanford, 1957.

Ziyaeddin F. Fındıkoğlu. *Ziya Gökalp: sa vie et sa sociologie.* Paris, 1936.

Louis Fischer. *The Soviets in World Affairs.* v. 1. Princeton, 1951.

Frederick W. Frey. *The Turkish Political Elite.* Cambridge, 1965.

M. V. Frunze. *Sobranie sochinenii.* v. 1. Moscow, 1929.

Avram Galanti [Abraham Galanté]. *Türkler ve Yahudiler.* Istanbul, 1947.

M. Tayyar Gökbilgin. *Millî Mücadele Başlarken.* vv. 1–2. Ankara, 1959–1965.

V. A. Gurko-Kriazhin. *Blizhnii Vostok i derzhavy.* Moscow, 1925.

George S. Harris. *A Political History of Turkey, 1945–1950.* Unpublished Ph.D. dissertation submitted to the Department of History, Harvard University, 1956.

Martin Hartmann. *Der Islamische Orient: Berichte und Forschungen.* v. 3: *Unpolitische Briefe aus der Türkei.* Leipzig, 1910.

Uriel Heyd. *The Foundations of Turkish Nationalism.* London, 1950.

Charles Hostler. *Turkism and the Soviets.* London, 1957.

Irandust. *Dvizhushchie sily kemalistskoi revoliutsii.* Moscow-Leningrad, 1928.

Server İskit. *Türkiyede Matbuat İdareleri ve Politikaları.* Istanbul, 1943.

Gotthard Jäschke. *Türk İnkılâbı Tarihi Kronolojisi, 1918–1923.* Istanbul, 1939 (translated by Niyazi Recep Aksu).

Feridun Kandemir. *Atatürk'ün Kurduğu Türkiye Komünist Partisi ve Sonrası.* Istanbul, n.d. [1966?].

Kemal Karpat. *Turkey's Politics.* Princeton, 1959.

Kâzım Karabekir. *İstiklâl Harbimiz.* Istanbul, 1960.

Sami Sabit Karaman. *İstiklâl Mücadelesi ve Enver Paşa—Trabzon ve Kars Hâtıraları: 1921–1922.* Izmit, 1949.

A. Karaev. *Iz nedavnego proshlogo.* Baku, 1926.

Bezmi Nusret Kaygusuz. *Bir Roman Gibi.* Izmir, 1955.

Ali Kılıç. *Kılıç Ali Hâtıralarını Anlatıyor.* Istanbul, 1955.

P. Kitaigorodskii. *Turtsii.* Moscow, 1929.

Gianes Kordatos. *Historia tou Hellenikou ergatikou kinematos, me base agnostes peges kai anekdota archeia.* Athens, 1956.

R. P. Kornienko. *Rabochee dvizhenie v Turtsii 1918–1963 gg.* Moscow, 1965.

Ahmet Bedevi Kuran. *Osmanlı İmperatorluğunda İnkılâp Hareketleri ve Millî Mücadele.* Istanbul, 1956.

Sof'ia Iosifovna Kuznetsova. *Ustanovlenie sovetsko-turetskikh otnoshenii.* Moscow, 1961.

Walter Z. Laqueur. *Communism and Nationalism in the Middle East.* New York, 1956.

———. *The Soviet Union and the Middle East.* New York, 1959.

Lenoid and A. Friedrich. *Angora: Freiheitskrieg der Türkei.* Berlin, 1923.

Bernard Lewis. *The Emergence of Modern Turkey.* London, 1961.

Ivan Maiskii. *Vneshnaia Politika RSFSR. 1917–1922.* Moscow, 1923.

A. Mel'nik [Anatolii Filippovich Miller]. *Turtsiia.* Moscow, 1937.

Anatolii Filippovich Miller. *Kratkaia istoriia Turtsii.* Moscow, 1948.

———. *Ocherki noveishei istorii Turtsii.* Moscow, 1948.

Mehmet-Zade Mirza-Bala. *Millî Azerbaycan Hareketi.* Berlin, 1938.

Petr Pavlovich Moiseev and Iuryi Rozaliev. *K istorii sovetsko-turetskikh otnoshenii.* Moscow, 1958.

Yunus Nadi. *Çerkes Ethem Kuvvetlerinin İhaneti.* Istanbul, 1955.

Gunther Nollau and Hans Jurgen Wiehe. *Russia's South Flank; Soviet Operations in Iran, Turkey, and Afghanistan.* New York, 1963.

Aron Davidovich Novichev. *Krest'ianstvo Turtsii v noveishee vremia.* Moscow, 1959.

Kenan Öner. *Öner ve Yücel Davası.* vv. 1–2. Istanbul, 1947.

Magdeleine Marx [Paz]. *La Perfide (par les routes d'Asie Mineure).* Paris, 1925.

———. *The Romance of the New Russia.* New York, 1924 (translated by Anita Grannis).

Nurettin Peker. *1918–1923 İstiklâl Savaşının Vesika ve Resimleri: İnönü, Sakarya, Dumlupınar Zaferlerini Sağlayan İnebolu ve Kastamonu Havalısı Deniz ve Kara Harekâtı ve Hâtıralar.* Istanbul, 1955.

Maurice Pernot. *La Question turque.* Paris, 1923.

Ov. Petrosian. *Bibliografiia armianskoi periodicheskoi pechati (1900–1956) s predisloviem i primechaniiami.* Erevan, 1957.

Richard Pipes. *The Formation of the Soviet Union.* Cambridge, 1964.

I. Raguza. *La vie de Staline.* Paris, 1938.

Joseph Rothschild. *The Communist Party of Bulgaria.* New York, 1959.

Necdet Sançar. *Gizli Komünist Belgeleri.* Ankara, 1966.

Hüseyin Avni Şanda. *Türkiye'de 54 Yıl Önceki İşçi Hareketleri.* Istanbul, 1962. [Reprint of his *1908'de Ecnebî Sermayesine karşı İlk Kalkınmalar.* Istanbul, 1935.]

Ervand Kazarovich Sarkisian. *Velikaia Oktiabr'skaia sotsialisticheskaia revoliutsiia i natsional'no-osvoboditel'naia bor'ba v Turtsii.* Erevan, 1958.

Aclan Sayılgan. *İnkâr Fırtınası.* Istanbul, 1963.

Lidiia Nikolaevna Seifullina. *Sobranie sochinenii.* v. 3: *Virineia.* Moscow-Leningrad, 1928.

Sabahattin Selek. *Anadolu İhtilâli.* vv. 1–2. Istanbul, 1963–1965.

Ivar Spector. *The Soviet Union and the Muslim World, 1917–1958.* Englewood Cliffs, 1962.

Elena Dmitrievna Stasova. *Stranitsy zhizni i bor'by.* Moscow, 1957.

Leften S. Stavrianos. *Balkan Federation.* Hamden, 1964.

Kemal Sülker. *Türkiyede Sendikacılık.* Istanbul, 1955.

Samih Nafiz Tansu. *İki Devrin Perde Arkası.* Istanbul, 1964.

Fethi Tevetoğlu. *Açıklıyorum.* Ankara, 1965.

———. *Faşist Yok Komünist Var.* 3d ed. Ankara, 1963.

Füruzan Hüsrev Tökin. *Türk Tarihinde Siyasî Partiler ve Siyasî Düşüncenin Gelişmesi, 1839–1965.* Istanbul, 1965.

Tonguç'a Kitap. Istanbul, 1961.

Tarik Zafer Tunaya. *Devrim Hareketleri İçinde Atatürk ve Atatürkçülük.* Istanbul, 1964.

———. *Türkiyede Siyasî Partiler; 1859–1952.* Istanbul, 1952.

———. *Türkiyenin Siyasî Hayatında Batılılaşma Hareketleri.* Istanbul, 1960.

Mete Tunçay. *Türkiye'de Sol Akımlar: 1908–1925.* Ankara, 1967.

Osman Turan. *Türkiyede Komünizmin Kaynakları.* Ankara, 1964.

Türk İnkılâp Tarihi Enstitüsü (ed.). *Atatürk'un Söylev ve Demeçleri.* vv. 1–3. Istanbul, 1945; Ankara, 1952–1954.

Türk Tarihi Kurulu (ed.). *Histoire de la république turque.* Istanbul, 1935.

R. Oğuz Türkkan. *Kızıl Faaliyet.* Istanbul, 1943.

Hilmi Ziya Ülken. *Türkiye'de Çagdaş Düşünce Tarihi.* Konya, 1966. vv. 1–2.

Veysel Ünüvar. *İstiklâl Harbinde Bolşeviklerle Sekiz Ay, 1920–1921.* Istanbul, 1948.

Vâlâ Nureddin Vâ-Nû. *Bu Dünyadan Nâzım Geçti.* Istanbul, 1965.

Dmitrii Ivanovich Vdovichenko. *Natsional'naia burzhuaziia Turtsii.* Moscow, 1962.

Mikhail Pavlovich [Velt'man]. *Revoliutsionnaia Turtsiia.* Moscow, 1921.

————. *Revoliutsionnyi Vostok.* Part I: *SSSR i Vostok.* Moscow-Leningrad, 1927.

Mikhail Pavlovich [Velt'man] et als. *Turtsiia v bor'be za nezavisimost'.* Moscow, 1925.

Ahmet Emin [Yalman]. *The Development of Modern Turkey as Measured by Its Press.* New York, 1914.

28–29 Kânunusani 1921 Karadeniz Kıyalarında Parçalanan Mustafa Subhi ve Yoldaşlarının İkinci Yıldönümleri. Moscow, 1923.

Hasan Âli Yücel. *Dâvam.* Ankara, 1947.

————. *Hasan-Âli Yücel'in Açtığı Davalar ve Neticeleri.* Ankara, 1950.

Z.A.B. Zeman and W. B. Scharlau. *The Merchant of Revolution: The Life of Alexander Israel Helphand (Parvus), 1867–1924.* London, 1965.

Dančo Zografski. *Za rabotničkoto dviženje vo Makedonija do balkanskata vojna.* Skoplje, 1950.

III. ARTICLES

Gregor Alexinsky. "Bolshevism and the Turks," *Quarterly Review* (London), 1923, v. 239, pp. 183–97.

Al'mukhamedov. "Kommunisticheskoe dvizhenie v Turtsii," *Kommunisticheskii Internatsional,* 1923, no. 25, cols. 7067–70.

Semen Ivanovich Aralov. "Diplomats Look Back: In the Turkey of Ataturk," *International Affairs* (Moscow), 1960, no. 8, pp. 81–87; no. 10, pp. 97–103; no. 11, pp. 96–102.

G. Astakhov. "Rabochee dvizhenie v novoi Turtsii," *Krasnyi Internatsional Profsoiuzov*, 1924, no. 2–3 (37–38), pp. 229–35.

———. "Sdvigi v Angarskom medzhlise i ikh smysl," *Izvestiia*, Aug. 17, 1922.

H. Baydour [Baydur]. "Chronique Internationale: En Turquie," *La revue communiste*, Dec. 1920, no. 10, pp. 373–77.

Abraam Benaroya. "Die Türkische Gewerkschaftsbewegung," *Sozialistische Monatshefte*, Aug. 11, 1910, v. 14, no. 16–18, pp. 1079–81.

Inal Butaev. "Ocherki vostokovedeniia," *Zhizn' Natsional'nostei*, March 22, 1922, no. 4 (10).

———. "Osnovnye momenty v razvitii natsional'nogo dvizheniia na musulmanskom Vostoke (Khalifatskoe Papstvo)," in Avestis Sultan-Galiev (ed.). *Kolonialnyi Vostok*. Moscow, 1924.

L. D——ii. "Pervaia konferentsiia predstavitelei fabrik i zavodov Kilikii," *Krasnyi Internatsional Profsoiuzov*, 1922, no. 12, pp. 1145–47.

Ahmet Cevat Emre. "1920 Moskovasinda Türk Komünistleri," *Tarih Dünyası*, no. 1–3, Dec. 1, 1964–Feb. 1, 1965, pp. 88–93, 146–51, 278–85.

———. "Kommunisticheskoe dvizhenie v Turtsii," *Pravda*, Oct. 26, 1922.

Yakub Demir (pseudonym). "Türkiye Komünist Partisi Birinci Sekreteri Yakub Demir Yoldaşın Konuşması," *Yeni Çağ* (Prague), Sept. 1965, no. 9, pp. 761–69.

Lütfü Eroğlu [Erişçi]. "Bizde Siyasî Cemiyet ve Partilerin Tarihçiliği," *Aylık Ansiklopedi*, Aug. 1948, no. 52, pp. 1489–97.

Enver Esenkova. "Le communisme en Turquie," *Est et Ouest*, Sept. 16–30, 1964, no. 326, pp. 14–21.

Fachri [Fakhri]. "Türkei: Die politische Lage und die Aufgaben der Kommunistischen Partei," *Rundschau*, April 20, 1933, no. 10, pp. 289–91.

———. "Kompartiia Turtsii v bor'be za massy," *Kommunisticheskii Internatsional*, 1933, no. 22 (364), pp. 42–46.

B. Ferdi. "Evoliutsiia Kemalizma ot natsional'noi revoliutsii k diktature burzhuazii," *Sputnik Kommunista,* 1927, no. 10 (43), pp. 30–38.

———. "Polozhenie rabochego klassa i kommunisticheskoe dvizhenie v Turtsii," *Kommunisticheskii Internatsional,* Nov. 12, 1926, no. 9 (67), pp. 43–45.

L. Geller. "Blizhnii i Dal'nii Vostok," *Krasnyi Internatsional Profsoiuzov,* 1923, no. 8 (31), pp. 212–13.

Vladimir Gordlevskii. "Iz zhizni sovremennoi Turtsii," *Vostok,* 1923, v. 3, pp. 203–206; 1924, v. 4, pp. 204–10.

V. A. Gurko-Kriazhin. "Politicheskie gruppirovki Turtsii," *Novyi Vostok,* 1922, no. 3, pp. 35–55.

———. "Rabochee i sotsialisticheskoe dvizhenie v Turtsii," *Krasnyi Internatsional Profsoiuzov,* 1925, no. 2–3, pp. 139–50.

———. "Voznikovenie natsional'no-osvoboditel'nogo dvizheniia v Turtsii," *Novyi Vostok,* 1928, no. 23–24, pp. 268–75.

George S. Harris. "The Role of the Military in Turkish Politics," *The Middle East Journal,* Winter 1965, pp. 54–66; Spring 1965, pp. 169–76.

Gotthard Jäschke. "Kommunismus und Islam im türkischen Befreiungskriege," *Die Welt des Islams,* 1938, v. 20, pp. 110–17.

———. "Neues zur russisch-türkischen Freundschaft von 1919–1939," *Die Welt des Islams,* 1961, new series, v. 6, no. 3–4, pp. 203–22.

———. "Le rôle du communisme dans les relations russo-turques," *Orient,* 1963, no. 26, pp. 31–44.

———. "Türkei" in Dr. Adolf Ehrt (ed.). *Der Weltbolschewismus.* Berlin-Leipzig, 1936, pp. 439–43.

———. "Der Weg zur russisch-türkischen Freundschaft," *Die Welt des Islams,* 1934, v. 16, pp. 23–38.

Hasan Jelal. "Communisti e Socialisti in Turchia," *Corrispondenza Socialista,* June 1965, no. 6, pp. 302–09.

A. de la Jonquière. "Angora et Moscou," *L'Asie française,* Sept.–Oct. 1924, no. 24, pp. 333–40.

Christo Kabaktschieff. "Letter from Constantinople: Kemal Pascha's Reign of Terror against the Labor Organizations," *International Press Correspondence,* June 28, 1923, no. 47 (27), pp. 459–60.

V. Kasparova. "The Women's Movement: The Women's Movement in the Near East: Turkey," *International Press Correspondence,* April 10, 1924, no. 24, pp. 222–23.

A. N. Kheifits. "Rol' missii M. V. Frunze v ukreplenii druzhestvennykh sovetsko-turetskikh otnoshenii," *Voprosy Istorii,* 1962, no. 5, pp. 90–104.

P. Kitaigorodskii. "Oktiabr'skaia revoliutsiia i natsional'no-revoliutsionnoe dvizhenie Turtsii," *Krasnyi Internatsional Profsoiuzov,* 1927, no. 10 (81), pp. 407–11.

———. "Rabochee dvizhenie v Turtsii," *Kommunisticheskii Internatsional,* 1925, no. 11 (48), pp. 165–74.

Will Kord-Ruwisch. "Die Arbeiterpresse in der Türkei," *Zeitungswissenschaft,* 1926, no. 4, pp. 53–55.

R. P. Kornienko. "Nachalo rabochego dvizheniia v Turtsii," *Narody Azii i Afriki,* 1964, no. 1, pp. 98–105.

D. Kuz'min. "Rabochee dvizhenie v Turtsii," *Novyi Vostok,* 1922, no. 2, pp. 154–59.

Sof'ia Iosifovna Kuznetsova. "Krakh turetskoi interventsii v Zakavkaz'e v 1920–1921 godakh," *Voprosy Istorii,* 1951, no. 9, pp. 143–56.

Bernard Lewis. "Communism and Islam." *International Affairs* (London), 1954, no. 30, pp. 1–12.

E. F. Ludshuveit. "Konferentsiia levykh turetskikh sotsialistov v Moskve letom 1918 goda," in Akademiia nauk armianskoi SSR. Sektor vostokovedeniia, *Vostokovedcheskii sbornik.* v. 2. Erevan, 1964, pp. 174–92.

———. "Posleoktiabr'skii revoliutsionnyi pod'em v Turtsii," in Moscow University. *Vestnik moskovskogo universiteta.* 1949, no. 7, seriia obshchestvennykh nauk, issue 3, pp. 39–54.

Sherif Manatov. "Turetskaia zhizn' v otrazhenii turetskoi pressi," *Novyi Vostok,* 1922, no. 1, pp. 354–59.

Anatolii Filippovich Miller. "Burzhuazno-natsional'naia revoliutsiia 1918–1923 gg. v Turtsii," in Moscow University. Otdelenie istorii stran zarubezhnogo Vostoka. *Noveishaia istoriia stran zarubezhnogo Vostoka.* Part I: (*1918–1929*). Moscow, 1954, pp. 274–88.

————. "Formirovanie politicheskikh vzgladov Kemalia Atatiurka," *Narody Azii i Afriki,* 1963, no. 5, pp. 65–85.

Zinniatulla Navshirvanov. "Sotsialisticheskoe dvizhenie v Turtsii," *Novyi Vostok,* 1922, no. 2, pp. 619–20.

————. "Turetskaia pressa," *Novyi Vostok,* 1923, no. 3, pp. 479–89.

A[ron] D[avidovich] Novichev. "Antikrest'ianskaia politika Kemalistov v 1919–1922 godakh," *Voprosy Istorii,* 1951, no. 9, pp. 56–75.

————. "Vliianie velikoi oktiabr'skoi sotsialisticheskoi revoliutsii na sud'bu Turtsii," in Leningrad University. *Vestnik Leningradskogo Universiteta.* 1957, no. 20, issue 4, pp. 95–107.

————. "Zarozhdenie rabochego i sotsialisticheskogo dvizheniia v Turtsii," in Leningrad University. *Uchenye zapiski Leningradskogo Universiteta.* 1962, no. 304, pp. 3–29.

Halis Okan. "Uslovija, pojava i razvitie na rabotničeskoto i sotsialističeskoto dviženie v Turtsija," *Istoričeski pregled,* 1960, no. 4, pp. 92–105.

H[enri] P[aulmier]. "Un complot bouffe à Constantinople," *La vie ouvrière,* May 18, 1923, p. 3.

————. "Le 'complot' de Constantinople se termine par un nonlieu," *La vie ouvrière,* June 29, 1923, p. 3.

————. "On arrête toujours en Turquie," *La vie ouvrière,* July 6, 1923, p. 3.

————. "The White Terror: Events in Turkey in July," *International Press Correspondence,* Sept. 13, 1923, no. 60(38), p. 670.

Maurice Pernot. "La nouvelle Turquie," Part III: "Le gouvernement d'Angora et les activités étrangères," *Revue des Deux Mondes,* March 1, 1924, v. 20, pp. 131–67.

"Pis'mo 'Mezhdunarodnogo Soiuza Rabochikh,'" *Krasnyi International Profsoiuzov,* 1922, no. 11 (22), pp. 1050–51.

B. Potskhveriia & Iuryi Rozaliev. "Trebovaniia rabochei gruppy na Izmirskom ekonomicheskom kongresse 1923 g.," in Akademiia nauk SSSR. *Kratkie soobshcheniia instituta vostokovedeniia,* 1956, v. 22, pp. 82–87.

Karl Radek. "The Assassination of Djemal Pasha," *International Press Correspondence,* Aug. 12, 1922, no. 68, pp. 507–508.

Dankwart A. Rustow. "The Appeal of Communism to Islamic Peoples," in J. Harris Proctor (ed.). *Islam and International Relations.* New York 1965, pp. 40–60; the Brookings Institution, Reprint 90.

Ervand Kazarovich Sarkisian. "Vliianie oktiabr'skoi revoliutsii na natsional'no-osvoboditel'noe dvizhenie v Turtsii (1918–1922)," in Akademiia nauk armianskoi SSR, *Izvestiia,* 1957, no. 10, pp. 7–22.

Shakir-Rassim. "Assotsiatsiia Rabochikh Turtsii," *Mezhdunarodnoe rabochee dvizhenie,* April 9, 1925, no. 3, pp. 1–2.

A. M. Shamsutdinov. "Oktiabr'skaia revoliutsiia i natsional'no-osvoboditel'noe dvizhenie v Turtsii (1919–1922)," in A. A. Guber (ed.). *Velikii Oktiabr' i narody Vostoka.* Moscow, 1957, pp. 384–407.

——. "Pervyi s'ezd Kommunisticheskoi Partii Turtsii," in Akademiia nauk SSSR. *Kratkie soobshcheniia instituta narodov Azii,* 1961, v. 30, pp. 227–37.

A. Skachko. "Agrarnyi vopros v Turtsii," *Zhizn' Natsional'nostei,* Sept. 2, 16, 24, Oct. 1, 17, 27, Nov. 3, 17, 25, 1920.

Mehmed Moustafa Soubhy [Mehmed Mustafa Subhi]. "L'organisation du crédit agricole en Turquie," in Institut International d'Agriculture. *Bulletin du bureau des institutions économiques et sociales,* Oct.–Nov. 1910, no. 2, pp. 59–76; English translation: International Institute of Agriculture. *Bulletin of the Bureau of Economic and Social Intelligence,* Oct.–Nov. 1910, no. 2, pp. 59–76.

Joshua Starr. "The Socialist Federation of Saloniki," *Jewish Social Studies,* Oct. 1945, v. 7, no. 4, pp. 323–36.

Avestis Sultan-Galiev. "Mustafa Subhi i ego rabota," *Zhizn' Natsional'nostei,* 1921, no. 14 (112).

———. "Politicheskie partii," *Izvestiia,* May 19, 1920.

Fethi Tevetoğlu. "Atatürk'ün Kapattırdığı Kızıl Teşekkül: Yeşilordu," *Türk Kültürü,* Nov. 1966, no. 49, pp. 62–74.

———. "Atatürk'ün Sovyet Politikası," *Türk Kültürü,* Nov. 1964, no. 25, pp. 28–31.

———. "Hafî Türkiye Komünist Partisi ve Türkiye Halk İştirâkiyûn Fırkası," *Türk Kültürü,* Feb. 1967, no. 52, pp. 255–68.

———. "Meclis-i Mebusan'da Gayri Müslim Sosyalistler," *Türk Kültürü,* Jan. 1967, no. 51, pp. 179–93.

———. "Türkiye'de Sosyalist ve Komünist Faaliyetler," *Türk Kültürü,* April 1966, no. 42, pp. 512–18; Aug. 1966, no. 46, pp. 903–909; Sept. 1966, no. 47, pp. 998–1011; Oct. 1966, no. 48, pp. 1129–34.

Sedat Toydemir. "Türkiyede İş İhtilâflarının Tarihçesi ve Bugünkü Durumu," in Istanbul University. İktisat ve İçtimaiyat Enstitüsü. *İçtimaî Siyaset Konferanslari.* Dördüncü Kitap. Istanbul, 1951, pp. 45–66.

Kh. M. Tsovikian. "Vliianie russkoi revoliutsii 1905 g. na revoliutsionnoe dvizhenie v Turtsii," in Akademiia nauk SSSR. *Sovetskoe vostokovedenie,* 1945, pp. 15–35.

"Turkey," *Current History,* Aug. 1923, pp. 895–96.

"Turtsiia: S'ezd rabochego obshchestva 'Amele-Teali,' " *Mezhdunarodnoe rabochee dvizhenie,* 1926, no. 44 (85), pp. 14–15.

S. Üstungel. "V tiur'me i na 'vole,' " *Novyi Mir,* 1951, no. 9, pp. 82–133; translated from Turkish: *Savaş Yolu.* Sofia, 1950.

Stefan Velikov. "Sur le mouvement ouvrier et socialiste en Turquie après la révolution Jeune-Turque de 1908," *Études Balkaniques* (Sofia), 1964, no. 1, pp. 29–48.

Eric Verney. "Under Kemalist Rule," *International Press Correspondence*, July 5, 1923, no. 48 (28), pp. 480–81.

W. "Les relations russo-turques depuis l'avènement du bolchevisme," *Revue du Monde Musulman*, Dec. 1922, no. 52, pp. 181–217.

" 'Yeşilordu' Cemiyeti," *Yakın Tarihimiz*, 1962, v. 1, pp. 69–72, 101–104, 133–35, 172–74, 215–16, 233–35, 281–83, 297–98.

A. Zhurbenko. "V Turtsii," *Zhizn' Natsional'nostei*, April 1, 1922, no. 5 (11), pp. 14–15.

IV. PERIODICALS AND NEWSPAPERS

Akşam, 1918, 1921, 1925

Alemdar, 1913, 1920

Anadoluda Yeni Gün, 1920–1922

Aydınlık, 1921–1925

Ayın Tarihi, Jan. 1947, no. 158

Le Bosphore, 1922–1923

Clarté, 1922–1925

Cumhuriyet, 1927–1931

Haber, 1923

Hâkimiyeti Milliye, 1920–1922

Hikmet, 1912

l'Humanité, 1919–1925

İdrak, 1919

İkdam, 1909–1910, 1919

İnsaniyet, 1910

İradei Milliye, 1920

İşçiler Gazetesi (Journal des Travailleurs), 1909.

İştirak, 1910, 1912

Izvestiia, 1918–1925

Kadro, 1932–1935
Kommunist (Baku), 1920
Kurtuluş (Berlin), 1919
Kurtuluş (Istanbul), 1919–1920
Medeniyet, 1910
Mezhdunarodnoe rabochee dvizhenie, 1923, 1925, 1926
Milliyet, 1933
The Nation, Sept. 7, 1921, v. 113
Orak Çekiç, 1925
The Orient News, 1922–1923
Oriente Moderno, 1921–1925
Pravda, 1918–1925
Peyami Sabah, 1920
Sabah, 1909–1910
Seyyarei Yeni Dünya, 1920
Son Saat, 1925
Sosyalist, 1910
Tanin, 1910, 1923
Le Tanine, 1924–1925
Tasviri Efkâr, 1919–1920
Teminat, 1912
Vakıt, 1919, 1925
Vatan, 1923
La vie ouvrière, 1920–1925
Vostok, 1922
Die Welt des Islams, 1934–1964
Yarın, 1931
Yeni Hayat, 1922
Yön, 1964
Zaman, 1918
Zhizn' Natsional'nostei, 1918–1924

Index

Note: In the index those individuals who never acquired a family name or whose family name is unknown are listed under their last given name. Diacritical marks are ignored for the purposes of alphabetization. Hence, for example, Şükrü precedes Süleyman instead of following as in normal Turkish practice.

214 THE ORIGINS OF COMMUNISM IN TURKEY

tegrates, 106, 126; and Second International, 163n8; and strikes, 163n9
Turkish Worker and Peasant Party (Türkiye İşçi ve Çiftçi Fırkası), 40, 163n10
Turkish Worker and Peasant Socialist Party (Türkiye İşçi ve Çiftçi Sosyalist Fırkası) : statutes, 33; founded, 41; leaders of, 41–42; outlook of, 42–44; and united socialist front, 45–46; and labor, 45–47, 98, 104–5, 120; and elections, 46–47, 121–22; suspended, 49, 105; revived, 98–99; and *Aydınlık*, 100; tactics of, 104; and Peoples Communist Party, 109–10, 115–16, 121; and Kemalists, 118–19, 123; and Izmir Congress, 120–21; leaders tried, 124; and Comintern, 180n29. *See also* Turkish Communist Party
Turkish Worker Association (Türkiye İşçi Derneği), 40, 104–6, 118–20, 177n14
Turkish Workers League (Türkiye İşçler Birliği), 178n20
Turkism, Turkists: in Salonika, 19; and Parvus, 26; in Istanbul, 28–29; and Greek invasion, 34; and Nejat, 41; and Subhi, 51; and Bebel, 160n6
Türkiye Amele Birliği. *See* Confederation of Turkish Workers
Türkiye Halk İştirakiyun Bolşevik Partisi. *See* Turkish Peoples Communist Bolshevik Party
Türkiye Halk İştirakiyun Partisi. *See* Peoples Communist Party of Turkey
Türkiye İşçi Derneği. *See* Turkish Worker Association
Türkiye İşçi ve Çiftçi Fırkası. *See* Turkish Worker and Peasant Party
Türkiye İşçi ve Çiftçi Sosyalist Fırkası. *See* Turkish Worker and Peasant Socialist Party
Türkiye İşçiler Birliği. *See* Turkish Workers League

Ukraine, 108, 131
Union and Progress (Peoples Soviet) Party, 103
Union internationale du travaille, 97
United States, 41
"University of the East," 108
Upmal-Angarskii, 79
Urals, 52
USSR. *See* Soviet Union

Vahideddin, Sultan, 34, 45, 54, 76, 97, 118
Vakıt, 142
Vanlı Kâzım. *See* Kâzım (from Van)
Vanoc, Neşir, 73
Vâ-Nû, Vâlâ Nureddin, 130, 185n4
Varınca, Ahmet Kemal, 164n1
Vazife, 126
Vehbi, Lt., 166n14
Velt'man, Mikhail Pavlovich, 63
Verbov (Verlov), 73, 170n9, n10
Vienna, 143

Workers Advancement Society, 133–34
"Workers and Peasants of Turkey," declaration to, 57

Yahya, 90–91, 94
Yakup, 57, 59, 166n14
Yeni Dünya (Oruç's paper), 107, 178n16. *See also Seyyarei Yeni Dünya*
Yeni Dünya (Subhi's paper), 53, 56, 59, 163n13, 165n5, 166n15
Yeni Felsefe Mecmuası, 19
Yeni Gün. See Anadoluda Yeni Gün
Yeni Hayat, 109–10, 114, 179n27
Yoldaş, 136
Young Turks: revolution of, 14–17 *passim*, 34, 142; and labor, 16, 36; and socialism, 21, 27, 32
Yozgat (Turkey), 76

Zeki, Salih, 59–61, 166n14, 166n18
"Zenon." *See* Navshirvanov, Zinniatulla
Zincirbend Gençlik. See Zincirli Gençlik